CORE EMUNAH:
HELLO?
G-D?

An Exploration of Life's Most Fundamental Question

Rabbi Shlomo Ben Zeev

PARTRIDGE

To order additional copies of this book, contact
Toll Free +65 3165 7531 (Singapore)
Toll Free +60 3 3099 4412 (Malaysia)
orders.singapore@partridgepublishing.com

www.partridgepublishing.com/singapore

DEDICATION

I have dedicated this book to the memory of my deceased grandparents:
Ze'ev Gavriel ben Menachem Mendel,
Ester Channa bas Gershon,
Noach ben Shlomo and
Itka bas Eliahu
It is also in memory of my late father-in-law Shimshon ben Michael.

May they see the merits of their descendants and rejoice in them
forever.

It is also to all of the people out there who, like me, would like to face
the truth of life and, with G-d's help, learn to live a life of meaning and
purpose.

CONTENTS

ACKNOWLEDGMENTS

O MANY PEOPLE have profoundly affected my life that I find it tough to choose whom to acknowledge. I will therefore simply say:

G-d, creator, guide, life bringer. He who has led me, sustained me, and brought me to this day. He who has given me everything that I have in life. I can only hope that this book can, some way, begin to "pay back" all the kindnesses that I have been given in life.

To my parents, who have also guided me, sustained me, laughed with me, cried with me and helped to make me into the man I am today. A special thank you to my mother, who took (a lot of) time in reviewing the original manuscript and giving me editorial advice. Thanks, Mom!

To my Rebbeim, both those alive and in the next world, who set me on the path to becoming the man that I am today.

I would also like to say a special thank you to Dr. Gerald Schroeder, Ph.D., to my good friend and student Dr. Yosef (Carl) Ashkenasi M.D., and to Rabbi Ben Tzion Schafier who gave of their time to review the book and to give me critiques and endorsements.

To my children and students, who have all challenged me and helped me hone much of my many (bad) character traits. (This includes you, too, Akiva!)

Lastly, to my loving wife. Throughout all the difficulties that we have been through, she has been there to support me. She who has raised our children to be true *menschim*, to love *Chessed* and go out of their way for others.

May it be His will that we have a long, happy and meaningful life together with lots of *GeFeN: Gedzunt, Parnassah*, and *Nachas*!

FOREWORD

What is it All About Anyhow?

 FEW YEARS AGO, when I was a young married fellow here in Israel, I was invited, like most Israelis, to take part in IDF reserve duty.

It was the best of times, and it was the worst of times.

I was the only religious soldier serving in a scouting unit, within a foot-soldier platoon, in a tank (armored) division. What this implies is that I stuck out like the proverbial sore thumb, as almost everyone else there was secular. In Israel, a nation divided between the religious and secular but full of Israeli Jews, who are always ready to tell you what is on their mind, (and what they think of yours), the topic of religion can sometimes be quite volatile.

As the only religious Jew in the platoon, I was the sole representative of all Torah observant life in Israel. If anyone held a grudge against the religious – for any reason whatsoever – then I was sought out as the figurative (or literal) punching bag to vent frustrations; but, more importantly, I was also sought as a source of explanation and understanding when it came to our religion. I took great pleasure in the latter, (not the former).

On one of those occasions, my company Sergeant approached me and asked if I could go on a walk with him to explain to him the issues of the laws of "Nidda" (the laws about a woman during her menstrual cycle). He wanted to talk to me about this as he came from a traditional family, he had a girlfriend, and things were beginning to heat up between them. We walked and talked for several hours going from the laws of Nidda and forbidden relationships (and the Mitzvah to marry a woman before having sexual relations with her) to the laws of Shabbat, the Sabbath day, and on to all sorts of issues under the sun. After a while, I turned to my Sergeant, a fine young Yemenite guy a little bit younger than me and said to him as follows. "Look, Sagiv, (his name), I'll be happy to sit with you whenever we have time to explore further any topic that you want concerning the Holy Torah. However, before we continue, there is just one thing that I must make absolutely clear: All of these things are Mitzvos, commandments because THE COMMANDER commanded them. So long as this is clear to you, that the reason that we fulfill these commandments is because they are on the authority of THE COMMANDER, then you will have a reason to keep them. However, if you don't accept this as fact, then all of the time spent explaining is pointless. You'll hear some "expert" on the topic give you a convincing explanation as to why you don't have to keep them, and that will be the end."

I'm happy to say that he got married to his girlfriend not too long after our conversation, (I like to assume that it was because of our conversation), and he has several kids today.

The point that I made to him is not only valid; it is the linchpin for the entire Torah. We refer to this as EMUNAH, (אמונה), which translates into English as "Faith" or "Belief". The issue of Emunah is so important, so fundamental, that our sages of blessed memory, the Rishonim[1], argue whether it's "one" of the 613 commandments in the Torah, or if it is too fundamental to be considered "a" commandment. Rather it's part and

---

[1]   Literally "the First Ones", a term referring to our sages who lived in the 9th to the 13th Centuries in the Gregorian calendar.

parcel of ALL of the commandments. However, no matter how we slice it, it is unquestionable that emunah is THE foundation of the entire Torah.

If a person's emunah is weak or lacking, then his or her complete adherence to the laws of the Torah is similarly weak. Weak emunah is comparable to a building with a shoddy foundation. Such a structure is more likely to collapse than to remain standing. All that is required, many times, is just one strong wind to knock it down!

So too in Torah: as long as the foundation, Emunah, is weak then the performance of Mitzvos and the continued practice of its commandments are constantly in danger of collapse. As long as it is not clear, there is a COMMANDER then it is similarly not clear that there are any COMMANDS, Mitzvos, as well.

With this as an introduction I would like to, therefore, posit the following axiom:

Any thinking human being, at some time in their lives, will ask him or herself life's most fundamental question. Depending on the answer to that first question, they will then ask the second question and depending on the answer they give, they would then ask a third. These are the fundamental questions regarding life. They are:

Question 1> Is there a G-d who created the universe?

If your answer is "no," then the questions stop here. If you answer "yes," then we must continue to ask question no. 2.

Question 2> Does G-d know me and desire a relationship with me?

If your answer is "no," then further questioning is pointless, as we are inconsequential. If you answer "Yes," then we must ask question 3.

Question 3> What is my relationship with G-d?

As with all relationships, this one, too, is a two-way street. If one side loves the other but the other side only likes the first, then the extent of the relationship is limited to the lesser of the two!

This book and, G-d willing, the books to follow, is written to help the reader explore – to the best of my knowledge and ability – the information required to make an informed decision about these three fundamental questions.

Having grown up in both the secular and religious worlds, I experienced both sides of the coin. I have, since I was young, always been fascinated by the sciences, (thank you Mrs. Tuvlin), and since my exposure to authentic Torah learning I have been deeply in love and enthralled by that as well.

Popular media would have us believe that these two worlds are in conflict. If we wish to follow Torah/Religion, we must do so despite the scientific data; and conversely, we are told, after exposure to the various fields of science no one can possibly be a believer.

Despite the fact that this is untrue, it has found its way into our subconscious in so many different ways.

Our great teacher the RAMBAM[2], one of the, (if not THE), greatest scientists and physicians of his day, while also being one of the greatest Torah scholars of his time, said as follows. If anyone feels that the Torah and science are at odds, unless faced with uncontestable proof, then it's the science that is incorrect[3]. Yet despite this, the foundation of a religious person's world - his emunah – if no investment is made into its development, is also not something that is powerful as well. It can be influenced both for better and for worse. Rav *Sa'adiyah Gaon*, writes[4] that for many people their emunah is weakened as the result of hearing the words of an *apikorus* (a denier of G-d) which then settled in his heart, or after having heard the

---

[2] Rabbi Moses Ben Maimon was a preeminent medieval Spanish, Sephardic Jewish philosopher, astronomer and one of the most prolific and influential Torah scholars and physicians of the Middle Ages. He was born in Córdoba (present-day Spain), Almoravid Empire on Passover Eve, 1135, and died in Egypt on December 12, 1204. For more information check out **http://en.wikipedia.org/wiki/Maimonides**

[3] Maimonides, *The Guide for the Perplexed*, 2:25. I did take some literary license here as the Rambam's real statement is that so long as the proof is not incontestable then we will follow the interpretation based on our masorah (=tradition). It has been my experience, however, that there is no such thing as incontestable science, as we will see – in great detail – within. See also *Emunot v'De'ot* by Rav Sa'adiya Gaon in his introduction and first chapter, where he discusses the true nature of scientific study.

[4] Emunot v'Deot - introduction.

words of a *ba'al emunah* (an adherent) who, in his attempts to strengthen emunah, brought weak proofs to do so[5].

Based on his words I found that there was a great need for this book.

The purpose of this book is to deal solely with the first question above: Is there a G-d? It is here to present a logical, fully developed argument, aimed to dispel the words of *apikorsuit* from our hearts, on the one side, while bringing strong proofs to G-d's existence on the other. We will discover that not only is the scientific data not at odds with the Torah, but rather, that without the Torah, as explained by the Creator, there is no way that the data can be understood.

Data, after all, is only information gleaned from experimentation. It is almost always open to more than one interpretation and therefore, cannot itself constitute absolute proof.

It is the goal of this book to help the reader, as the saying goes, "see the forest despite all of the trees." Meaning, when we consider the whole picture presented by the information – what does it show, and in which direction does it point? Theist or Secularist?

The information and sources are available to all, but many people will not have sufficient motivation to explore them on their own, or to do a complete and thorough job in the analysis of the information. Therefore, I have tried to crystallize and organize this data into a short, yet coherent, logical and readable form. Life is a gift given to all the world's people – why should this essential information not be as well?

It is my fervent hope that the information contained in this volume will help to remove obstacles from in front all my fellow Jews and all of those Gentiles (=people not of the Jewish faith) who believe in the Creator of the universe but suffer from a sense of inferiority or confusion due to the stigma of mass media.

Please read and enliven your soul!

One caveat, however.

---

[5]   I pray to HaShem that I don't suffer from this in my words!

As most of the information presented in this volume is brought to give the reader all of the pertinent information relevant to the existence of The Creator, I must also point out that most of it does not actually tell me *who* He is. The purpose of this volume is only to remove the obstacles that have been preventing us from exploring faith-based religions. None of it can, in any way, act as a proof for one religion or another in any shape, way or form.

As with all rules, the one exception to this one will be the chapter entitled "In the Beginning," as it is organized based on the first several verses of the book of Genesis to deal with the topics of cosmology, physics, botany and more. Exploration of reality based on an ancient religious text clearly sets a precedent for the authenticity and truth of the "OLD" Testament. However, proving the Old One says nothing and proves nothing about the content of the new one or of any other book for that matter[6].

G-d willing, in future volumes I will present the reader with even more pertinent information that is required to make informed decisions concerning the Jewish faith as we explore the further questions presented above "Does G-d know me?" and "What is my relationship with G-d?"

Having said that, this book is the product of my own investigation, utilizing the gifts that HaShem ("The Name" =G-d, used interchangeably during the book) gave me to the best of my ability. However, I remain a human being, capable of making mistakes and it is possible that, despite my best efforts and those of the people who gave their time to review my work, that there still remain errors. I would greatly appreciate it if you, the reader, do find any - please let me know. My contact details can be found at the back of the book.

---

[6]   As I told one person of the Christian faith "If I would print the Old Testament as the prelude to my book, does that mean that my book is also the Divine word of G-d, as well?"

1

Emunah vs. Faith: Identical Twins?

What Does "Emunah" Actually Mean?

S I STATED IN THE FORWARD, the purpose of this book is to lay the foundations for emunah. However, before we can begin to explore the realm of emunah, first we have to quantify JUST WHAT IT IS WE ARE TALKING ABOUT. Just what is emunah?

Faith

In English, EMUNAH translates as "faith" or "belief". What exactly does "faith" mean?

According to the Oxford Online Dictionary,[7] the definition of faith is:

Complete trust or confidence in someone or something

---

[7]   http://oxforddictionaries.com/definition/english/faith

> *Strong Belief in the doctrines of religion, based on spiritual*
> *conviction rather than proof.*
> *A particular religion*
> *A strongly held belief*

According to dictionary.com[8] the definition of faith is:

> *Confidence or trust in a person or thing: Faith in another's abilities*
> *Belief that is not based on a proof*
> *Belief in G–d or the doctrines or teachings of religion*
> *A belief in anything as a code of ethics standards of merit etc.*
> *A system of religious belief*

Merriam-Webster[9] also includes a similar definition of faith as:

> *A firm belief in something for which there is no proof and*
> *something that is believed especially with strong conviction;*
> *especially: a system of religious beliefs <the Protestant faith>*

Most definitions of faith include this conception of "belief without proof". In my opinion, this basic definition of faith as a belief not based on proof is erroneous. We arrived at this misconception because of improperly understanding how we use "faith" in real life. Here is a simple example illustrating the operation of our current definition of faith (belief without proof).

Let's say that I need to go somewhere, and I entrust my dear friend with my delicious chocolate bar to hold until I return. After I have finished doing my business, I come back and find that my chocolate bar has disappeared and that my friend happens to have a smear of chocolate around his mouth. I ask my friend what happened, and he says, "I just couldn't stop myself, and so I ate it!" In this instance, I believe/have faith

---

8   http://dictionary.reference.com/browse/faith?s=t
9   http://www.merriam-webster.com/dictionary/faith

in my friend's answer even though I don't honestly know if that is what happened. This is an example of a belief in something without proof or evidence. After all, it could be that my young son ran into the room, saw the chocolate bar in my friend's hand, grabbed it, opened it, took a bite and then, just before leaving the room, shoved it in my friend's face and said, "You want some too"? Maybe my friend didn't want to incriminate my son. Do I know what happened? No. So, therefore, I have to have faith that what my friend told me is what happened, even though there is no proof or evidence.

Ergo: Only when I have, NO KNOWLEDGE is there room for faith.

This belief became ingrained further into society's collective mind because almost all religions make use of precisely that claim: believe in X without proof. It's just they take it one step further.

True Believers

Let me illustrate the real problem here with a story:

Once upon a time, I was forced, (for lack of a viable alternative), to sit next to a missionary on a plane trip to the States. (I mean I could have jumped out of the aircraft at 30,000 feet going 800 miles an hour, without a parachute, endangering all of the other passengers. It just didn't seem to realistic, though). I knew what was coming. I was ready. Therefore, when my neighbor turned to me and struck up a conversation concerning the truth of the Christian faith, I was ready. "Jesus," he said, "was the Messiah of the Jews"! "How do you know that to be true?" I asked him. "Well," he said and began quoting me from the New Testament as to Jesus's ancestral lineage.

Why did he do that? It's because the Torah (also called "the Bible" or "the Old Testament") says clearly that the Messiah is going to come from the house of David; so anyone claiming "Messiah"-hood, must be David's descendant. He then proceeded to quote to me from the Gospels, which refer to Joseph of Nazareth as a descendant of David. "But wait a minute,"

I said, "Don't all Christians hold that he wasn't Jesus's real father? G-D was Jesus' dad! If that's the case, then who cares what the lineage of Joseph was? He wasn't Jesus's dad"! "That's true," he said, "But in Luke 3:23–38 it says that Mary, Jesus's mom, was a descendant of the house of David, so his claim to messiah-hood is through his mom." I looked at him in utter disbelief. "How could you even think such a thing?" I said. "It is clearly written in The Torah (Numbers 1:2) that a person's lineage comes from his father only, not from his mother. I'm afraid to tell you that no matter how you slice it; Jesus can't be a descendant of David"!

There was quiet for a few minutes. Then, after a short while, he turned to me and said the following "Those are difficult points you raise. BUT THAT'S THE STRENGTH OF FAITH!"[10]

Then he said as follows, "Even though I have no proof and even though it makes no sense … I have faith that it is true!"

That is what I meant by "a step further."

IF the meaning of Emunah, "faith", is to believe despite a lack of proof; THEN the greatest act of faith and a real test of the extent of a person's faith is when his faith is in conflict with empirical evidence.

The more absurd or far-fetched – the greater the feat of belief, and so much greater still is the believer!

Does that sound right to you? It doesn't to me! But if you feel it does - don't worry, you're in good company.

It is precisely this conclusion, which so confuses us in the realm of Emunah. Taken to its logical conclusion, it is possible to say that in matters where there *is* knowledge – it's no longer subject to faith at all.

Therefore, our dictum, thus far, is faith = no proof; science = lots of proof, no faith. GREAT FAITH = follow regardless of, and in spite of, the evidence.

The result of all of this, which bothers me the most, is that we assume that this definition applies just as much when we are dealing with Emunah,

---

[10] At this point I immediately took a quick look at his hands to see if he would do the "Yeshivish Thumb" when he gave me his explanation. He didn't. Clearly a non-Jewish Christian. Sorry, this is an inside Jewish joke.

which, as I said previously, is THE foundation of everything that we do in keeping the Holy Torah. This has been so ingrained that I have even heard Torah scholars who have said that Emunah, (faith), means exactly that: to believe regardless of the facts or in spite of them. Which, of course, bothers me deeply, as I will explain.

I also discovered that this is not the only way that we see this misconception is utilized. I found that when I would question my secular friends about mutual acquaintances of ours who had become religious, there was an observable pattern to their answers. I'd ask, "Why do you think that they would take such a step in their life, to change their lifestyle so drastically?" The answers that I received went something like this: "He always was a little weird," "He had an accident in life," "He broke up with his girlfriend" or "He was depressed." Something along that line. Meaning: It can't be that there is a LOGICAL reason for a person to become religious. It must be that due to some tragedy, some upset, (temporary insanity), some *emotional issue* that caused him to change his mind and his ways. After all, faith doesn't follow logic; it's entirely foundation-less!

Nothing could be further from the truth.

However, as the purpose of this chapter is not to set before you the logical evidence for faith, G-D willing we'll do that during future chapters, I do want to clarify the misunderstanding concerning Emunah so that from now on it is evident WHAT we are talking about.

However, before that – one more point.

Cold, Hard Facts... or Not?

This mistaken notion has led many people to follow blindly anything that was discovered by "scientists" using "scientific methodology" regardless of the veracity of the proofs that they bring. The assumption is that since science, supposedly, is based on cold, hard facts, then this isn't an issue of belief at all! Just the opposite! This is the clear and concise truth. No faith involved. ... NOT!

However, science, even when backed up with methodological testing, is many times more faith-based than empirical proof based. It is the faith, the preconceived notions, that drive the interpretation of the data. G-d willing, I will quantify and present the proofs to this assertion more fully in the later chapters (you'll just have to have faith!). In the meantime, let me give you two examples:

Have you ever been on a diet? Well then, let's ask, which one are you following? Are you on the "Grain Brain Diet" (low carbohydrate, high fat, moderate protein)? Are you on the Atkins diet, (mainly proteins and no carbohydrates)? Maybe you're doing the Zone diet, (part protein, part carbohydrate, part veggies)? Or maybe, just maybe, you're on the Bread Diet, (a diet that states that it's important that the mainstay of your diet is bread based)! Perhaps, some of you are on the China Study diet, (a diet of vegetables and legumes, no meat or milk).

Do you know that all of these diets were created and extensively studied by scientists using scientific methodology? They all have "science" on their side! They all claim that all of the evidence shows that their diet is THE correct diet for at least 95% of the planet! So, whom should you follow? Well, I guess that just depends on who offers you the better "spread" in their diet; OR... on with whom you have the most ...(i.e. blindest) faith.

Another issue where we find this is in the realm of general health and which foods best promote it. Who knows just what it is that you need to have healthy bones and teeth? (Milk, of course!)

Ask any dairy farm and they will bring you out truckloads of data and drop it on you, (not killing you, of course, after all, the one actually getting "milked" here is you, the consumer). All of it is supposed to prove to you beyond any doubt that there was not, is not and never will be anything as healthy for you as cow's milk.

However, if you speak to other scientists, say, perhaps, Dr. T. Colin Campbell, author of "The China Study" and a well-respected Doctor and scientist, he would tell you that you are drinking liquid poison! "Milk is for cows," as the naturalists say!

So, whom do you follow here? The dairy industry, which clearly has a financial interest in your continued use of their product, (say "Moo!" everyone!), or the naturalists, who also have scientific studies on their side to prove their point? I guess it depends on WHO you have the blindest faith in, (or what flavor the ice cream is).

Many times, science, despite having arrived at some cold-hard facts, interprets the data, and assumes the interpretation is correct, based less on cold hard evidence, and more due to warm, squishy bias, which is rooted in deep, blind faith.

Enough on this for now. As I said, we will come back to it later. Getting back to the topic at hand:

What is Emunah?

Well, first and foremost, it's a word.

Emunah is a Hebrew (Semitic) word and, therefore, we have three ways in which to check its precise definition. Either using:

It's context in the Holy Torah, our fundamental source of all Hebrew; or

The root of the word. Many Hebrew words are "built" by using a root word with "plugin" forms into speech frames. We can, therefore, use the root word to find commonality between one word and all other words that share the same root. Or

Usage of the word in stories or figures of speech

Let's take these concepts for a spin:

Context in the Torah

Let's take a look at several places in the Holy Torah where the word emunah is used. (I'm only bringing three, but there are plenty of other instances – look them up!):

Exodus 17:12

And Moses' hands were heavy, and they took a stone and placed it underneath him (Moses), and he sat on it, and Aaron and Chur stabilized his hands, on this side one and on this side one, and his (Moses) hands were EMUNAH until the sun set.

This passage from the book of Exodus was said concerning the war that the children of Israel waged against the Amalekites in the desert. Moshe sends his student Joshua to battle against them, while he proceeded to go up on a mountain and raise his hands in prayer to heaven. The Torah tells us that when he would raise his hands – Israel would win, but when they lowered, Israel began to lose. So, Moses sits down on a rock (not a comfortable chair, because the people of Israel were in distress) and Aaron, Moses's brother, and Chur, Miriam's son, propped up Moses' hands. The Torah tells us that then Moses's hands were "Emunah" until sundown. What could that possibly mean? Well, if, as we have understood up until now, it means to believe in something without proof does that mean that Moses's hands were down, but he said, "I have faith that they are up"? I think not. Rather here the usage of the word means "strength" or "stable". The verse is telling us that before Moses sat on the rock and rested his hands on Aaron and Chur his hands were unstable, whereas NOW that his hands were resting on Aaron and Chur his hands were stable and secure. They had strength and vitality. We are talking clarity here, not doubt.

Chronicles 2 34:12

And the people were working with EMUNAH in their labors.

Literally "and the men were performing their tasks with Emunah". Here the verse is talking about King Josiah, a pious and righteous king of Judah, who, when he saw the dilapidated state of the Mikdash, (the Holy Temple in Jerusalem), immediately commanded: "Make a collection so that we can rebuild the Mikdash." They collected the money during the

Festivals and then gave it to the artisans, to start the repairs that were so desperately needed. This verse states, "the artisans performed their duties with Emunah." If we "plug in" the explanation of Emunah that we had until now this would seem to imply that the artisans were doing their duties believing that they were doing their job without any real proof. It's kind of like talking to a modern-day contractor: when you ask him if everything is ok he says, "Everything is perfect! Trust me"! What do you think? Should you trust him? I wouldn't!

No! That can't be the meaning of the verse! Rather the verse is relating that which was evident and discernible, that the artisan's performed their work with strength and vitality.

Proverbs 14:15

> *A fool (peti) will make/call "Emunah" all things, but a wise-crafty person will understand things to its fullest.*

Here Emunah is used in its future tense as a verb, ya'amin, whereas up until now we have been looking at it as a noun or an adjective, emunah.

Here, if we apply the "plug-in" explanation that we had originally, it really makes no sense! "A fool will have faith in something without proof by anything" which, structurally, is a double negative. If the word Ya'amin means to believe without evidence, then the words in all things become superfluous. Rather, the verse is speaking along the same vein we saw earlier: that a fool makes robust and vital anything, even something which isn't, whereas a wise-crafty person will apply his mind to ensure that he fully understands what he is dealing with: whether robust and vital or weak and frail. Only that which is healthy and vibrant will be considered by the wise person to be so.

It would seem, therefore, that the true meaning of the word Emunah as used in the Torah refers to STRENGTH and VITALITY.

Let's see if that holds true in the other tools.

The ROOT-WORD.

The root word of the word emunah is א.מ.נ. If we want to try to understand a word by using its root the way to do so is to see what other words there are with which we are familiar that utilize the same root. When I put my mind to it, I came up with the following terms:

Ne'eman, Oman, Iymun, and Emunah.

Now, what are these words?

Let's start, for example, with the word Iymun (אימון). What is iymun? It means "practice." For example, when a person learns to be a sharpshooter or an artist, the more he shoots or paints – the better he becomes. That is an act of strengthening knowledge and capability.

Iymun, practice, leads a person to become an oman, an artisan, a professional in his or her trade. This title belays a level of proficiency that one receives once he has proven himself – strengthened his standing in his field of choice – in the eyes of his friends and neighbors.

Another word that uses the same root is the word Ne'eman, נאמן. Ne'eman refers to the base believability and reliability that a person has in the eyes of others. 9 out of 10 times, it is the result of proving oneself in the eyes of others, thus strengthening his moral character in the eyes of his peers.

So, it seems that here, too, the correct interpretation of the concept of Emunah denotes strengthening [something] and making [something] more vital. The common denominator would seem to be that a person utilizing "Amen" (the root of Emunah) is going through a process of taking something that he already has, not that he has baseless faith in, and improving, strengthening and vitalizing it!

Usage in Stories and Metaphors

Let's take a look at one example. It's a story that our sages tell us about one of the people that the Torah calls a Tzadik, (an upstanding, righteous man), Noah. The Torah tells us many things about Noah; however, I want to stress something on which our sages zero in. A piece of extraneous verbiage, (extra words) that the Torah uses to describe Noah's entering the famous ark, (Genesis 7:7):

> *And Noah came and his sons and his wife and his son's wives along with him into the ark in the face of the waters of the flood".*

Our sages ask themselves "Why did the Torah have to tell us this extra detail, that they entered the ark "because of the floodwaters"? Wouldn't it have been enough to say that they entered the ark, and that's all? Wouldn't we have understood that the reason he went into the ark was the floodwaters?

The answer that they give is astonishing, (see RaSh"I ad loc.): that by adding these words they are telling us something about Noah. It's telling us that he was counted among the smallest of Emunah, (mi'ketanei emunah), those of little faith. Just what does this mean exactly?

Well if we were to use our "plugin" explanation here what would be the meaning of the words of our sages? The meaning would be that we learn from here that Noah was the smallest of believers without any proof!

Does this explanation make any sense whatsoever?!

Is it possible, according to the Biblical account, to say that Noah believed in G-D without any rhyme or reason? Absolutely not! He SPOKE to G-D! Does it mean that he, as opposed to the "great" believers, (i.e. even flying in the face of fact), didn't act based on his faith? Absolutely NOT! Noah did far more on his faith than most "true believers" ever will! For 120 years he slowly, painstakingly, built the ark with his two hands! Our sages tell us that he did this publicly as well and that during the 120 years of building he was approached, on almost a daily basis, in the following manner:

Here's Noah slaving away, building the ark and someone wanders over to him and asks "So Noah! What are you doing?" and Noah tells him "I'm building an ark." The guy then asks, (giggling and winking at his friends), "What do you need an ark for?" Noah answers "Because G-D is going to bring a flood to the world, and you are going to die in it, and I am going to live because I built this here ark!" At which point the other guy bursts out laughing, "HA! Noah and his ark! You really think that G-D's going to drown us? What an idiot!"

So, NO; Noah – it would seem – had plenty of faith upon which to act.

SO HOW IN THE WORLD COULD OUR SAGES CALL HIM "AMONG THE SMALLEST OF BELIEVERS"?

The answer, (at least the only one that makes sense to me), is that G-D, like a man, is a multifaceted Being and that the measure of our Emunah is based on just how well we know HIM. Noah, despite his obvious piousness and faith, lacked faith in G-D in one area, and that is the aspect of G-D called TRUTH.

What do I mean by this? I mean to say that G-D has many attributes: truth, justice, mercy, and more. We enumerate 13 attributes of G-d that we beseech on the High Holidays, asking for forgiveness and mercy for our iniquities. However, the one characteristic which we experience the most, (usually without paying any attention), is the attribute of MERCY. G-D has mercy on all of the creation. G-D feeds and sustains the entire universe. G-D loves everyone with a love that is beyond human understanding. He also forgives with a forgiveness that is beyond human understanding.

Having said that, it would seem that Noah's mistake was as follows. Noah, who for 120 years worked his hands to the bone building the ark, despite all the ridicule and jeering of his friends and neighbors; who stood fast in the face of his generation, did so while thinking that all he was building... was a prop. Background scenery. It was only a means to "set the stage" so that the people of his generation would "get the picture" and change their evil ways. To Noah, the ark was, essentially, unnecessary. In other words: Noah didn't think that G-D, the merciful, the compassionate, had it in Him to carry out His words when HE told him that He was going to wipe out the world with a flood. Noah thought that G-d just didn't have it in Him.

THAT is a lack of Emunah! It is for this reason that Noah was called "of the smallest of believers" because he failed to understand something fundamental. The TRUTH that is G-D: if He says it – He means it!

So, when the time set for the flood came near, and it started to rain, (our Sages teach us that the rain started one week before the beginning of the flood so that if the people did repent then the rain would have turned into a blessing), Noah said to himself "Wow! G-D knows how to set the stage so that people will think it's real!" On day 7 when the waters started to rise Noah was thinking "Any minute now, they'll repent!" and yet the waters continued to increase! "Wow!" Noah thought, "That's showing them G-D! They'll think you mean business now!" When the waters were up to his knees, Noah began to wonder what the story is! Finally, our Sages explain, the waters got so high and grew so violent that the waters themselves forced Noah to enter the ark and shut the door behind him.

All of the above is what the Torah means when it says that Noah entered the ark "because of the flood waters."

This explanation is in harmony with the definition that we have said up until now. The reason that our Sages call Noah "of the smallest of believers" is because, in a certain very critical area of Emunah, Noah was totally lacking! His trust in G-d, which is what truly needs strengthening in life, was fundamentally lacking, he couldn't imagine G-d, the merciful, actually doing what He said He would do, and therefore he is called "among the smallest of believers."

In summary, we have learned in this chapter:

There is a misconception in the world that Emunah, (loosely translated as "faith"), means to believe in something in spite of the lack of evidence. Which led to:

That the greater the absurdity and lack of proof, the greater the feat of Emunah of the believer. Which resulted in:

Something that has proof is not subject to faith (however, we disputed this).

Emunah does not mean "faith" as is commonly interpreted.

The correct explanation of Emunah is "strength and vitality".

It is not an abstract concept but rather a verb that describes a process.

We strengthen our trust in G-d (=Emunah, to make stronger and more vital) in the following manner. We first take that which we know (the knowledge that G-d exists, (I know! I know! We're getting there! Patience!) and that He commanded that we perform mitzvah x, and what to expect as a result (wait for book 2!)) and we then strengthen it, by living it, thereby strengthening, and making more vital our connection to G-d and His word.

True Emunah, real strength, and vitality, living our lives based on that which we know to be true, is needed to increase our steadfastness in following G-D. It's like exercising a muscle: the more we use it, the stronger it gets!

So, when we speak of Emunah vis-a-vis G-D, as the verse says in Exodus 14:31 "And they had Emunah in HaShem and in Moses, His servant," just what does this mean?

It means the following: If G-D tells us something and it's written in black and white, either handed down in the written Torah or explicitly in the Oral Torah, then I have to strengthen and vitalize my acceptance that everything HE told me is what will transpire exactly. The word "Emunah" and the word Ne'eman (trustworthy) are synonymous. If a person is trustworthy, (ne'eman), then by trusting him and having faith that what he says He will do – He will do, that is Emunah! As we say before the recital of the SHEMA, E-1 Melech Ne'eman, (He is a Trustworthy G-D King). If He says it – I can trust that that is what will be. THAT is Emunah!

Let me give a story to solidify this point:

Fifteen years ago, as of this writing, we were in the midst of getting prepared to accept the Holy Shmitta (Sabbatical) year. The Shmitta year is a year where, in the land of Israel, no crops are grown, and no ground work is done, (plowing, seeding, weeding, etc.) unless the tree/plant, etc. would die without it.

At the time, I was working in an IDF army program, called "Nahal Charedi" (today Netzach Yehudah), and I was supposed to go and be with the men on the program for Shabbos (the Sabbath day); it was the summer already, and the weekly Torah portion was called Bahar, ("on the mountain" of Sinai), where the Torah discusses the Commandment of Shmitta. What else could I do but speak about this particular Mitzvah? So I said to myself, "Self, you need to go talk to your neighbor, Reb Moshe Kahanai, and get a good story about keeping the Mitzvah of Shmitta." So that's what I did! Let me tell you a little bit about my pious neighbor Reb Moshe Kahana: He is one of the larger farmers in the *Nahal Soreq* area of Israel, where I live, and he is a shining example – all year round – as to what an average Jew is supposed to be like. To me, this means that he works very hard for his living and almost all of his free time is spent in the Synagogue learning Torah. If he finishes working at 10 in the morning at 11 am, he is in the synagogue. If he ends at 4, he is there by five. If he ends at 9 or 10 in the evening – he is there until 11 PM at least. THAT's a real Jew[11]! He also is one of the bastions of the Mitzvah of *Shmitta* in our area. He keeps it to the "t"!

---

[11] Let me make clear: When I speak of "a real Jew" I am talking about your average Jew, the ones who feel that they are not on the level of full trust in HaShem to provide them with a livelihood no matter what. This is not, however, intended to say that *anyone* who feels that Torah is his profession and spends as much of his time as possible learning Torah is NOT a real Jew. Just the opposite! I wish that I had that

In any case, so I go up to him, and I see that he is on and off the phone all of the time. I approached him and said "Reb Moshe! How are you? What's going on?" He tells me that he is on the phone now with the Beis Din (Rabbinical Court) of the *Eidah Chareidis* (the Orthodox Community) concerning the wheat that he has in his fields. "Why?" I asked. "Because," he said and proceeded to explain his situation and told me the following story:

The way that things are in Israel is that there is a very particular, very precise planting cycle. Everything planted takes something from the ground and gives something to it in return. The next crop planted takes from the nutrients left by the first and gives new nutrients to be used, in turn, by the crop that will follow. This is how it works year-round. So, based on this system, this year, the year preceding *Shmitta*, was a year in which the farmers in the area all planted wheat from the beginning to mid-winter so that the rains, (which only fall in the winter in Israel), should water them. Otherwise, it is ridiculously expensive to irrigate. What happened was that that year was a drought year, only a small amount of rain fell, and the farmers waited... and waited... and waited! In the end, experts came to the area, dug up the ground and discovered that the wheat had rotted. So, most of the farmers of the area went to their respective insurance companies, opened up their right pocket and said, "Do you see this pocket? Please fill it with money to replace the lost crops!". They then proceeded to the government, opened up their left pocket and said, "Do you see this pocket? It needs to be filled with subsidies so that I can afford to overturn the ground and plant something new!". They then took the money, turned over the soil and planted something new.

Reb Moshe was also approached by both his insurance company and the government and was given the same offer: turn over your grounds,

---

level of Emunah as well! But seeing as my level of faith is not that strong, *and so is that of most people,* therefore I call the average working man who spends as much of his "free" time learning Torah as is available to him "a real Jew". Unfortunately, there are those who *don't have* the level of pure Emunah and spend their days learning *and regret it and are bitter towards HaShem.* We'll have to discuss this at a different time.

plant something new and take some money! Reb Moshe heard them and said, "No, but thank you." When these people heard that, they considered calling the men with white coats and to get a padded room ready! "NO?" they said incredulously, "Why not"? I'm sure they were thinking "Bucks, Dollars, Shequels, Cash" and the names of any other forms of currency. Who, in their right mind, turns down money?

Reb Moshe calmly looked at them, proceeded to open up his Torah to Leviticus chapter 25:3, and read it to them.

> *Six years you shall plant your fields and six years you shall trim your vineyards, and you shall collect their produce. And on the seventh year, it shall be a Sabbatical year for the land, a sabbatical for HaShem, etc.*

The guy looks at him and goes "Yeah? So, what! That's next year! What does that have to do with now?" Reb Moshe looks at him, says "Patience!", and continued to read: (verse 20)

> *And if it shall come that you ask just what will we eat during the seventh year if there is no plowing and gathering of produce?...*

Here he picked up his voice a little bit and said:

> *And I shall command my blessing unto you in the sixth year and it, (the land), shall produce the grain required (to sustain you) for the three years."*

(Years 6, 7 (Shmitta) and 8, until we can grow new food).

"Don't worry," he said, "I'm just waiting to see HaShem's blessing."

When I approached him on that day, I asked him "Do you have a good story about Shmitta for me?" he told me all of the above and said, "From where do you think that I have all of this wheat? It's the grain that everyone said would never grow! And do you know what?" he asked. "According to the survey that was done, it's the finest, fattest wheat that has grown in the past seven years!"

So why was he fretting about the grain in the field? Because he had sold the whole lot for the sake of baking matzos for Pesach. This grain is guarded against water so that it shouldn't become Chometz (leavened). Because the wheat in the fields was so dry already and the summer sky was overcast, as it was about to rain, he was worried maybe he would have to rush and reap it all before the rains came so that it would not get wet from the rain!

That, ladies and gentlemen, is Emunah. When G-D states explicitly, in either the Written or the Oral Torah, a promise or makes a commitment: do I strengthen my connection with HIM, voraciously clinging to HIS words... and do as HE instructs... or not?

There is blind faith in the world... but it's not Jewish Faith; it's not Emunah.

There is another aspect of belief in G-D called BITACHON, and we'll explain what that is, G-D willing, in a later volume, so be patient!

2

The Basis of Faith and Trust

What Do I Really Need to Believe Something?

S WE LEARNED IN THE PREVIOUS CHAPTER real Emunah, true faith and trust, are not baseless things. They begin with a foundation of knowledge that must continually be reassessed and improved. That's what Emunah is all about: living my life based on the clarity of that which I know to be true.

Nevertheless, the question remains: how do I start? What is, or should be, the criteria upon which I base my core knowledge? But even more so, how do I know what I know?

To understand that, we must first understand the following:

Amazingly, we have all the necessary utensils at our disposal to weigh accurately and assess all aspects of life. It's called the human mind. All people on this earth have the G-d given ability to analyze, criticize and speculate almost any matter under the sun. We are all capable. However, we must at the same time recognize our shortcomings in this regard. Many times, despite our ability to make judgement calls, we don't do so for one of two reasons. Either because we choose not to, for whatever the reason might be, or even if we choose to analyze a certain topic we don't know, or have not been taught to recognize what constitutes a good proof and what does not[12]. This chapter assumes that the reader wants to do the work, and therefore, is geared to help define what constitutes real proof.

There are a few limits, prerequisites, and fine-tunings, which must be recognized and scrutinized before we can rely upon the conclusions of our mind. Just what do I mean by this?

Limits of the human mind

First, the mind is limited by its experience.

As we will discuss in future lessons, although we know that space is limited and we are told that it is expanding,, we have absolutely no way of comprehending or describing into WHAT it is expanding. Why is that? Very simple, because it is beyond human experience. Everything that we do know, as of today, is based on the sensory knowledge that we acquired using the five senses of taste, smell, touch, sound, and sight. If we have not experienced it with any of these five things – we know nothing about it in any way. Our human senses are limited by our very limited nature.

Also, even those things that we have experienced are further limited by the extent of the experience that we have had. Having seen, for example, the American Bald Eagle only once – I really can't tell someone else that much about it other than it's got white feathers on its head and neck and a mean stare! How would I be able to understand more about it? By further observation, of course!

The assumption, therefore, is that if I have two people that have observed the American Bald Eagle, one watched him for 1 hour and the other one for 10 hours, then clearly the one who has observed him for

---

[12]   The above is an adaption from the words of Rav Saadia Gaon, in his book *Emunot v'De'ot* in the first chapter.

10 hours is the one with the better understanding of the American Bald Eagle. Correct?

Maybe.

It depends on what is the information that I would like to learn about the Eagle. If I want to know about its behavior – clearly the one who has more hours of observation is more likely to be the one with that knowledge. However, if I want to know more about, say, its feeding habits and the one-hour guy happened to have used his time watching him while he fed, whereas the other guy only saw him feed for 10 minutes then the one-hour guy is the one to go to for that information. Assuming, of course, that the two of them are equally capable.

Which brings us to the next issue, concerning the limitations of the human mind.

It is quite likely, due to human nature, that the guy with the 10 hours of observation, but only 10 minutes of feeding observation, could say to himself "Hey! I know a lot more about the eagle than that guy!" and proceed to produce a detailed conclusion concerning the feeding habits of the eagle based on the other 9 hours and 50 minutes of observational knowledge that he has.

Now in truth, as the student of the aforementioned observational experts of American bald eagles, I am in dire need of this knowledge, so that I know what to feed my pet American bald eagle and how to prepare it for him. Now I need to know: which one of these experts can I trust?

To me, it makes the most sense to say the guy with the full hour of observation! Why? Because in addition to the incredible powers of the mind, is something called "visualization" and "speculation." I "consult" my general knowledge concerning the bald eagle and I improve upon the experience that I have concerning the feeding habits of the eagle using my powers of imagination.

Now imagination is a very remarkable power of the mind! Not all things "imagined" or "imaginary" is necessarily untrue. What it is, is unobserved!

You see the power of imagery in the mind is so great that, essentially, if we have visualized it – it's as if we did it! It is for this reason that the power of visualization is given such praise nowadays, as it is the key to a person's personal success in practically any endeavor. The better a person can visualize him-or-her-self as having already achieved the goal or having overcome that obstacle, the more likely it is that he will make that goal and hurdle that obstacle. Why? Because, even if, in reality, I have only done it in my mind's eye, to my mind, I actually did it.

So too we tend to assume that if I can imagine it – it's true. Many times, that is not the case!

Therefore, a secondary limitation to the human mind is to know how to distinguish between that which is real and that which is imaginary. Sometimes the line between the two is fragile, and we might assume that what we imagined is true, or that something true is only imaginary.

To state it succinctly: You cannot utilize imagination as proof.

The Prerequisite for Knowledge

In three words: "Seek the Truth".

Having said that we have to realize that there are one of two reasons why we don't live up to this ideal: Either because I am not a seeker, or because I am biased, and therefore not objective.

We would all like to assume that we are objective, and the truth is that we are… some of the time. However, most of the time we are running on pre-conceived notions that we have concerning many things under the sun. Much of the time we are not even aware of our biases.

Our sages, ob"m, tell us – based on the Torah's prohibition against a judge taking bribes – that when the Torah says, *"Bribes blind the eyes of the wise and slur the words of the just[13]"* that this is true under all circumstances.

---

[13]   Deuteronomy 16:19

Even if the person receiving the bribe is given it with the understanding that he should rule as he feels is just!

So, the next question that we need to ask ourselves is "am I biased in my judgment? Am I accepting a sort of bribe?"

"Bribe?" you're surely thinking, "From whom, per se, am I receiving a bribe"?

Answer: From your very own self! How? Let's bring a few examples:

There is no-one in the world today who doesn't know that there is a connection between smoking cigarettes and increased likelihood of sickness. (Come on guys! It's even written on the box in big letters!) Despite this fact, there are still many millions of people today who smoke. How can they ignore the facts? Simple! They're biased! They tell themselves "I am the exception to the rule" or "One more won't hurt me" (they then repeat this to themselves as they slowly, but surely, finish the box and the carton).

It has similarly been demonstrated that there is a clear connection between obesity and health as well. Yet despite this, there are many people who can't stick to a diet or exercise regimen. It's not because they didn't come to such a decision. Many times, we have no problem shaking our addiction to food ("I'm not addicted Rabbi" my students tell me about their smart-phones, "why I can quit whenever I want to. In fact, I quit every single day." Hmm. Not addicted?). However, their conviction lasts… until they meet the ice-cream or the chocolate cake. Why? What changed? Their desire for "X" overcomes their logic and therefore, the litany of excuses begins.that

So, too, in the realm of G-d.

We all know that, at the end of the day, the conclusion that there IS a G-d is one that has consequences. Except for the philosopher's creed, also called the Deist philosophy, there wasn't, isn't, and never will be anyone who claims that there IS a G-d… but no consequences. If there is a G-d, He has expectations of you and in not fulfilling those expectations, you can expect to get what's coming to you! If there is no G-d, however, then there are also no "divine" consequences to your actions. Effectively you can do what you want, when you want, to whomever you want without any real or eternal effects. (More on this in the chapter entitled *The Twilight Zone*).

So, the question is: am I willing to accept the consequences of my conclusions concerning the subject at hand? Will I follow through with the consequences resulting from my search for understanding and knowledge? Am I a seeker of the Truth?

If the answer is "Yes," then you are objective. If the answer is "No" then you must understand that you are biased, as you don't want to "give up" on whatever it is that might be affected by possibly believing in a G-d.

Your body and its desires have bribed you[14].

A Little Fine-tuning

Lastly, we have to realize that, many times, part of the difficulty of objectivity is that the definition of our search is not so clear. What do I mean? Let me explain with a parable:

If I were to go somewhere with my son, a friend's house, for example, and I would tell my son on the way "I expect you to be a good boy when we get there" – what should I expect to occur when I get there?

Well, knowing my son, I can expect him to turn over the plants, take apart the furniture and track mud everywhere because – to him – that's what a good boy does! What's the problem? A lack of definition.

When I say "good" what do I mean? If I ask my child "did you have a good time at the party," then they will answer, (if, indeed, they deign to

---

14   In a coaching course that I took while working on my degree in Education, I was taught the following life lesson. One of the first stages of coaching a person is stating the goals and the gains that I would make by their achievement. However, in order to affect a change, the person that is being coached he must also recognize what are the benefits he is getting in his current situation. Once we have these two things the coach then turns to his trainee and says, "Which of these gains do you prefer? Those of the goal or those of your present situation"? Only when I realize that I am willing to give up the "gains" and "benefits" that I have in my present situation in favor of those of the goals is there hope for change and progress.

answer. Darn teenagers!), based on what their definition of "good" is. If that means to them that there was good food, and that they sat together and did something meaningful, then their definition is similar to mine, and I will have correctly understood the various grunts and "hmm"s which comprises a teenager's answers. The problem, therefore, is when we have different understandings as to what "good" means. In which case, although I seem to be using the same words as the child, they would have an entirely different meaning, and I would misconstrue their intent. The same applies to so many things. Think of your relationship with your spouse, for example.

Therefore, when searching for truth, we must have a clear definition as to what we are searching for, for only then can we truly understand if we have found it.

How Deep is Your Love?

In addition to the issue above of objectivity as to our purpose in our search, we also have to be truthful with ourselves concerning the results of our search.

We must be truthful as to the scope of our knowledge: Just how much information do I have at my disposal concerning X? Furthermore, we must be truthful, even in the face of vast and in-depth knowledge, as to how much of that knowledge I actually understand and comprehend. Having information and understanding it, are two different things altogether.

The Definition of Proof

Based on all of the above we can now understand what constitutes evidence. It must be:

- Something specific,

- Based on clear and relevant observational knowledge, (no imagination involved).
- Not injecting a reading or bias into the interpretation of the information so that we can be sure of our objectivity concerning the results of our search.
- We must recognize the real extent of the information at our disposal.
- We also must be truthful as to how much of the information available to us we understand.

However, even when we have all of the above, we still have to ask ourselves the following question:

Does the information point conclusively to said conclusion?

As I like to teach my students, there are two ways to disprove any proof. Either we can show that the person didn't understand the evidence he brought in the first place, OR we can show that there is more than one way of looking at the evidence. As long as the information is not conclusive – it's also not a proof.

There is, however, one exception to the above rule. If I have some facts concerning a topic and in all of them the simplest understanding is X, yet there is room, based on the information to say Y. Eventually, it becomes ridiculous to argue and object that "No! It's Y" when clearly X is the simpler answer. This rule of logical argument is referred to as "Occam's Razor" and it is a fundamental tenet of debate.

Therefore, the answer that:

- Answers the most issues; and
- Does so in the simplest fashion

is also, most assuredly, the correct answer.

(With G-d's help, we will explore this topic more extensively later on in this book).

Clearly, another addendum to the veracity of my information is that of outside verification. Outside verification can be achieved either by consensus if the issue is not one that is clearly observable or the sheer number of people who can testify concerning a historical event.

We will explore this last issue, with G-d's help, in the next volume.

In summary:

The prerequisites for knowledge and proof are that it is:

Based on actual relevant experience.

Not influenced by the imagination.

The observer is not biased/bribed in his reading; and

The observer is willing to live based on the conclusion. This shows that he's searching for the truth.

That the objective of the observation is clearly defined so that there is no room for error and misinterpretation; and

That the information is clear enough so that there is only one possible conclusion.

Now that we understand this, we are now ready to delve into the world of proofs of G-d's existence or lack thereof.

However, before we continue, I would like to make one last statement. I am a fan of the scientific method. However, I am not a fan of it when applied to the creation sciences for the numerous reasons that will be made clear in this book. However, the most basic reason is because all of the criteria discussed above cannot be utilized concerning the creation sciences. For more on this – see the footnote[15].

---

[15] On my blog I have three articles entitled "How to be Jewish, Scientific, and Sane" where I encapsulate my reasoning. For more information look them up at www.rabbibz.com

3

Into the Twilight Zone

What Are the Ramifications of Answering the Question "Is There a G-D" With "No"?

FOR THOSE OF US BORN IN THE 1970'S, like myself, and certainly those born earlier, remember a television show called "The Twilight Zone." The show was of the "horror" genre, and the underlying theme was always the same: Person X thinks he's going to have a regular day. He's wrong. He's going to do/see/experience something today that will change his life (horribly) forever.

The issue is that many times we do, or experience, something without ever considering the consequences such an action has and in so doing... we enter ... the Twilight Zone.

It is my contention that if anyone decides to answer question #1 "Is there a G-d?" with the answer "No" then they are entering the twilight zone. In this chapter, we'll explore why.

<u>Yeah, but what does it DO?</u>

Nowhere is this lack of concern for consequences more evident than when we explore the theory of evolution and its ramifications for humanity. This chapter is not an exploration of the validity of the theory; I reserve that for a different chapter. In this chapter, I will explore how it has affected (i.e. ramifications to) humanity over the past 55 years, since first being taught publicly as "Darwin's" own truth.

So as not to confuse the reader with extraneous details let's sum up the theory of evolution as "survival of the fittest[16]". As far as a significant amount of the scientific community is concerned, G-d did not have a hand in the creation of, and the advancement of, the various species. It is all controlled by the laws of biology, chemistry, and physics and what-have-you. The only thing that matters in the evolution of the species is that the species with the "stronger" genes is the one that survived until today.

Despite the difficulties with the theory, which we will see in a later chapter, for which it will ever remain just that – a theory[17] – the real

---

[16] Despite the fact that this statement is not Darwin's, rather it was penned by Herbert Spencer some 6 years prior to the printing of "The Origin of the Species" by Darwin, it has become clearly connected in the understanding of the theory. If there are any pure Darwinist's out there – deal with it.

[17] This is a jab. I know it. Evolutionists get all in a huff when the issue of "theory" is mentioned and they begin a long tirade about what the power of a theory is ... blah, blah, blah. However, it is, at the end of the day, only a theory and it will forever remain so. Why is this? Very simple: it's impossible to prove it beyond a shadow of a doubt. The problem can be summed up by the short spoof movie "Bambi meets Godzilla", one of my childhood favorites. Assuming Bambi is the mutant, of course. Basically, the movie is about 3 minutes of credits followed by a short animation in which we see Bambi playing when all of a sudden, he is crushed by a giant foot. The film pans out and we see it's Godzilla who has just crushed Bambi. (Then 3 more minutes of credits). Clearly, despite his superior genes he didn't survive. In addition, not all survivors are the fittest, but rather they are the survivors! "Fittest" "Strongest" and any other "est" that belays superiority over something else will always remain an iffy thing. More on this in the chapter entitled "The Emperor's New Clothes".

question is this: if I am a proponent of this theory how does it affect my life? Is it just one of those quirks in the world and therefore meaningless, or does this conclusion have ramifications on how I view and how I live my life?

The answer is clear: of course, it has ramifications! Many of them quite obvious!

To say that life develops from the simple to the advanced means, conversely, that the farther away we are from the point of the "beginning" the more advanced is the new development.

Now, I have always wanted to present an evolutionist with the following: his picture, two chimpanzees, two wildebeests, two lizards, two fish, two amoebas and a pile of slime. Why do you ask? According to his theory, this is his family tree: him, his parents, grandparents, great chimpanzees, great wildebeests, great lizards, great fish, great amoebas and great-great-great slime! What a beautiful family tree! According to his world-view if you call him a monkey's uncle – you are not far from the truth!

Essentially, as the "pinnacle" of advancement in the world, we are all just more capable sacks of slime! Nevertheless, let's say that we accept that. We're good. We can handle existence in the form of advanced slime and live with it. What then?

Well then, we move on to the next issue.

If I posit that there is no Creator, no Commander, to the world – then there are also no commandments. If there are no commandments, there are also no absolutes in the world. No absolute "good" and no absolute "evil", as at the end of the day these are human contrivances.

If that is true, then the next step is to conclude that – honestly – it doesn't matter what I do, to myself or anyone else. There are also no real consequences to my actions as well. But I'm jumping the gun. Let's take this one step at a time.

Just another animal????

One of my teachers, Rabbi Akiva Tatz, told a story of how he was once traveling on an airplane when he overheard the following conversation:

Flight attendant: "Hi. We're serving the meal now. Would you like the chicken?"

Female Passenger: "No. No chicken. I don't eat other animals".

Upon hearing this strange response, Rabbi Tatz asked, "What do you mean you don't eat other animals? Why not? It doesn't seem to bother *them*"!

From where did this life-view come?

In my opinion, there is no doubt that it emanates from the theory of evolution. How so?

Since the theory of "E" posits we are all animals, just that some animals happen to be more advanced than others, in the end, a chicken is just "another animal".

However, this woman, and people like her, take it – incorrectly – one step further. Why do I say this? Well, just ask your local lion if he has any qualms about eating other animals! Ask the fish! Ask most of the animal kingdom if there is any problem whatsoever in eating other animals and they'll tell you – with no hesitation – that there is absolutely no problem whatsoever in eating *you* while you ask this ever so important question!

So why do WE seem to assume that there is such a problem?

It's the right thing to do!

Well, it's because we human beings know intuitively that there is a problem in killing another person. So, if another person is just another animal – then killing and eating a chicken is a moral question. It, therefore, follows that just as much as there is a problem killing a super advanced animal, (i.e. man), so too there is a moral dilemma to kill an animal, (i.e. your barbecue chicken).

It is for this same reason that we have moral qualms concerning the usage of animals in testing ... anything! If it's immoral to use super-advanced slime animals, (i.e. humans), then that selfsame morality should show me that it is just as immoral to do so to mere slime animals, such as bunny rabbits. Especially since bunny rabbits have a fluffy tail. If humans also had a fluffy tail ...

See, that's the thing about morality; you can't have your cake and eat it too. That is, if evolution is true. If there is such a thing as morality and there is no G-d – then it should apply equally to all of "Natures" creatures.

However, this notion is absurd for several reasons:

Consider this: one of the most liberal nations in the world concerning this issue of animal rights is the country of New Zealand[18]. They are so forward thinking on this issue that it was voted on in their parliament as to whether or not humanity's closest cousins, the chimpanzee's, who are only a few genes off in the genome tree, should be awarded rudimentary people's and legal rights[19]! Despite this, even in New Zealand, we do not find that laws have been enacted to deal with the following scenario:

"All rise for the honorable Judge!" "What's today's case, bailiff?" "Today's case is the people against the African lion. Your Honor, I would like to present the court with graphic evidence as to the premeditated murder of the gazelle by the African lion. Murder in the 1st degree!" "What evidence do you have?" "An entire documentary series by the BBC your honor! Here! You see: here's the lion preparing to pounce and... there he goes and ... ooh! You see your Honor! Murder in the 1st degree!" "What does the defense have to say?" "ROAR," says the lion, who is in the middle of finishing off the leg of his defense attorney.

---

[18] http://en.wikipedia.org/wiki/Great_ape_personhood "New Zealand granted basic rights to five great ape species in 1999."

[19] Who knows? Maybe a few chimpanzees in parliament would improve the world's situation! Despite the above even they have not considered giving chimps a driver's licenses!

If morality holds for all animals under the sun then why is no one arraigning the BBC and any other similar television channels, who clearly filmed the whole thing and never once tried to stop an act of 1st-degree murder? Not only that but they're apparently making a bundle from these documentaries. Otherwise, they wouldn't make them in the first place! Isn't this a classic case of accessory to murder[20]?

If morality applies to all animals, then it must be a two-way street! Why DON'T we prosecute the lions for murder and the chimpanzees for stealing bananas from their fellow chimps? Why don't the animal rights activists open up schools for the teaching of etiquette to lions and tigers and bears, oh my!? The answer is clear: there is a different standard to which we hold human beings.

Well, why is that? I think that we humans got things all mixed up during "human evolution" and really, the law of the jungle is the only law that should apply! Why should we hold people to a different standard? Who made the standard and why should it/can it bind me?

For this reason, when Rabbi Tatz heard the woman say that she didn't eat other animals he said, astounded, "Why not? It's what other animals do!" Why not take it a step further? Why not just live like an animal? I mean, when you think about it, they seem to lead a much more stress-free life than we do!

Hungry? No problem! Just pounce on the neighbor's kid, or his schnauzer, and eat them!

Need the bathroom? Don't hold back! Go on the fire hydrant like all of the other animals! Better yet: mark your territory at the same time!

Clothes? Who needs 'em? When was the last time you saw a poodle put on a sweater? Besides, it seems that society urges all people nowadays to walk around without clothes, just like the animals! At least this way there won't be any stigma: you're no different than any other animal!

What do YOU think Mr./s. Reader? What would we do to a person who acts in this fashion?

---

[20] http://en.wikipedia.org/wiki/Accessory_%28legal_term%29

One of two things: either we lock them up in the loony bin, as clearly, they have lost their mind! OR we would put them down, just like a rabid dog!

Why is this? Because no thinking person would ever consider this person as normal! There is something wrong with them. They have lost their mind. They are a threat to society. They belong in a straitjacket inside a rubber room! However, ...

If it were evident to us that this person is 100% sane, if he undertook his actions in a thought-out pre-meditated fashion, then we would have a different name for this person: evil. Then we would consider putting him down just like a rabid dog.

Social Conditioning

However, when looked at in another light – none of the above makes any sense! Who is it that defines someone as "sane" or "insane"? Is there a rulebook definition? If there is – why should it be binding? Is this another case when we say the "majority rules"? If so, then why don't we follow the majority of all animals, in which the consumption of the child or schnauzer of the neighbor is the norm? After all, in the eyes of Darwinism, we are all just different types of animals! Why shouldn't we just chalk it up to "survival of the fittest"?

The answer? Social conditioning, pack mentality and a slew of other "ism's" produced in an attempt to provide a real answer as to why we hold a man to a different standard.

What they all mean is this: really, there is no real reason as to why we persecute this dog-like individual! The only reason is so that we can have a living, breathing, "society" in which I can fool myself into thinking that I am, in some way, actually different and better than the rest of the animals in the world... when, in reality, I am not! The individual should suffer for the delusions of the masses.

However, as we stated earlier if the individual is in the category of "sane" and his/her actions were cold and calculated, based on his/her worldview that man is just another animal then we have a different name for him: evil. What, exactly, is "evil"? Who made up the term? What does it mean and what difference does it make if we give this person the despised title of "evil"?

According to the theory of evolution, the only real ramification is that this person is branded a social pariah. Outside of that, there is nothing. There is no soul to be affected for the better by using "good" (i.e. socially acceptable and "moral" behavior) and no effect to one's detriment based on the acts of "evil". It's all social/societal, and these are only words that have no other weight than social/societal ones.

Therefore, if a person does not care what society thinks of him – they have no weight or function.

If evolution is true then, meaning social/societal pressures aside, (as their only merit is within the constraints of society), none of the above matters. Just the opposite is true! If I buck society, that's when I actually become a free man!

Now we can finally begin to understand how society has arrived where it has today.

Modern man

Now it becomes apparent what has happened to the modern man. It is not just the advent of new technologies that have changed man. It is not only that we have more time for rest and relaxation that has done it to us. It is the injection of a world-view that supposes to explain the possibility of a world and a universe that doesn't have, or need, a Creator.

The minute that this ever-so-important part of life goes out the window – so does life itself[21].

It wasn't until the early to mid-20th century that Darwinism became a real world-view. It was only then that most of the influential societies on the planet accepted it. Among them it took root, and from them, it grew and thrust its tendrils into all parts of society, where it sits and festers to this very day.

When we look at the youth of today: confused, disillusioned, disrespectful and violent, can we blame them for who they have become? They are victims of social and societal conditioning that have led them to this point[22]!

When we teach them that, in reality, the only real rule that is of any value is "survival of the fittest" then all we are teaching them is that if you want to have what passes for a "good" life in this world – then you must be the fittest.

It doesn't matter what area of human experience you are the most fitting in – so long as you are the fittest in something. It also doesn't matter exactly how you become the fittest. At the end of the day, the last one standing is the survivor and therefore, by default, he is the fittest. Moreover, no. It doesn't, and shouldn't, make a difference in the world if he became the survivor by hook or by crook.

If Darwin is right, then the only thing that matters in life is to survive it, no matter what the cost. There is no G-d, no good or bad, no right or wrong. There is only survival… of the "fittest" in the contest, we call "life."

---

[21]   Indeed, the first recorded instance that we know of this is the "famous" "conversation" of Cain and Able recorded in the Genesis 4·8. Except that it is not recorded, as the Torah text only tells us that a conversation takes place that was followed, immediately, by Cain killing Able. The Targum Yonatan *ad loc* fills in the blank by telling us that in order to justify the murder of his brother the first thing that Cain did was to deny the existence of G-d.

[22]   This topic is somewhat explosive as it touches the topic of "free will" and just how much "freedom" we have within it. This topic is beyond the scope of this book. The reader can certainly look it up in the appropriate Jewish sources

Is it any wonder that since this theory went mainstream that the homicide rates tripled between the 1950's and the 1980's[23]?

Is it any wonder that since the corrupting influence of this theory based, as it is, on a simple philosophy[24], and taught as if it were G-d's own truth, found it's way into the minds of our youth that many of the foundation stones of society, such as marriage and family, have been in steady decline[25]?

State Sponsored Darwin And Its Effects

Modern history has shown us conclusively that all of the above is a direct and unavoidable result of the Darwinist theory. Of this, we have two clear examples: Eugenics and Nazism.

Eugenics was the practice of "improving human genetics using selective breeding". As everything stems from genetics and as there are "weaker" and "stronger" traits among the human population, therefore through selective breeding, a "more powerful" being could be created. Essentially, it is the same as breeding thoroughbred horses and "pure-bred" dogs and the like.

This theology led to the formation of two new worldviews, both based on the theory of Darwinism when taken to its full logical conclusion. As we

---

[23] http://www.cdc.gov/mmwr/preview/mmwrhtml/su6004a13.htm?s_cid=su6004a13_w When we take into consideration that evolution was not regularly taught in US public schools until the 1960's (see http://en.wikipedia.org/wiki/Creationism#United_States). More on this later in the chapter. See also appendix I concerning worldwide figures of homicide, suicide, marriage and divorce rates as compared to the rates of religious peoples.

[24] Despite all claims to the contrary by those who espouse the theory, (i.e. that it is only a tenet to explain biological phenomenon and does not espouse a philosophy) you cannot give a reason as the foundation of the theory that is entirely philosophical (as it certainly is not empirical) and deny that it has any philosophical ramifications!

[25] http://www.cato.org/sites/cato.org/files/pubs/pdf/pa364.pdf "There have been worrisome increases in family breakup, abortions, illegitimate births, and teen suicide, for example. Violent crime rates have drifted upward—in the 1920s, 1960s, 1970s, and 1980s, for example... with no immediate sign of long-term improvement"

said before since the theory of evolution states that G-d is not a necessary component in the "creation" of man, therefore, there is neither good nor evil in a person's actions[26]. Once this underpinning was solidly in place the following two extensions of eugenics occurred:

The removal, forcibly or otherwise, of undesirables from within the genome. One way that this was done was by the separation of, and/or the forced sterilization of people who didn't fit the norm of society: the insane, the infirm, those suffering from genetic diseases and the like[27]. This form of eugenics was practiced all around the world, including the United States of America, from the early 1900's up until just after World War 2.

Nazism, as an ideology, was based almost exclusively on Darwin's theories and also on eugenics. The Nazi's took the eugenics ideology even further by removing the weak of society regardless of the strength of their genes. This included the elderly and the infirm, even if their infirmities were the result of fighting on behalf of the Fatherland. They did this in a program called "euthanasia," which means "Good death."[28] Many of the above were the original "test dummies" during the perfection of Zyklon B gas.

Also, they took the ideology one step further in segregating the human race into "strong" races and "weak" races. Based on this ideology the Nazi's were able to carry out their program of genocide, as those who were murdered were not even "human" in the first place. The prime examples of which were the Jews, who in Nazi ideology were no more than ticks and parasites who weakened the world by sucking out its lifeblood[29].

None of this would have been possible if not for the theories of evolution. Up until this point, no one in the Western world would have

---

[26] Our sages, ob"m, refer to this as "There is no judge nor any judgment", meaning there is no cosmic law which I am bound to keep whether I want to or not. The only laws are societal, human laws, which I can choose to disregard when and if I feel like it.

[27] **http://en.wikipedia.org/wiki/Eugenics#History**

[28] http://en.wikipedia.org/wiki/Euthanasia#Nazi_Euthanasia_Program .28Action_T4.29 see also **http://en.wikipedia.org/wiki/Action_T4**

[29] **http://en.wikipedia.org/wiki/Nazism#Racial_theories**

considered doing such reprehensible acts, as all men were made in G-d's image[30]. Granted that didn't stop wars from happening, but those were for ideological reasons (G-d vs. G-d, or vs. oppressors), not because the enemy was not human.

In the aftermath of World War 2, the American army conducted a study to discover what caused so many of its soldier's deaths on the field of battle. The conclusion was that despite the training that the soldiers received, many times the cause of death was that when they got the enemy in their sights... they couldn't bring themselves to pull the trigger! That was another human being that they were going to kill[31]! The average American soldier, pre-brainwashing of Darwinism and "survival of the fittest"[32], held this belief strongly. Many died because of it.

---

[30] Even slavery, that has existed in the world up into nearly the present day, originally was justified in the Judaeo-Christian world as being the outcome of the curse of Ham/C'naan, who was cursed by Noah (Genesis 9:25) that he would be the "slave of slaves". Eventually it underwent an "evolution" to justify the immoral treatment of the slaves themselves, as they were sub-human anyway. The Torah has strict laws concerning slaves and the treatment they are supposed to receive and even considers one who murders a slave as a murderer. This was not, however the position of idol-worshiping cultures, which this book is not – in any way – trying to understand or defend.

[31] **http://www.americanheritage.com/content/secret-soldiers-who-didn%E2%80%99t-shoot**. I also heard this from Glenn Doman of the Institutes for the Achievement of Human Potential in one of his lectures.

[32] My intent in this statement is not ignoring the negative effect of both television and video games, both of which didn't really exist in those days. However, in addition it was the moral teachings of the day that made the difference in the average American as people. Darwinism, on the other hand, has no morals to teach at all. It is as a result of the affluence and publicity that Darwinism received in being taught in the school system that led to the erosion of morality in general. My point being that in the 1950's and the early 1960's there was a concept of a "moral authority" and strong censorship, so much that the violence of the video games of today and the TV programming would never have been allowed due to the moral authority and censorship. My parents have told me that for them an R rated movie was if the lead female actor would kiss the lead male! All of this began to erode on a massive scale since the 1960's... when Darwinism began to be taught publicly in schools. Coincidence? ...I don't think so.

So, we see that when taken to its next logical conclusion the "no G-d" theories of Darwinism and its ilk lead to either the "stronger" races ensuring that it is not in any way affected by the "weaker" ones; or that "survival" be the goal regardless of one's present strength. After all: the survivor is de facto the fittest.

But it doesn't stop there. Oh no!

Monty Python's the Meaning of Life

For those of you who are "in the know", you recognize that this movie is just a bunch of skits which only vaguely touch upon the meaning of life. However, it is important insomuch as it relates to a point that is the ultimate result of the "no G-d" world: lack of meaning.

One of the incredible developments in the latter half of the 20th century was the invention of Logotherapy by Holocaust survivor Viktor Frankl. In his book "Man's Search for Meaning" Frankl explains Logotherapy as follows:

> *Logotherapy is founded upon the belief that it is the striving to find meaning in one's life that is the primary, most powerful motivating and driving force in humans.*

In other words, a man with a purpose, whose actions have meaning, is a man with a reason to live. However, a man without such a purpose is, therefore, a man… without a reason to live.

What does a person without a reason to live, do? Well considering that his options are limited, he can only do one of the following two things. He can either choose to find some meaning… or not.

However, there is an extreme problem with the world based on Darwinian Theory: what thing of real meaning can you find that will give you long-term purpose? Helping others? Although pleasurable – it goes against the survival of the fittest. I mean clearly, this would be a case of the fit equipping those who are not with the means of survival!

In reality, what did the giver gain by his giving if there is no G-d to reward him for his act of kindness? Nothing. He loses. He gave away what he had that makes him better and therefore, fitter to survive!

So that means that the average Darwinian is more likely to be self-centered than other-centered. And that leads to a very crooked road indeed.

It leads to husbands and wives with no real responsibility to one another and no commitment. It leads to parents who are more interested in themselves than in their children. It leads to people without any real sense of community.

In short, it leads to individuals with no sense of purpose in their lives, and that leads to boredom.

Boredom is a state that a human being cannot cope with, (why? Darwin will never be able to answer), he, therefore, seeks out what to do with the time that he has on his hands.

At first, he fills it with whimsical, nonsensical things, such as music, art and theater. With the advent of movies and video games, he moves on to these. But there is only so long that these things can cover one's lack of meaning.

We then move on to the next level: sensory changing. It starts out "innocently" with alcohol; perhaps some "light" drug use, loose sex. But these things only last for a short while. So, he then moves on to the harder drugs and, perhaps, more dangerous activities to give his life some "thrill". But even these things, which at first give a person a lot of pleasure, eventually wear off, and he is left with what he has been avoiding, which now must be dealt with, the glaring emptiness of a meaningless existence.

After having gone through it all and having experienced it all, he then asks himself the ultimate question.

The Ultimate Nothing

If there really is no G-d and there is no reward or punishment for one's actions; and if, as we posited earlier, there is no real meaning, no pot of gold at the end of this rainbow, then why survive at all? If there truly is no purpose to life why, indeed, should I take part in the competition at all?

Why should a person go through the heartache, the sickness and all of the various other "little" things of life, just to have a little bit of "fun" and a smidgen of pleasure? Why not just end it all right now?

It is for this reason that we find that the rates of suicide are rising globally. Let's take a quick look at the Wikipedia article on the epidemiology of suicide:

> *Globally, as of 2008/2009, suicide is the tenth leading cause of death with about 800,000 to one million people dying annually, giving a mortality rate of 11.6 per 100,000 persons per year. Rates of suicide have increased by 60% from the 1960s to 2012, with these increases seen primarily in the developing world. For every suicide that results in death, there are between 10 and 40 attempted suicides.*

What the article is saying is that a grand total of roughly 41,000,000 people annually try to commit suicide!

The correlation between the proliferation of the teachings of Darwinism in the 1960's and the rise in suicide rates should be noted. It should also be pointed out that the real increase is in "the developing world". Meaning the more developed they become – the more likely they are to commit suicide.

As a side-note is an especially scary trend that I have heard about from my students, but that I have not, in fact, succeeded in finding any information about. It is their claim that there is a form of cult-worship, or hero-worship, among teens around those who actually found the courage to commit suicide. I was told by my students about a movie starring Robin Williams called World's Greatest Dad. In this film, Robin plays an unsuccessful English teacher and writer who found his way to fame when his son, who accidentally died, is "framed" as having committed suicide for ideological reasons that were provided by his father (Robin Williams) in a "Suicide note." It then goes on to portray how his son was considered a hero figure for having found the courage to commit suicide.

I ask you, why wouldn't this be the case? Granted adolescents are not prone to do anything for a particular reason or ideology, but if you tell me that, really, life has no meaning and that there is no afterlife to look forward to anyway – then why, indeed, should one live it? If after my 120 years in this world, whether they be full of joy or sorrow, I have nothing to look forward to and – in the cosmic balance of things – it makes no difference if I live or not, then why suffer living? If the fact that I am alive today is due to some cosmic accident, then what does it matter if something happens that cancels out my accidental life?

If I don't matter, and my actions don't matter; if there are no "cosmic scales" in which my actions and I are weighed, why bother?

Therefore, if the answer to question #1 is "No, there is no G-d", then you might as well just end it now. Why go through the heartache and the sorrow? Unless, deep down, you know that there really might be more to life, both the world's continued life and your own?

It is my fervent hope that the information that I will present in the coming chapters will help you to reconsider the question and to come to a different conclusion in which we deal with the ever so important question of the meaning of life in a way that will help you to understand that – yes! – you and your life have meaning in this world.

But let me end this chapter with a story:

It was the 1970's and the great Rabbi and Tzadik (saint) Rabbi Yaakov Kaminetzky ztvk"l[33] was traveling by airplane to the Holy Land of Israel. Due to his advanced age, he was in business class, whereas his family and grandchildren were flying coach. During the flight, both his children and his grandchildren came back and forth constantly to either speak to sabba, ("Grandpa" in English) or to check on him and make sure that he had everything he needed. Sitting next to Rabbi Kaminetzky was the general secretary of the Histadrut in Israel, (a major governmental body), Mr. Yerucham Meshel. Mr. Meshel was watching the scene as it played out on the plane and finally, he could wait no more! He turned to the Rav and said, "Pardon me, Rabbi. I couldn't help but notice the way that your family behaves with you. So full of intent and respect! I have to ask you, Rabbi, why is it that your children treat you with such great respect whereas my kids won't give me the time of day"?

Without hesitation, Rabbi Kaminetzky looked at him sternly and said "It's simple, sir. My entire life I have taught my children that the Torah was given to us by G-d Himself on Sinai. To my children, that means that I am one generation closer to Sinai than they are, and to my grandchildren, I am two generations closer. This is why they respect me. You, however, have taught your children and grandchildren that man comes from a monkey. This means that you are one generation closer to the apes than they are and two generations closer than your grandchildren. They are the more advanced animal, therefore, so why should you, the more primitive monkey, deserve their respect [to which I add "unless the more primitive monkey has a banana]"?

Think about it.

4

Logical and Philosophical

How Human Logic Drives Us to The Understanding
That the Universe Is a Divine Construct

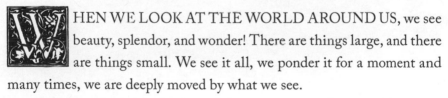HEN WE LOOK AT THE WORLD AROUND US, we see beauty, splendor, and wonder! There are things large, and there are things small. We see it all, we ponder it for a moment and many times, we are deeply moved by what we see.

Then... we look a little closer. We take a piece of the world, we put it under a microscope, and we get a new picture of the world. There is so much going on here that we have yet to comprehend!

The more powerful the equipment developed – the more we find out about the world on levels that we never thought possible.

This leads us to believe that there is an infinite amount of information and an infinite number of pieces yet to be discovered. If we only had the technology to do so. Just that thought, by itself, leads me to understand the greatness of creation!

However, this issue aside, we must stop ourselves a moment and consider the following: Is the conclusion above correct? Is it actually possible to divide anything into an infinite number of parts? Accordingly, it stands to reason that within the space of 12 inches, (30 cm), of dirt there is an infinite number of parts and within the area of a football field, there is an infinite number of parts! So why is it that when we stack the infinite parts of 12 inches of dirt next to the infinite parts of a football field that we find there is a terrible discrepancy in their lengths? Why is the football-field longer if it also is infinite in its components? What would drive me to say that a football field is infinite when clearly it is finite as I can easily measure it?

The answer, of course, is that neither the 12 inches nor the football field is infinite. Neither the one nor the other contains infinite parts. Rather both the football field and the 12 inches can be divided up into an incredibly large number of finite parts. We are just too lazy, or unable, to count that high!

The Finite World Around Us

The entire known universe is finite. There is no such thing as a measurable entity that is not finite. Regardless of the sheer volume of parts, so long as it is evident to us that it has a starting point and an ending point – it's finite, despite the distance or the number of parts between them.

Even the known universe, that scientist's measure today as being 40,000,000,000 light years[33] across, is finite. This is true despite the fact that you, me and all of our friends will never walk, run or in any way traverse it. It's all finite.

---

[33] A "light year" is the amount of space that it would take a beam of light one year to travel. Considering that light travels at 300,000 km (187,500 miles) per second that means its speed times 60 seconds times 60 minutes times 24 hours a day times 365 days in a solar year. In short: it's kind of big.

I realize that this creates a logical conundrum: for if the universe is finite and, as all discernable data points, it is also expanding, into what, exactly, is it expanding? Space? Space is finite!

However, that topic is irrelevant to our issue.

Despite the logical, rational, clear truth of the above, science is only now beginning to consider this conclusion.

The following is an excerpt of an article from New Scientist magazine (August 17, 2013, pg. 32) entitled The Infinity Illusion:

> *INFINITY. It is a concept that defies imagination. ... Just thinking about it can make you queasy.*
>
> *But we cannot avoid it. Mathematics as we know it is riddled with infinities. The number line stretches to eternity and beyond, and is infinitely divisible: ... Whether geometry, trigonometry or calculus, the mathematical manipulations we use to make sense of the world are built on the idea that some things never end.*
>
> *The trouble is, once unleashed these infinities are wild, unruly beasts. They blow up the equations with which physicists attempt to explain nature's fundamentals. ... Worst of all, add infinities to the explosive mixture that made up the infant universe and they prevent us from making any scientific predictions at all.*
>
> *All of which encourages a bold speculation among a few physicists and mathematicians: can we do away with infinity?*

It's a good thing that science is finally catching up with the core principles of logic and observational data. Although not quite mainstream ... it'll get there soon enough!

The Rational World of Cause and Effect

Not only is the world finite, but it also is clearly a world of cause and effect. There is not one thing in any of the universe, known or unknown, which is not bound by that physical law. In Newtonian physics, this is quantified as "to every action, there is an equal and opposite reaction". The Zeroth law of physics, the law of equilibrium, quantifies the very opposite of this law when it states (and I paraphrase) that if there is something upon which no outside forces are acting – nothing will ever happen to it.

Everything in existence has a cause.

Children are born from parents, who were born from parents and so on. Water is the result of the bonding of chemicals that are released from various sources that emanate from different other sources and so on and so on. The solar system is the result of the countless forces in the universe acting and reacting. Despite the fact that we may not (ever) be able to actually comprehend them – that's the fact, Jack!

Cause and Effect in A Finite Universe

When we consider these two axioms together, what comes out is this: there must have been a First Cause that itself had no cause.

For if the universe is, indeed, finite. And:

If the universe is the result of cause and effect. THEREFORE:

It must be that there is a First Cause that itself has no cause. There is no such thing as an infinite chain of cause and effect, just as there is no infinite time or infinite space[34].

Based on the above premise, and as we will see when we revisit the topic of the infinite in later chapters, we can, therefore, reject outright the

---

[34]   For more on this topic see the chapter entitled "In the Beginning" about the first four days of Genesis.

postulation of some philosophers that dismiss this logical proof. They do so by asking why is the First Cause unique that it does not require any causes[35]?

Honestly, we are not bothered by this skepticism, as there is a plain and straightforward answer to it. The reason is because the First Cause IS infinite; it is not limited to the finite physical world and its foibles, it doesn't need any outside force to make it do something, it's not bound by time or space, and therefore it also has no cause.

Will the Real First Cause Please Step Forward?

So, the real question that everyone is pondering is this: What, exactly, IS the First Cause? Is it chaos, or is it Intelligence?

This is one of the difficulties raised against the "cosmological argument".

> *Even if one accepts the cosmological argument as a proof of a First Cause, an objection against the theist implication of the proposition is that it does not necessarily identify that First Cause with God[36].*

This is true, as I stated in the foreword of the book, that if all I have to my name were scientific and philosophical data and knowledge, it would tell me nothing about who or what the First Cause is. However, having stated that there is at least one deduction that we can make.

---

[35] **http://en.wikipedia.org/wiki/Cosmological_argument#Objections_and_ counterarguments.** In the first of the objections "What caused the first cause" is the product of skepticism for the sake of being a skeptic. Logically, since we have found no cases of "infinite" in all of existence that means that all of the physical world must be finite. If it's finite it has a beginning and therefore a cause which itself has no cause.

[36] Ibid. Question no. 2 "Identity of a first cause".

As we will see in later chapters,[37] the known universe and all realms of human knowledge seem to point to one thing unanimously: the universe is orderly and screams that it is made with intelligence.

In truth, there is no known arena of human endeavor in which randomness and chaos play a role!

For example: if a person were to throw the dice and roll double sixes consistently there could only be one of two possible reasons that explain this occurrence. Either the dice are fixed, (the more likely reason); or they are somehow consistently reproducing all of the factors involved in rolling the double sixes the first time. The speed, the spin, the angles, the sides, the air factors, such as humidity and wind speed, and all other related factors, if they realign and are consistently reproduced, they will also have the exact same results. It is because of the extreme unlikeliness that these factors will come together again to produce the same results that dice games are referred to as "games of chance".

Furthermore, the entire scientific method is based on this principle, that the result will be the same if all of the pertaining factors are. Only something that is observable, repeatable and measurable is considered scientific fact. Otherwise – it's either an interesting idea or a piece of fiction, labeled either "hypothesis" or "theory" for the foreseeable future.

Even things as "chaotic" as the waves in the ocean or sand dunes are subject to the laws of physics and chemistry and are, therefore, not random. Not understood, maybe. But not random.

In fact, outside of claims based on sheer ignorance, some of which we will explore in later chapters; there are no proven instances of randomness at all in the universe. Please be patient, as we will get to it!

Ergo: The First Cause was not random, It was/is Intelligent.

---

[37]　See, for example, the lesson entitled "World of Care and Wonders".

Rabbi Akiva and Turnus Rufus

The Midrash[38] tells a story of one of the many arguments between Rabbi Akiva (RA) and Turnus Rufus (TR), the Roman ruler of Israel of his day, as follows:

TR says to RA "Prove to me that G-d created the world." RA says, "Come back tomorrow and I'll do so[39]." TR comes back the next day, and RA says to him "What is that that you are wearing"? "A garment," responded TR. "Where did it come from?" asked RA. "A tailor," replied TR. "Prove it to me," said RA. "Prove it to you?" said TR, "Clearly it could only have been made by a tailor"!

To which RA responded, "Just as the garment testifies to the tailor – so, too, the creation testifies concerning the Creator"!

In later chapters, we will explore the enormity of the order that is inherent in nature and see how it testifies to the unfathomable intelligence of the Creator. The enormous amounts of energy needed to sustain the universe are incalculable, which attests to the limitless (i.e. infinite) power of the Creator.

Ergo: the universe is the result of the Will and Intelligence of the First Cause, the Creator of the universe. He who we call "G-d".

The Model Universe

I remember as a child that there was many a time that I had purchased a model, say a plane or the like, and after a while, I got bored with it, and it just stayed around.

---

[38] *Otzar haMidrashim, Midrash Temura* pg. 583. In some editions it is just a "non-believer" (*kofer* in Hebrew)

[39] Yes, even great Rabbi's don't always have all of the answers at their fingertips.

There is a philosophical postulation in a similar vein. It states that even if one chooses to accept God as the First Cause, one could argue that God's continued interaction with the Universe is not required[40].

This was the philosopher's creed for hundreds of years[41], and it is even more ridiculous today than it was in their time! Today we know that there is no such thing as a perpetual motion machine[42] [43]. Yes, indeed all good things must end! Yet despite that this is a well-known phenomenon apparently, philosophy still has not caught up with this fact! If there were not a constant influx of energy into this great ball of wax – the universe would have come to a grinding halt forever ago[44]! Furthermore, as we will explore in detail in the rest of this book and in those to follow, there is plenty of evidence as to G-d's interaction with the universe.

In Summary:

Because we live in a finite universe, and because the entire known universe is the effect of some cause, therefore, there must have been a First

---

[40] http://en.wikipedia.org/wiki/Cosmological_argument#Objections_and_counterarguments

[41] See the *Kuzari*, written by Rabbi Yehuda HaLevi (c. 1075 – 1141) who was a Spanish Jewish physician, poet and philosopher. In the first part, first chapter he describes in great detail the philosopher's position on existence.

[42] **http://en.wikipedia.org/wiki/Perpetual_motion. Perpetual motion** describes motion that continues indefinitely without any external source of energy. This is impossible in practice because of friction and other sources of energy loss. Furthermore, the term is often used in a stronger sense to describe a perpetual motion machine of the first kind, a "hypothetical machine which, once activated, would continue to function and produce work" indefinitely with no input of energy. There is a scientific consensus that perpetual motion is impossible, as it would violate the first or second law of thermodynamics.

[43] The funny thing is that Richard Dawkins brought up this point in his book "*The Greatest Show on Earth*" and yet didn't fully understand the full implications of what he was saying when he did so!

[44] G-d willing we will explore this issue more fully in the chapter "In the Beginning…"

Cause. He/It constitutes the only infinity in all of the existence. The Cause that itself doesn't have a cause.

The First Cause was, and is infinitely powerful and intelligent, as we deduced by our exploration of the world. Therefore, the First Cause was G-d.

As far as what logic and philosophy can teach us about G-d – we'll touch upon that in a later chapter.

5

World of Care and Wonders

An Exploration of The Complexity and Interdependence of The World's Life and Eco-Systems.

How great are Your actions, HaShem (i.e. G-d), You made them all with wisdom, the land (i.e. the world) is full of your acquisitions (the works of Your hands).
Psalms 104:24

HEN ONE TAKES A CLOSE LOOK at the world around us, I mean a really good look, one can't help but notice the great splendor inherent in the world. It's a beautiful world, full of wonders and majesty and most of us stand in awe in the face of its beauty.

But beyond the world's beauty, and in many ways one of the foundations upon which that beauty and majesty lie, stands the incredible co-operation and interdependence of the world's various pieces. They work hand-in-hand to make the splendor happen. Every thinking person in the world today recognizes this fact regardless of his or her upbringing and/or personal philosophy. The question, therefore, is not whether there is tremendous cooperation and interdependence among the systems of the biosphere, but rather how did this come to be?

Modern science of the evolutionary persuasion would have us believe that this all happened by "accident", the result of life rushing to fill in the "vacuums" created via the mechanism of evolution. However, upon close inspection, this claim falls away like the dust that it is.

Indeed, the degree to which the world's ecosystems not only help one another but, rather, REQUIRE one another is so great that even some scientists believe that the Earth itself is a living entity. This has been given the title "the Gaia Hypotheses"[45].

> The concept that the biosphere is itself a living organism, either actually or metaphorically is known as "the Gaia hypothesis". James Lovelock, an atmospheric scientist from the United Kingdom, proposed the Gaia hypothesis to explain how biotic (meaning biological organisms) and abiotic (meaning non-biological, such as water, air, etc.) factors interact in the biosphere. This hypothesis considers Earth itself a kind of living organism. Its atmosphere, geosphere, and hydrosphere are cooperating systems that yield a biosphere full of life. ... Ecosystems occur when communities and their physical environment work together as a system. The ... biosphere is the term we use [that encompasses] everything in general terms.

---

[45] http://en.wikipedia.org/wiki/Biosphere

To understand why Dr. Lovelock found no other explanation to understand our world, that the only frame of reference he had was abiological entity, we have to understand the extent to which the world's systems rely on one another! Therefore, let's take a look at the systems listed above, the atmosphere, the geosphere, and the hydrosphere, to understand just how complex the world's systems really are.

The Atmosphere

The atmosphere of Earth is a layer of gasses surrounding our planet that is held in place by Earth's gravity. The atmosphere protects life on Earth by absorbing solar ultraviolet radiation, warming the surface through heat retention (greenhouse effect), and reducing temperature extremes between day and night (the diurnal temperature variations).

In general, air pressure and density decrease in the atmosphere as height increases (i.e. the entire atmosphere is made of the same chemicals, the layers differ only in the compound density).

However, the temperature has a more complex profile with altitude, and may remain relatively constant or even increase with height in some regions.... [Based on the temperature-pressure profile] ... Earth's atmosphere can be divided into five primary layers. From highest to lowest, these layers are[46]:

Exosphere (outer layer, very thin composition from 10,000km down to 700km above the Earth's surface), Thermosphere (between 700 km to 85 km), Mesosphere (between 85km to about 50km), Stratosphere (50km to 20km) and Troposphere (20km to 0). (See illustration)

One of the first things to consider concerning the atmosphere is the issue of its density. Consider this: What would happen if the composition of atmospheric gasses were more or less dense? What would be the result be?

What would happen if the Earth's atmosphere was 50 times denser than it is? ... an atmosphere [that dense] would have to differ from ours in many factors ... it would always be cloudy (like the atmosphere of Venus is), so you'd never see the sky[47].

The density of the Troposphere, the level of atmosphere in which we live, is fine-tuned so as to allow for gasses of just the right density and properties to mix into a breathable mist (i.e. breathable oxygen). Also, due to the nature of the mixture of gasses at this

46   http://en.wikipedia.org/wiki/Earth's_atmosphere
47   http://www.physicsforums.com/showthread.php?t=535011

level, the temperature at ground level starts high (17 degrees Celsius on the average) and slowly cools off towards the "ceiling" of the Troposphere.

At higher altitudes, the properties of the gasses change just slightly, to become part of the protective system of the planet. If from ground level up until the top of the troposphere, the temperature starts out high and slowly drops, once we hit the next higher level, the stratosphere, temperatures begin to rise due to the ultra-violet absorption capacity of this layer (the ozone, O_3). This means that the stratosphere is a layer of insulation for the world! This change in temperature and density creates a "barrier" that actually locks the breathable atmosphere near the planet while at the same time allowing for mixing and re-mixing of the gasses via temperature change. (As hot air rises, slowly cooling at the top of the Troposphere, and then drops again, only to repeat the process once re-heated). Furthermore:

Atmospheric circulation, which takes place within the Troposphere, is the large-scale movement of air, and the means, (together with the smaller ocean circulation), by which thermal energy is distributed on the surface of the Earth[48].

In the next level of the atmosphere, the Mesosphere, the consistency of the atmospheric gasses is still significant enough to form another layer of protection (via friction) in which meteorites burn.

> *Millions of meteors enter the atmosphere, an average of 40 tons per year. Within the mesosphere, most of them melt or vaporize as a result of collisions with... gas particles[49].*

Here, however, the properties of the atmospheric gasses change their composition and no longer retain heat, making this layer of the atmosphere the coldest on earth with temperatures reaching -100 degrees Celsius (-150 degrees Fahrenheit). It is in this cold temperature at the highest level of the Mesosphere where the next layer of protection for the planet is created: the reflective atmosphere. It is in this layer that the most harmful radiative

---

48   http://en.wikipedia.org/wiki/Atmospheric_circulation
49   http://en.wikipedia.org/wiki/Mesosphere

spectrum of the sun's rays is blocked from the world while simultaneously allowing the harmless spectrum (i.e. visible light) to pass through almost entirely unhindered. As mentioned before, much of the rest of the radiation is absorbed in the stratosphere's ozone.

Due to the reflective nature of the Mesosphere, and to the negligible density of the Thermosphere the Earth has a second layer of insulation. The Thermosphere takes its name from the extreme temperatures that it contains, estimated as rising up to around 1500 degrees Celsius (2700 degrees Fahrenheit). The intense heat is the result of the double exposure from the sun, as here the sun's rays radiating towards the Earth are combined with those rays reflected off the Mesosphere. Due to the sparseness of the atmosphere's composition at this height, there is almost no mixture of air at this level, which is why it retains an almost constant temperature throughout.

The outer layer is the Exosphere in which the temperature once again drops due to the scattering of the radiative light of the sun and the sparseness of the last vestiges of the atmosphere.

So, in a nutshell: Without the Troposphere, there would be no breathable gasses and no dispersion of thermal energy via circulation. Without the Stratosphere, which locks in the relatively warm air of the Troposphere, allowing for air circulation, the gasses would escape into the higher layers of the atmosphere and from there into space leaving a dead planet and/ or a burnt one, due to the dangerous UV radiation from the sun that it blocks. However, the Stratosphere wouldn't exist if not for the Mesosphere,

whose job is to reflect most of the sun's radiative light, allowing in only the visible light spectrum, and protecting the planet from various projectiles (meteors). Yet only together with the lower Stratosphere does the Mesosphere achieve its reflective properties. Because of

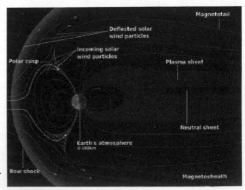

the reflection of the Mesosphere, the Thermosphere is created, which creates a further level of insulation for the planet from the absolute cold of space.

However, all of this would be useless if not for the existence of the MAGNETOSPHERE. The magnetosphere is the field of magnetic force that the Earth "naturally" generates which protects it from the SOLAR WINDS of the sun. Without the magnetosphere, the solar winds would blow away most of if not all of, the ozone, and – most likely – all of the breathable atmospheres from the Earth leaving behind nothing but a dead planet.

Atmospheric Composition

Now that we understand what the parts of the atmosphere are, and how they interact, now it is time to ask the next fundamental question. Where did the atmosphere come from? What is required to make an atmosphere, and how precise of a mixture does it need to be?

I mean, obviously, life on the planet cannot survive without an atmosphere. However, which came first? The atmosphere or the gasses that created it? The magnetosphere or the atmosphere?

Just where does the atmosphere come from[50]?

Scientists tell us as follows:

> *Air is mainly composed of nitrogen, oxygen, and argon, which together constitute the major gasses of the atmosphere. The remaining gasses are often referred to as "trace gasses", among which are the greenhouse gasses such as water vapor, carbon dioxide, methane, nitrous oxide, and ozone[51].*

---

[50] This issue will be explored more fully in the chapter entitled *"In the Beginning"*.

[51] **http://en.wikipedia.org/wiki/Earths_atmosphere**

That's all good and well, but it still begs the question: where does the atmosphere get the chemicals that make it up?

The truth is that despite all of the ink spilled in attempted estimation, this remains one of the (very many) great mysteries in science today. From where DID the atmosphere really come from? Let's see why:

Oxygen, But Not Just Any Oxygen, O_2

By mass, oxygen is the third-most abundant element in the universe, after hydrogen and helium and the most abundant element by mass in the Earth's crust, making up almost half of the crust's mass[52].

Good! Amazing! Got lots of that O stuff! Wonderful! ... Or is it? Does that answer the question?

No.

This is because pure Oxygen (O) isn't usable for atmospheric purposes! Due to the volatile nature of Oxygen, it must be mixed and diluted so that the air doesn't catch fire every time someone lights a match[53].

OK! So pure O is bad. Only a double atom, O_2, (atmospheric oxygen) will do! How do we get that? Well, that's a source of argument:

Elemental O_2 only began to accumulate in the atmosphere after the evolutionary appearance of these organisms, roughly

---

[52]   http://en.wikipedia.org/wiki/Oxygen.

[53]   http://en.wikipedia.org/wiki/Oxygen. Free oxygen (O) is too chemically reactive to appear on Earth without the photosynthetic action of living organisms, which use the energy of sunlight to produce elemental oxygen (O_2) from water. Meaning that the plants take the O molecule from H_2O (water) and combine 2 of them together to make O_2? Nope! Photosynthesis uses the CO_2, during which it breaks off the C(arbon) molecule for its own use and then releases the O_2 into the atmosphere as a "waste product" (so called as the plant has no need for it). It is amazing though that land-based life does need it... maybe it's not so wasteful after all?

2.5 billion years ago[54]. In the process of photosynthesis, phytoplankton releases oxygen into the water. Half of the world's oxygen is produced via phytoplankton photosynthesis. The other half is produced via photosynthesis on land by trees, shrubs, grasses, and other plants[55].

What this means is that vegetation, whether land-based or water-based, is the primary source of elemental, or atmospheric, oxygen production. Yet plants, to produce oxygen, requires a steady source of CO_2, carbon dioxide, to allow for the process of photosynthesis. Say what????? Yes, you heard correctly. Plants don't make O_2; they just release it into the atmosphere.

Now granted that the main ingredient of existence, carbon, (the C of CO_2), according to all opinions, is to be found "naturally[56]" as it is the backbone of all carbon bonds. However, for there to be CO_2, which the plant-life, via photosynthesis, break into carbon and O_2, (2 molecules of Oxygen), we first have to have a source of O_2! So, we have to ask ourselves: since, clearly, we were not around at the beginning of the world exhaling and providing the CO_2, which was then broken down via photosynthesis – then where did it come from?

Also, there is another problem: plants cannot exist without liquid water, which means that it is impossible that plant life preceded the existence of water on the planet! If you don't have the foundation to sustain plant life, then it's impossible for plant-life to exist! Or, to put it bluntly: no H_2O – no vegetation! No vegetation – no atmospheric oxygen!

---

54   http://en.wikipedia.org/wiki/Oxygen

55   http://news.nationalgeographic.com/news/2004/06/0607_040607_phytoplankton. html. This, of course, totally ignores the issue that we mention in the later chapter entitled *"Abraham and A-biogenisis"* that oxygen and early life have tremendous difficulties *living* together, as both water and oxygen tend to destabilize chemical bonds.

56   http://en.wikipedia.org/wiki/Carbon#Formation_in_stars take a look there and we find that despite it's being the 4th most common element in existence it's not so simple to say that it "just happens". Apparently, it requires the heart of a sun to make it!

In my search, I found only one person who gave a real answer as to the question of the source of the world's oxygen:

Despite the common belief that vegetation is responsible for the presence of oxygen in the atmosphere, this is not stoichiometrically (or logically) sound. There is simply not enough reduced carbon in the vegetation on the planet to balance out the vast amount of oxygen in the air[57]. Put simply, the life cycle of plants is a part of the carbon cycle, but they are really dependent upon the atmosphere rather than the other way around. Burning off (oxidizing) all the plant life on earth would use up only a small fraction of all the oxygen in the atmosphere – less than 1%.

Chemistry must balance out its elements that is what "stoichiometry" is. Trees cannot 'create' oxygen because matter is never created or destroyed, it merely changes form. When a tree absorbs CO_2, it uses the carbon to build its structure and such, releasing the oxygen back into the air, but it does not 'create' it.

The vast ocean of oxygen in our atmosphere is a direct result of the fact that we have vast oceans of water. Water vapor is abundant in the atmosphere (where, incidentally, it is by far the most relevant greenhouse gas), and when it rises to the upper levels it is dissociated by high energy UV light into H_2 and O_2 gasses. The hydrogen gas is extremely light, and much of it boils into space, leaving the stable O_2 behind to enrich the atmosphere.

---

[57] What this means is that pound for pound the Carbon absorbed by the vegetation into the plants cannot account for the sheer volume of O_2 in the atmosphere. This is contrary to the more popular stipulation that at today's rates of photosynthesis (which are much greater than those in the land-plant-free Precambrian), modern atmospheric O_2 levels could be produced in around 2,000 years. (http://en.wikipedia.org/wiki/Great_Oxygenation_Event)

Which leads us to the question: if the Earth's water is constantly boiling away then over hundreds and thousands of years why isn't Earth a waterless planet?

> *Yet, it appears that there is no net loss of water from the earth due to the constant bombardment from micro-comets. (What a miracle!) These bodies are generally the size of houses, and the earth is peppered with tens of thousands of them daily. When they strike the atmosphere, they shatter into water vapor, adding water, and oxygen, to the ecosystem.*
>
> *All life on earth is totally dependent upon the atmosphere, and it is dependent upon the supply of water on earth[58].*

In effect, this says that it is the existence of liquid water, its processes, and the hydrosphere, which contribute to the free oxygen that makes up the Earth's atmosphere. This can explain to us how we get O_2, but it still begs the question: since the vegetation cannot account for the existing volume of oxygen.

For all this is wonderful when you HAVE an atmosphere, however, if there is no atmosphere, does that mean that instead of rising to the stratosphere the UV rays are absorbed directly by the water thereby producing O_2 without first changing to its gaseous form? OR, do the UV rays boil away the water existent on the planet, leaving behind a barren rock? Let's explore – potentially – what that would do:

> *With regard to plants, UV-B impairs photosynthesis in many species. Overexposure to UV-B reduces the size, productivity, and quality in many of the crop plant species that have been studied (among them, many varieties of rice, soybeans, winter wheat, cotton, and corn). Similarly, overexposure to UV-B*

---

[58]   http://www.strangequestions.com/question/208/Where-does-Earths-oxygen-come-from.html

impairs the productivity of phytoplankton in aquatic ecosystems. UV-B increases plants' susceptibility to disease. Scientists have found it affects enzyme reactions that conduct fundamental biological functions, it impairs cellular division in developing sea urchin eggs, and it changes the movements and orientation of tiny organisms as they move through ocean waters. Since some species are more vulnerable to UV-B than others, an increase in UV-B exposure has the potential to cause a shift in species composition and diversity in various ecosystems. Because UV-B affects organisms that move nutrients and energy through the biosphere, we can expect changes in their activities to alter biogeochemical cycles. For example, reducing populations of phytoplankton would significantly impact the world's carbon cycle, because phytoplankton store huge amounts of carbon in the ocean[59].

In short: the more exposure to UV rays – the less likely the earth is to produce anything life-sustaining!

Now, remember: the above was researched under modern conditions, and despite all the UV protection that the atmosphere gives us the amounts of UV penetration due to a reduction of ozone in certain areas has clearly affected the viability of oxygen production by phytoplankton. How much more so if there were no atmospheric UV protection whatsoever?! Well, just what would happen if we were missing, say, only the ozone layer?

The ozone protects us from deadly types of UV that we would normally be protected against. This kind damages your skin and deeper tissue's DNA causing various types of cancer. Basically, we'd all die of cancer.

Well, not "die of cancer", but we'd burn to death. The Earth and all of its inhabitants would burn because the Sun's powerful

---

[59] http://earthobservatory.nasa.gov/Features/UVB/uvb_radiation2.php

UV rays would come at us and we'd have no protection. Cancer
happens now while we still have 80 – 95% protection from the
sun's UV rays because of the ozone layer. Without the ozone
layer, the rays would literally fry us[60].

Getting back to the question above: can this process of freeing O2 occur in water exposed to direct UV? Maybe. But then again, in all likelihood it would not! Even though photo-disassociation, (the process discussed above, through which H2 and O are separated), occurs under modern conditions, we must remember that we are looking at a "controlled" picture, as seen through the eyes of our multi-level atmosphere. Were it not for the atmosphere, we would not only be exposed to UV radiation (of unprecedented measures) but other radiative spectrums as well.

So far, all we have looked at is the O_2 of the atmosphere, but what about the most abundant chemical, Nitrogen?

Nitrogen, But Not Just Any Nitrogen, N_2

Nitrogen is a common element in the universe, estimated at
about seventh in total abundance in our galaxy and the Solar
System. It is synthesized by fusion of carbon and hydrogen
in supernovae. Due to the volatility of elemental nitrogen[61]
and its common compounds with hydrogen and oxygen[62],
nitrogen is far less common on the rocky planets of the inner
Solar System, and it is a relatively rare element on Earth as
a whole. However, as on Earth, nitrogen and its compounds

---

[60] **http://wiki.answers.com/Q/What_would_happen_if_the_Ozone_layer_was_destroyed**

[61] According to all of the sources that I have seen "Elemental Nitrogen" is just plain old "N".

[62] Hydrogen-Nitrogen= Ammonia or N_2O (laughing gas), Hydrogen-Oxygen=water.

occur commonly as gasses in the atmospheres of planets and moons that have atmospheres[63].

This means that pure nitrogen (N) is basically non-existent on our planet, (Thank G-d!), which is a good thing because if it were it would cause the world to explode!!!! Luckily, the major concentration of nitrogen on earth exists in its gaseous form in the atmosphere as N_2, which is relatively non-reactive, odorless and colorless. It also allows perfectly for a transparent atmosphere.

But is there a reason for this? Is nitrogen really a necessary component of the atmosphere? At first glance, it would seem that it is not!

The air is 78% nitrogen and 21% oxygen, plus a few trace gasses, but there would be nothing wrong in breathing a helium/oxygen mix (other than having squeaky voices). As long as there is at least about 5% oxygen, and if the other major component is not poisonous and/or flammable, we humans would be OK[64].

According to the above, it would seem that there are other possible mixes of gasses, which would make a breathable atmosphere. As long as they contain within them the right concentration of oxygen. In fact, many other types of gasses are used by divers to facilitate diving that does not contain nitrogen! For example, Helium, Neon, and Hydrogen are also perfectly acceptable when mixed with oxygen in a diver's tank[65]!

However, it's a good thing that we don't have an atmosphere made of Helium because, although breathable – due to its ability to conduct heat – we would be in serious trouble from the heat of the sun[66]! Neon, in large amounts, although considered less toxic than nitrogen in diving, is also

---

[63] http://en.wikipedia.org/wiki/Nitrogen

[64] http://www.newton.dep.anl.gov/askasci/gen06/gen06753.htm

[65] http://en.wikipedia.org/wiki/Breathing_gas

[66] This aside from its small atomic weight, which causes it to drift off into space!

considerably more volatile. It is for this reason that it is thought to be so scarce on almost all planetary bodies[67]. The same goes for Hydrogen[68]. It's a good thing that hydrogen "happens" to make covalent bonds very easily, (i.e. it quickly bonds with many other atoms), as otherwise, we would really be in trouble here on earth!

SO, although other chemicals might have done the trick, thank G-d the one we have just "happened" be the best! But that's not all for nitrogen! Wait until we get to the nitrogen cycle later in this chapter!

How Much Room is There for Play?

So now we have a fantastic atmosphere with "just the right" chemical makeup to support life, utilizing the major compounds oxygen and nitrogen (with a few others). Is that all there is to say about the atmosphere? Of course not! Just mixing Nitrogen, Oxygen, and Argon doesn't necessarily make for a breathable life-sustaining atmosphere[69]!

If there is too much oxygen in the air, it can cause burning and damage to the tissues of the lungs, and we would still die - quite slowly and painfully[70]. If there were too much nitrogen in the air, we would all

---

[67] http://en.wikipedia.org/wiki/Neon. The reason for neon's relative scarcity on Earth and the inner (terrestrial) planets, is that neon forms no compounds to fix it to solids, and is highly volatile, therefore escaping from the planetesimals under the warmth of the newly-ignited Sun in the early Solar System. Even the atmosphere of Jupiter is somewhat depleted of neon, presumably for this reason.

[68] At standard temperature and pressure, hydrogen is a colorless, odorless, tasteless, non-toxic, nonmetallic, highly combustible diatomic gas with the molecular formula H2. ... Hydrogen gas (dihydrogen or molecular hydrogen) is highly flammable and will burn in air at a very wide range of concentrations between 4% and 75% by volume http://en.wikipedia.org/wiki/Hydrogen

[69] http://en.wikipedia.org/wiki/Breathing_gas#Helium

[70] http://www.osha.gov/SLTC/etools/shipyard/shiprepair/confinedspace/ oxygendeficient.html states the following: *Oxygen-deficient atmospheres are the leading cause of confined space fatalities in the shipyard. While normal atmosphere contains between 20.8 and 21 percent oxygen, OSHA defines as oxygen deficient any atmosphere that contains*

asphyxiate from lack of oxygen! The same would happen if there were too much argon around due to argon's toxicity[71].

So clearly, it's not just that we "have" these chemicals floating around in the air. Something must continually be controlling things to prevent the levels from being unbalanced! The amounts of chemicals in the air must constantly remain "just so"!

Not only that but, as we mentioned earlier, there is also a lot of CO_2 in the air as well, produced from various sources and considered to be one of the primary reasons for global warming today!

A mixture of Oxygen and carbon dioxide would be poisonous. If there is too much carbon dioxide in the mix, it blocks our ability to absorb oxygen and we would lose consciousness quite quickly[72].

So there also must be some form of control over the amounts of CO_2 in the air. Otherwise, we would not be around to ponder it! (Wait for it in the water cycle (hydrosphere)).

---

less than 19.5 percent oxygen, and as oxygen enriched, any atmosphere that contains more than 22 percent. Oxygen-deficient atmospheres may be created when oxygen is displaced by inerting gases, such as carbon dioxide, nitrogen, argon, or the ship's inert gas system or firefighting system. Oxygen can also be consumed by rusting metal, ripening fruits, drying paint, or coatings, combustion, or bacterial activities. Oxygen-enriched atmospheres ... present a significant fire and explosion risk.

[71]   http://archive.rubicon-foundation.org/xmlui/handle/123456789/2768,   http://zidbits.com/2012/11/can-we-breathe-other-gasses-mixed-with-oxygen/   http://en.wikipedia.org/wiki/Breathing_gas#Argon

[72]   There are so many living creatures all breathing out CO_2, there is decomposition of living matter and many other sources of CO_2 being released into the air all the time and mixing with the oxygen. Why is the ratio of oxygen to CO_2 still so low? Why are we not all dying of asphyxiation? Well, for two reasons: 1> because the waters of the ocean trap CO_2; and 2> because the Earths vegetation is constantly "eating" the CO_2 and releasing it as O_2. More on this shortly. Amazing, isn't it?

In Summary of the Atmosphere

To sum up the issue of the atmosphere: The atmosphere is an integral part of the biosphere in that it protects the planet from temperature extremes, disperses and absorbs harmful radiation, provides a breathable gas within life-sustaining parameters and is instrumental in the dispersion of thermal energy

Therefore, it turns out that atomic/elemental oxygen, O_2, one of the cornerstones of the atmospheric gasses, can't exist without the atmosphere. Yet the atmosphere cannot exist without VEGETATION, and vegetation can't exist without WATER, (whose chemical formula, H_2O, uses a single Oxygen molecule).

In summary: it would seem that both organic life and water would have a genuinely troubled existence if not for the presence of the atmosphere according to modern scientific methods[73].

Which brings us to the next issue:

---

[73] G-d willing we will explore this issue more in the lesson entitled "In the Beginning", an exploration of creation as laid out plainly in the Holy Torah.

Water and the Water Cycle

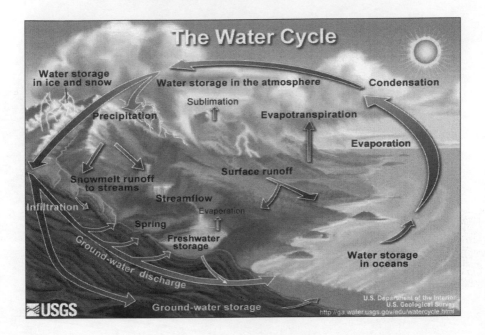

I have always been fascinated with the stuff! You can drink it, wash in it or with it, throw it at friends inside of balloons. It's really impressive stuff! One of the things that always struck me though is that water's chemical makeup, H_2O, in many ways parallels its Hebrew name מים, the word (pronounced "*My-Eem*") is made up of 2 letter Mem's and 1 Yud. The word also parallels the chemical makeup of the molecule where we have the two hydrogen atoms connected to a central oxygen molecule. Coincidence? I don't think so.

> *Liquid water, necessary for all known life, is not known to*
> *exist in equilibrium on any other planet's surface. At present,*
> *the other planets in the Solar System are either too hot or too*
> *cold to support liquid water on the surface in vapor-liquid*
> *equilibrium. As of 2007, water vapor (the gaseous form of*

water) has been detected in the atmosphere of only one extra-solar planet, and it is a gas giant[74].

There are many reasons why water vapor, and/or liquid water, are not found on other planets. To name a few[75]:

Liquid water cannot exist in either extreme heat (turns to gas) or extreme cold (freezes solid). Therefore, the following conditions must be met to allow for the existence of liquid water:

The planet's orbit must be not too close (=too hot), yet not too far (=too cold), from the central star (i.e. the sun).

The planet's orbital path must be elliptical, not circular, to allow for slight temperature variance (summer-winter).

The planet must rotate on its axis. Otherwise, it would be locked in orbit around the sun with one side locked facing the sun (burning hot) and the other permanently facing the darkness of space (freezing cold).

The planet must have a single moon to help both create said planetary rotation and to regulate tides.

The earth's rotational axis must be at an angle relative to the sun, again, to allow for temperature variance.

The planet must have a protective atmosphere, to prevent collisions with asteroids and meteorites flying through space.

Also, the existence of other planetary bodies (Jupiter being a major contributor in this regard) in the relative "flight path" of the planet also protects our planet from large traveling space-debris.

As mentioned earlier the conditions on the said planet must also be conducive for the proper combination of hydrogen and oxygen to become H_2O (water).

The atmosphere of said planet must contain greenhouse gasses, but only a limited amount, so as not to trap too much heat in the air. That would increase the ambient temperature of the planet (which would then

---

[74] http://en.wikipedia.org/wiki/Earth

[75] See Hawking's book *"The Grand Design"* chapter 7 for a nice list of things in the galaxy that are "Just Right".

boil away the water, further increasing the amounts of greenhouse gasses in the air)! Yet there also cannot be too little greenhouse gasses, which would allow too much of the heat to escape into space.

Amazingly, despite all of the above required conditions, we have, thank G-d, lots of the stuff on our planet!

Water, a Vital Resource

Water covers 70.9% of the Earth's surface and is vital for all known forms of life. … Water on Earth moves continually through a cycle of evaporation or transpiration (evapotranspiration), precipitation, and runoff, usually reaching the sea. evaporation and transpiration contribute to the precipitation (i.e. snow, rain, and dew) over land.

If it were not for this ever-so-important cycle, there would be almost no available water on land as all rivers and streams are fed using precipitation. Without rain, there would be no vegetation or life on the land.

Yet despite the water cycle, during which much of the liquid water is evaporated and then broken down into H_2 and O, the world's water supply remains a constant and the salinity levels, (the levels of salt in water in the water), of both fresh and sea waters, remains at roughly constant levels (3.4%). This is clearly to our benefit, as most life cannot live at levels of 5% or more[76]!

---

[76] http://en.wikipedia.org/wiki/Gaia_hypothesis/Regulation_of_the_salinity_in_the_oceans. This issue is also a clear refutation of one of the many means of "measuring time" based on the ocean's salinity levels. Since life cannot abide salinity of more than 5% this means that this level has roughly been maintained throughout history. It is estimated that the rivers and streams flowing from the United States alone discharge 225 million tons of dissolved solids and 513 million tons of suspended sediment annually to the ocean. Throughout the world, rivers carry an estimated four billion tons of dissolved salts to the ocean annually. (**http://oceanservice.noaa.gov/facts/riversnotsalty.html**) if it is true that the earth is billions of years old then – clearly

As stated previously the reason for this is that meteorites, whose main composition is frozen water, are constantly bombarding the Earth[77]. Because these meteorites break-up upon entry into the atmosphere, (more specifically the Mesosphere, as noted earlier), they enter earth in the form of water vapor which is then quickly dispersed via the water cycle mentioned above.

Also, it is via the hydrosphere's processes that the excess hydrogen is released. Once the water (H_2O) evaporates, it goes up into the upper atmosphere where it is broken into H_2 and O, as mentioned previously. It's good that this happens there as most of the excess Hydrogen then floats off into space. Were it to stay in the earth's atmosphere we would be in trouble, as we mentioned earlier!

However, after having said that, we realize that if there were no atmosphere (Mesosphere) in which thue meteorites were destroyed then, instead of falling to earth harmlessly, they would impact on the planet, each of them with the force of several megaton bombs! If we consider that there are millions of meteorites entering the atmosphere per year, in all likelihood instead of helping to sustain the equilibrium of water on the planet, they would probably do more to destroy it, despite their watery composition!

In addition to initiating the evaporation cycle above water does so many more things for the ecosystems of our planet!

Water is a good solvent and is referred to as "the universal solvent" ...[78]. Water is called the "universal solvent" because it dissolves more substances than any other liquid. This means that wherever water goes, either through the ground or through our bodies, it takes along valuable chemicals, minerals, and nutrients.

– there should be nothing alive in the oceans today as the salinity levels should have exceeded the threshold of life a long time ago! Somehow, it hasn't!

[77] Isn't *that* a miracle! Just what The Doctor ordered!

[78] http://en.wikipedia.org/wiki/Water. See http://www.hbci.com/~wenonah/hydro/h2o.htm for many interesting facts about water. See also http://ga.water.usgs.gov/edu/waterproperties.html.

However, not only does water "take along" useful chemicals and the like – but it also leaves behind many valuable chemicals and minerals as well. This is one of the main reasons that it is possible for us to grow new crops year after year. If not for the ability of water to replenish the sources of plant growth in the soil – no new plants would ever grow!

Also, the properties of water, this ever-so-important substance, are unlike those of any other elements in existence!

Pure water has a neutral pH of seven, which is neither acidic nor basic. Which is why it is used in the base functions of all life on the planet. If it were acidic, it would negatively affect the processes of all life. If it were a base, it would halt vital chemical processes. But that's not all!

Water is unique in that it is the only natural substance that is found in all three states -- liquid, solid (ice), and gas (steam) -- at the temperatures normally found on Earth. Earth's water is constantly interacting, changing, and in movement.

Water freezes at 32° Fahrenheit (F) and boils at 212° F (at sea level, but 186.4° at 14,000 feet). In fact, water's freezing and boiling points are the baselines with which temperature is measured: 0 degrees on the Celsius scale is water's freezing point, and 100 degrees is water's boiling point.

Water is unusual in that the solid form, ice, is less dense than the liquid form, which is why ice floats. When you think about it, this fact about the unique properties of water is one of the most important ones! For if water were, in this regard, like all other substances, whose solid form was denser than its liquid form, then during the cold seasons much of life would die from hypothermia! If ice sank, instead of floating, then what would happen is that all of the lakes and bodies of water would freeze into solid blocks of ice. If they turned into ice then not only would all life in the waters freeze to death but also all life on the ground, which requires water to survive, would die, as they would have no access to liquid water.

But that's not all! For once a body of water has "frozen over", a lake, for example, the ice not only doesn't drop to the bottom but remains on the top where it now provides a layer of insulation to trap the heat of the lower layers of water. This insulation allows for a livable "atmosphere" for the inhabitants of the waters.

Water has a high specific heat index. This means that water can absorb a lot of heat before it begins to get hot. This is why water is valuable to industries and in your car's radiator as a coolant. The high specific heat index of water also helps regulate the rate at which air changes temperature, which is why the temperature change between seasons is gradual rather than sudden, especially near the oceans.

Water has a very high surface tension. In other words, water is sticky and elastic and tends to clump together in drops rather than spread out in a thin film. Surface tension is responsible for the capillary action, which allows water (and its dissolved substances) to move through the roots of plants and through the tiny blood vessels in our bodies.

So, this magical compound is "just right" and provides for all of our life needs. If this ever-so-important substance didn't have all of the unique properties that it does – life would not exist!

Even that's not all! There are so many amazing things to talk about when it comes to water that it boggles the mind!

However, water is another one of those (great many) scientific mysteries. The most fundamental question concerning water being: where did it come from? I mean if the early earth was – basically – a fireball, then it had no water in its early stages! So where did the water come from? (For more on this see the lesson "In the Beginning").

But we have it, so why worry? Well, one reason to worry is that really, we should not have any water in the first place[79]! Another reason is due to the "Faint Young Sun Paradox":

The "Faint Young Sun Paradox" describes the apparent contradiction between observations of liquid water early in

---

[79] WATER'S life-giving properties exist on a knife-edge. It turns out that life, as we know it relies on a fortuitous, but incredibly delicate, balance of quantum forces. http://www.newscientist.com/article/mg21228354.900-waters-quantum-weirdness-makes-life-possible.html

the Earth's history and the astrophysical expectation that the Sun's output would be only 70% as intense during that epoch as it is during the modern epoch. Astronomers Carl Sagan and George Mullen called attention to this issue in 1972. ... In the then current environmental conditions, this solar output would have been insufficient to maintain a liquid ocean[80].

So really, the science of the evolutionary persuasion is kind of looking for some (Divine) help to try and "explain away" the amazing "coincidence" and "just right"-ness of the known universe when it comes to the earth and the universe as we know and understand it!

Co-dependency of the Water Cycle

How is the water cycle dependent upon the other cycles? Well, when we take into account that without an atmosphere, (as we discussed above at length), there is no real hydrosphere, and in all likelihood no water to speak

---

[80] http://en.wikipedia.org/wiki/Faint_young_Sun_paradox. This means that a sun with 30% less heat output would not be hot enough to prevent the oceans from freezing over, whereas all the known data shows emphatically that earth has always had a liquid ocean. "There has been no dearth of theories, however. Over the last 40 years, climate scientists have offered a range of explanations — everything from high concentrations of insulating greenhouse gases in the atmosphere to changes in Earth's proximity to the sun. Some ideas are more plausible than others, but even the most probable hypotheses present roadblocks for scientists". http://www.sciencenews.org/view/feature/id/349771/description/Faint_Young_Sun. For an update of all of the thinking on the topic – look there. See also http://www.sciencedaily.com/releases/2010/03/100331141415.htm the article entitled "Why Earth Wasn't One Big Ball of Ice 4 Billion Years Ago When Sun's Radiation Was Weaker" and leads with the words "Scientists have solved one of the great mysteries of our geological past". The funny thing was that on the same page was a link to an article from 2012 (http://www.sciencedaily.com/releases/2012/05/120530152034.html) whose title is "Why Earth Is Not an Ice Ball: *Possible Explanation* for Faint Young Sun Paradox"! What happened to "problem solved?

of due to the amounts of UV, so apparently the hydrosphere depends upon the atmosphere. As we will see, the nitrogen and carbon cycles, both rely on the hydrosphere and the atmosphere for them to work and to provide the groundwork for all life.

Considering that Carbon is the building block of all organic life, it makes sense for us to start our next look at the interdependence of life from its cycle.

The Carbon Cycle

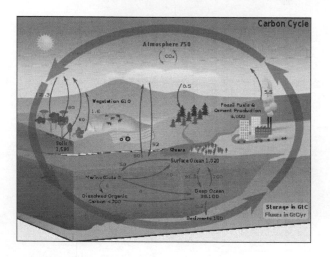

The carbon cycle is the biogeochemical cycle by which carbon is exchanged among the biosphere, pedosphere, geosphere, hydrosphere, and atmosphere of the Earth. It is one of the most important cycles of the earth and allows for carbon to be recycled and reused throughout the biosphere and all of its organisms. ...

Carbon exists in the Earth's atmosphere primarily as the gas carbon dioxide (CO_2). Although it is a small percentage of the atmosphere (approximately 0.04% on a molar basis), it plays a vital role in supporting life. ... Trees and other green plants *such as grass convert carbon dioxide into carbohydrates during photosynthesis, releasing oxygen in the process[81].*

As we mentioned previously in the process of photosynthesis, the Carbon of CO_2 is removed from the gas O_2 to be used by the plant for itself. This releases the "useless" O_2 into the air where it goes on to make an atmosphere.

[There is a] ... correlation between the carbon cycle and formation of organic compounds. In plants, carbon dioxide [via] carbon fixation[82] can join with water in photosynthesis (green) to form organic compounds, which can be used and further converted by both plants and animals[83].

This means that the plants then use the C, in combination with water (H_2O) to create carbohydrates (= Carbon + Hydrate (Latin for water)).

After the plants use the carbon to make the organic molecules creatures in the biosphere, then eat them. There they are employed in biological processes only to be expelled back into the atmosphere during respiration (breathing out that good old CO_2)!

However, excess CO_2 in the air, as stated earlier, is a no-no. It just won't do. So, if the production of CO_2 exceeds the intake of the vegetation – then what happens? Well, one of two things: either we all die from lack of breathable oxygen or we die from excess heat trapped by greenhouse gasses, or... it gets absorbed into the oceans (i.e. the hydrosphere) where it is taken care of.

Carbon dioxide dissolves readily in water. Once there, it may precipitate (separate from the water) as a solid rock known as calcium carbonate (limestone). Corals and algae encourage

---

[81] **http://en.wikipedia.org/wiki/Carbon_cycle**

[82] A fancy name for the production of organic compounds via photosynthesis.

[83] http://en.wikipedia.org/wiki/Carbon#Organic_compounds

this reaction and build up limestone reefs in the process. ...
"Chemistry"[84] regulates this dance between ocean, land, and
atmosphere. If carbon dioxide rises in the atmosphere because
of an increase in volcanic activity, for example, temperatures
rise, leading to more rain, which dissolves more rock, creating
more ions that will eventually deposit more carbon on the ocean
floor[85].

What this tells us is that there just happens to be a non-thinking, non-programmed, accidental something-or-other that we will call "chemistry" (the great and powerful god – Chemistry!!!!!) which is regulating the amounts of CO_2 in the air throughout history at levels that just happen to be those which all organic life need to survive. Wow! Quite the coincidence, isn't it?

So, the carbon cycle is connected to the atmosphere, the atmosphere is connected to the biosphere; the biosphere is connected to the hydrosphere, which in turn is connected to the... atmosphere!

The Nitrogen Cycle

Nitrogen is essential for many processes and is crucial for any
life on Earth. It is a component of all amino acids... and is
present in the bases that make up nucleic acids, such as RNA
and DNA. In plants... nitrogen is used in chlorophyll molecules,
which are essential for photosynthesis and further growth[86].

---

[84]   The quotation marks are my own addition.

[85]   See http://earthobservatory.nasa.gov/Features/CarbonCycle/page2.php for a full account of how this happens.

[86]   http://en.wikipedia.org/wiki/Nitrogen_cycle#Ecological_function

Clearly, then, Nitrogen is a very necessary factor to have at our disposal. It's a good thing that we have loads of the stuff in the atmosphere, isn't it? Well... no. In its present state, it's not really helpful at all!

> *Although Earth's atmosphere is an abundant source of nitrogen, most of it is relatively unusable by plants. Chemical processing, or natural fixation (through processes such as bacterial conversion—see rhizome), are necessary to convert gaseous nitrogen into forms usable by living organisms, which makes nitrogen a crucial component of food production. The abundance or scarcity of this "fixed" form of nitrogen, (also known as reactive nitrogen), dictates how much food can be grown on a piece of land. The nitrogen cycle and the carbon cycle work together to maintain an ecosystem. (ibid)*

Let's explain the above: N_2, the form of nitrogen available in the atmosphere, is almost entirely unusable for any sort of life. However, if there was an abundance of regular nitrogen in the atmosphere, our goose would be cooked! Or, rather, there would never have been a goose to cook in the first place!

Therefore, what can we do to ensure that we have a "we"? Well, nothing really. It's a "good thing" that there "just happens to be" a chain of bacteria that take the N_2 from the air and does something with it to make it usable for life!

> *The nitrogen cycle is the process by which nitrogen is converted between its various chemical forms. ... Nitrogen is present in the environment in a wide variety of chemical forms including organic nitrogen (N as in aNimal feces), ammonium (NH_4+), nitrite (NO_2-), nitrate (NO_3-), nitrous oxide (N_2O), nitric oxide (NO) or inorganic nitrogen gas (N_2). ... The processes of the nitrogen cycle transform nitrogen from one form to another. Many of those processes are carried out by microbes, either in*

their effort to harvest energy or to accumulate nitrogen in a form needed for their growth. (ibid)

There are, however, two types of cycles that go on, both of which are crucial for all life. They are the land-based nitrogen cycle and the oceanic nitrogen cycle. Let's quickly describe how these two cycles work.

The Land-Based Nitrogen Cycle

Basically, there are 2 ways for nitrogen to enter the soil: either using nitrogen fixation (for the atmospheric nitrogen, N_2)[87] or by means of being directly absorbed into the ground from "fixed" nitrogen found in, for example, "cow pies".

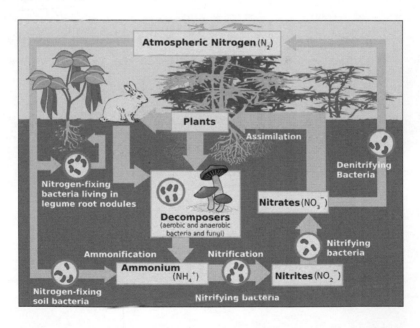

---

[87] Atmospheric nitrogen must be processed, or "fixed" (see page on nitrogen fixation), to be used by plants. Some fixation occurs in lightning strikes, but free-living or symbiotic bacteria do most fixation. http://en.wikipedia.org/wiki/Nitrogen_cycle#Nitrogen_fixation

Once the nitrogen enters the soil, that's when the real fun begins!

Why is that? Well because that is when the nitrogen "just happens" to be converted into its other forms using ammonification, nitrification, assimilation and finally denitrification.

What AMMONIFICATION means is that the unusable atmospheric nitrogen (N_2) and organic nitrogen (feces) are changed, mostly using bacteria in the soil, into ammonium. Ammonium is a primary source of nitrogen for many plant species, especially those growing on hypoxic (oxygen-deficient) soils. However, it is also toxic (=poisonous) for most crop species and is rarely applied as a sole nitrogen source[88].

Lucky for us, there is ANOTHER type of bacteria that is prevalent in the soil that takes the ammonium and, via NITRIFICATION, converts it into nitrates. Which is good. I mean magnificent. I mean ESPECIALLY SUPER GOOD. Why is this?

It's because plants use nitrates to make proteins, or they make 'amino acids', which are then used to make the proteins. They are the building blocks of all the plant material and enzymes. In other words, no nitrates – no plants!

However, there is a bit of a problem! If the soil and the plants are regularly robbing the atmosphere of its N_2, (atmospheric nitrogen), then – how is it that we are still breathing? I mean, as we stated earlier if the volume of oxygen were to become much greater than the 20% it is now then it would be disastrous! Yet despite the absorption of N_2 into the soil and plants – the atmosphere has always remained with the same oxygen-nitrogen volumes! How is that?

That is due to the following two things:

The final stage of the ground-based nitrogen cycle DENITRIFICATION. And:

The oceanic nitrogen cycles!

What is Denitrification, you ask?

---

[88]   http://en.wikipedia.org/wiki/Ammonium

> *Denitrification is a microbially facilitated process of nitrate reduction that may ultimately produce molecular nitrogen (N_2) through a series of intermediate gaseous nitrogen oxide products*[89].

So there "just happens to be" another stage of specific microbes that "come to the rescue" by reconverting the nitrites and nitrates produced during nitrification back into atmospheric nitrogen (N_2).

WHEW!!!!! If it weren't for all of the "accidents" that "just happened" we wouldn't have an atmosphere to breathe!

What about the oceanic nitrogen cycle? Let's now look at that.

The Oceanic Nitrogen Cycle:

Nitrogen enters the water either through precipitation, runoff or as N_2 from the atmosphere. In its present form, it is unusable, and mostly toxic, to all marine life.

Luckily there is something called cyanobacteria in the water which performs the job of NITROGEN FIXATION that we mentioned earlier, (i.e. the conversion of the atmospheric nitrogen (N_2) into a more usable source of nitrogen). Cyanobacteria are able to fix nitrogen gas into ammonia (NH_3), nitrites (NO_2) or nitrates (NO_3) which are then absorbed by plants and converted into proteins and nucleic acids[90].

When you think about it, the cyanobacterium is a miracle! Without the cyanobacteria to convert the N_2 of the atmosphere into fixed nitrogen, the fixed nitrogen (extant in the water) would get used up in about 2000 years[91]. Why? Because it is needed by the life forms in the ocean to build them!

---

[89]   http://en.wikipedia.org/wiki/Denitrification

[90]   http://en.wikipedia.org/wiki/Cyanobacteria#Nitrogen_fixation

[91]   http://en.wikipedia.org/wiki/Nitrogen_cycle#Marine_nitrogen_cycle

Once in this form the other wonders of the sea, (phytoplankton[92], for example), can start their work of producing oxygen via photosynthesis and building themselves and their numbers using the fixed nitrogen from the cyanobacteria. Now the process of AMMONIFICATION can commence as Ammonia and urea are released into the water by excretion from plankton.

> *Nitrogen sources are removed from the euphotic zone (the area of water that in which sunlight reaches fully) by the downward movement of the phytoplankton. ... This can occur in a number of ways. ... The sinking [of nitrogen] results in ammonia being introduced at lower depths below the sunlit zone. Ammonification or Mineralization is performed by bacteria to convert the ammonia to ammonium.*
>
> *At this point NITRIFICATION can occur, as the bacteria prevalent below the sunlit zone are able to convert ammonia and ammonium to nitrite and nitrate[93]...*
>
> *... Nitrate can be returned to the euphotic zone by vertical mixing and upwelling, where it can be taken up by phytoplankton to continue the cycle.*

N_2 is then returned to the atmosphere through Denitrification[94] (that final reconversion of the nitrites and nitrates back into N_2 using those

---

92   Phytoplankton are photosynthesizing microscopic organisms that inhabit the upper sunlit layer of almost all oceans and bodies of fresh water. They are agents for "primary production," the creation of organic compounds from carbon dioxide dissolved in the water, a process that sustains the aquatic food web. http://en.wikipedia.org/wiki/Phytoplankton

93   As they are inhibited by light from doing so in the euphotic zone

94   http://en.wikipedia.org/wiki/Nitrogen_cycle#Marine_nitrogen_cycle Shellfish seem to play an important role in the process of denitrification in the oceans http://en.wikipedia.org/wiki/Nutrient_cycling#Ecosystem_engineers

specialized bacteria). Once again providing the atmosphere with that much need N_2 stuff that is so necessary for our survival.

NEXT, ... the phytoplankton is eaten by different oceanic life, proliferating life in the oceans!

Wow! Just think about it! IF there were no nitrogen cycle – there would be no micro and macronutrients for the phytoplankton. If there were no phytoplankton, there would be no oxygen to create an atmosphere. If there were no atmosphere, then – in all likelihood – there wouldn't be any liquid water. Yet without liquid water, there can be no... Phytoplankton! (And without the phytoplankton, the very basic staple of much of aquatic life, most marine life would not exist as well).

It's enough to make your head spin (round and round, and round...).

Plate Tectonics

It is a well-known fact today that the world isn't flat. Hate to be the one to break that news to you, if you didn't already know by now.

Not only is the world round but it is a vibrant, dynamic, constantly changing place. One of the reasons for that is the issue of plate tectonics. The earth's crust isn't airtight or anything like that. Just the opposite! It's comprised of many "plates" that are constantly on the move! In fact, it is due to the movin' and the shakin' of the plates that we have mountains and valleys, earthquakes, tsunamis and many, many other things.

In fact, we are told that at one point in time, there was only one major landmass[95]. Scientists refer to this landmass as "Pangea," and it was because of the forces of plate tectonics that the continents drifted apart until we have the seven landmasses that we find today.

---

[95] This is an issue that is addressed in both the written and oral Torah's, which I discuss at length in the lesson entitled *"In the Beginning"*.

In this chapter, I don't want to discuss the history and the assumptions made as to how plate tectonics work[96], rather I would like to focus on the effects of tectonics for all life on the planet.

Although tectonics is responsible for the destructive forces that accompany volcanic activity, earthquakes, and tsunamis, it is also responsible for many positive side effects as well:

> *Volcanic ash, although problematic for many things, has a positive side effect in that it lowers global temperatures. This is because the sulfur dioxide (SO_2) in the cloud created by the eruption combines with the water that is in the air to form droplets of sulfuric acid. The sulfuric acid then proceeds to block some of the sunlight from reaching the Earth and thereby cooling global temperatures[97].*

Also, the volcanic soils formed from the breakdown and weathering of the volcanic rocks are among the most fertile in the world. They are necessary to provide new minerals and other vital ingredients for productive vegetation growth.

Tectonic plate movement also facilitates this, as the older strata are destroyed and recycled via subduction and new strata are created out of the earth's molten magma to replace the part that was "dragged" by the subduction.

Ore deposits, such as gold, silver, bronze and others, fuel deposits such as natural gas and oil, and many other such deposits found in the earth all are available because of tectonic movement and the heat and pressure created thereby.

In short, the action of plate tectonics is vital for the existence of vegetation and life on earth. Still, that's not all!

---

[96] I do that on my blog at www.rabbibz.com in an article entitled "*Noah, Tectonics and Continental Drift*"

[97] http://pubs.usgs.gov/gip/dynamic/tectonics.html

There is still a great debate as to what it is that makes tectonics work? Is it the sheer weight of the slabs that causes their subduction? Is it the boiling of the molten core that moves the plates? Or is it the water that exists in the earth's core that makes it happen? Think about it: to the best of our knowledge Earth is the only planet that has both liquid water and plate tectonics – is it coincidence... or are the two connected?

Ecosystem Engineers

Although everything that G-d made is wonderful, it is the Jewish Torah's outlook that there are still certain aspects of the creation that He left to be perfected by others. The Midrash[98] relates that although the wheat that G-d makes is great, He left room for a man to take that base ingredient and make it into something better: bread. The same thing is true in many of the earth sciences but nowhere quite as spectacularly as when it comes to the ecosystem's engineers!

What, you ask, is an ecosystems engineer? I'm glad you asked that question! Let's take a look at one: the minuscule earthworm!

---

[98]   Midrash Tanchuma, Parashas Tazria, 8

At first glance, we ask ourselves: How can this tiny, little creature, with no brain or any real limbs, have ANY importance whatsoever in this world? The answer might astound you!

> *Earthworms travel underground by the means of waves of muscular contractions, which alternately shorten and lengthen the body. The shortened part is anchored to the surrounding soil by tiny claw-like bristles (setae) set along its segmented length. ... The whole burrowing process is aided by the secretion of lubricating mucus. ... They also work as biological "pistons" forcing air through the tunnels as they move. Thus, earthworm activity aerates and mixes the soil, and is conducive to mineralization of nutrients and uptake of them by vegetation. Certain species of earthworm come to the surface and graze on the higher concentrations of organic matter present there, mixing it with the mineral soil. Because a high level of organic matter mixing is associated with soil fertility, an abundance of earthworms is generally considered beneficial by the organic gardener. In fact, as long ago as 1881 Charles Darwin wrote: "It may be doubted whether there are many other animals which have played so important a part in the history of the world, as have these lowly organized creatures."[99]*

What the above means is as follows:

Worms aid in the mixing of the topsoil with other various ingredients, such as rotting vegetation and animal feces. This makes the topsoil very fertile and is called "hummus" in the scientific jargon.

In addition, they also bring vegetation and other substances deeper into the ground via their burrows. There these materials are digested and deposited as casts, (i.e. worm feces). These casts are of even greater biological significance as they are even more nutrient-rich than the aforementioned hummus.

---

[99] http://en.wikipedia.org/wiki/Earthworm#Locomotion_and_importance_to_soil

Their burrowing acts to aerate and soften the ground. This allows for better water perforation, for better plant root penetration and the expulsion of ground gasses that would otherwise be unproductive.

Perhaps you think that all this sounds like fiction, I mean, just HOW MANY worms might there possibly be? The answer: a lot more than you think!

Recent research estimates that even in a land that is not very arid there are as many as 250,000 per square acre. In more fertile land it is estimated that there are as many as 1,750,000 per square acre[100]. In other words: the more worms – the more fertile the ground is!

The more fertile the ground is the more vegetation.

The more vegetation, the more oxygen, and the more grazing animals.

The more grazing animals, the more "food" there is for the worms and the more worms... and the process goes around and around again!

---

[100] http://en.wikipedia.org/wiki/Earthworm#Benefits

<u>Cross-Pollination</u>

(a.k.a. Biotic Pollination)

Another fantastic example of the complex interactions of this world is that of cross-pollination. This refers to the simple fact that most of the world's vegetation (about 90%[101]) cannot reproduce without help from an outside – biotic (i.e. some lifeform) – source. This is because the plants are divided into male and female plants and in most instances, the males and the females do not reside next to one another.

So how do the male spores find the female ones to facilitate reproduction? They hop a ride on the backs of a creature who brings the one to the other[102]! The most well-known instance of this phenomenon is that of bees and flowers, but that is far from being the only one. Insects, bats, mice and many other animals are also involved in spreading the pollen all over the place as well!

---

[101]   http://en.wikipedia.org/wiki/Pollination#Abiotic
[102]   http://en.wikipedia.org/wiki/Pollination#Biotic

This process, therefore, is vital to the existence of almost all plant life. It is so essential that there is an entire sector of agriculture, pollination management, whose sole purpose is to compute and provide for the pollination needs of most of the agriculture industry[103].

The value of bee pollination in human nutrition and food for wildlife is immense and difficult to quantify.

It is commonly said that about one-third of human nutrition is due to bee pollination. This includes the majority of fruits, many vegetables (or their seed crop) and secondary effects from legumes such as alfalfa and clover fed to livestock[104].

ERGO: if there are no pollinators – there is no vegetation. If there is no vegetation – there would be nothing freeing the CO_2 from the atmosphere. If there is an abundance of CO_2 in the atmosphere, global temperatures increase. If global temperatures increase too much, the water would evaporate. If the water evaporates temperatures rise precipitously ending all life on the planet.

In Summary

The more we learn about our world, the more we understand just how complex and interdependent all of its facets are. The various spheres, the vegetation, and all life forms, all have their own part to play in the continued existence and balance of all of the planetary spheres. The more we learn – the more wonder we find!

---

[103] http://en.wikipedia.org/wiki/Pollination#In_agriculture see also http://en.wikipedia.org/wiki/List_of_crop_plants_pollinated_by_bees and http://en.wikipedia.org/wiki/Pollination_management

[104] http://en.wikipedia.org/wiki/Pollinator_decline#Consequences

So... is it live... or is it Memorex? Is the planet just another example of a living breathing being, Gaia; or are we to look at the truly amazing sphere that is our planet and recognize that there is immense, unmeasurable wisdom and intelligence here?

Is the precipitous balance that these incredible cycles make just one more case of beating all the odds; or does the balance and symmetry required of them, display the inklings of recognition of the thumbprint of the Creator?

In my experience, what all life seems to be screaming at us is that intelligence shows the work of an Intellect. Moreover, intelligence is the product of an intelligent Being.

6

The Emperor's New Clothes? Or: Would You Buy a Car from A Guy Like this?

A Close Look at The Evidence for The Theory of Evolution.

HROUGHOUT HISTORY, or rather, until recent history man looked at the heavens, the land, sea, and all of their inhabitants and stood in awe of the majesty and complexity of the universe and its creations.

As far as the quest for the source of all of this, where it all came from, there really was no doubt in anyone's mind at all: a complex construct can only be the made via a Being, (minimally), with intelligence and the power to make it happen. Ergo the universe and all of its complexity were made by a Being of unlimited power and knowledge. We called this Being "G-d".

Then, (a slight over-simplification will follow. Just roll with it please), an individual came along by the name of Charles Darwin, who threw a monkey(-wrench), into things, changing the face of human thought up until the present day.

Darwin, in his famous book *The Origin of the Species*, presented humanity with a new way to look at it all. "It's not Divine," said Darwin, "it's ... accidental, the result of random, un-managed, undirected natural forces and nothing else."

As with all matters of intelligent argument, we try not to argue just for argument's sake, (although we do that on occasion as well!). Therefore, it makes sense that if we are to consider the arguments in any realistic way, they must be accompanied by a> proofs, that must; b> actually demonstrate the point being made!

If we can bring counter-proofs to the argument, or even better, if we can show that the proofs produced, do not definitively prove the point made, then what we are left with is an empty claim and no more.

The goal of this chapter is to examine, logically, the proofs brought by the adherents of the Darwinian/Neo-Darwinian movements to see if, in fact, they actually demonstrate the points for which they were brought. As it is my intention here to deal with the main issues of the topic, I will not address many of the details that are brought up in the context of the issue. That goes beyond the scope of this book and misses the point. I try to stick to the main points, because if they are incorrect - so, too are all of the details surrounding them. However, this does *not* mean that I have a complete understanding of how to explain everything. That isn't the point of this chapter nor of this book. In this regard I'm in good company because science doesn't have all of the answers either.

To make this topic more palatable, I will divide this issue into the following topics, based on the categories of proof that are brought by evolution's adherents:

- The Observable Sciences of Archeology and Anthropology
- Observable Biology and its related sciences: Micro-Evolution
- Biology and its related sciences: DNA
- Biology and its related sciences: Mutations

The Observable Sciences of Archeology and Anthropology

There are a few key topics that Darwin had at his disposal during the 1800s in the creation of his theory of evolution. The lowest common denominator is that all of them were based on the observable sciences available in his day, (microbiology and even most of biology didn't exist!). They were Archeology, Anthropology, (the science of comparative anatomy), and some practical experience which we will discuss in the 2nd part concerning microevolution.

The Proofs from Archeology

During Darwin's day, archeology was going at full steam, exploring the farthest reaches around the globe to find the scraps of pre-history available in the new world. A pretty complete archeological record was compiled in which the following was discovered:

At the lowest earth strata, there were no apparent signs of life whatsoever. Higher up there were remnants of simple life. As we continue to progress upwards through the various layers, we find that life becomes progressively more complex.

However, it also was noted that although there was a clear progression of complexity in the archaeological remains, there were no signs of apparent development. Rather the complex nature of life would change as if the event occurred instantly. If, for example, the first layer was mollusks the second layer was fish, the third lizards and so on.

The people at the time did not regard this as a theological difficulty, but rather took it as a sign of the words of G-d at the beginning of Genesis, who commanded the creation of life – and it was! (More on this in a later chapter, G-d willing).

However, what was clear in the archeological records was that there was a progression of life from simple to complex, and that it occurred at different periods of time.

The Proofs from Anthropology

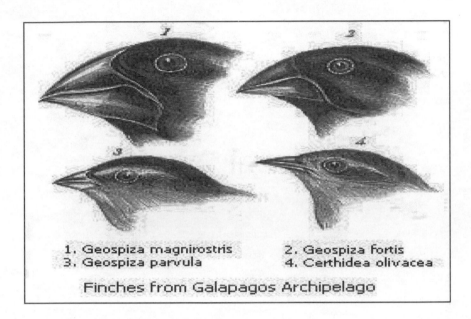

1. Geospiza magnirostris
3. Geospiza parvula
2. Geospiza fortis
4. Certhidea olivacea

Finches from Galapagos Archipelago

During his youth, Darwin took part in an expedition on the boat The Beagle during which he gathered specimen samples upon which he formulated the basis of his theory. One of his most famous findings concerned the varying types of finches found on the mainland of South America upon comparison with the finches that he found on one of the outlying islands, the Galapagos.

Darwin noted the difference in the size of the beaks, and other of the birds' features, which made him ask a question. Since, in all other aspects, these birds are finches, what was it that caused their beaks to become so different one from the other?

His conclusion: It was the result of "Natural Selection". Effectively "Natural Selection" means that certain forces of nature are always affecting the development of the species, in an uncontrolled and undirected way. What decided how a certain trait would develop? Darwin hypothesized that the deciding factor was whether the animal possessed a quality that gave it survival advantages relative to his peers. This also has been referred to as "survival of the fittest".

Now, this hypothesis got him thinking: if this force of "nature" can cause small changes within a single species perhaps, it could, as the result of numerous small, incremental, changes also lead to large-scale changes? Maybe … to one species evolving into an entirely different species?

These were, (together with the issue of selective breeding, AKA "micro-evolution", which we will speak about in part 2), the founding ideologies behind Darwin's thinking that led to his hypothesis that is known today as "evolution", or more precisely "MACRO-evolution".

Now that we know what we are looking at we can start to scrutinize.

The Depth of Proof

From the outset, we must realize that we are dealing with the EXTRAPOLATION of information to formulate a hypothesis. This means that there is no actual OBSERVABLE, MEASURABLE information here, only an assertation that was made based on the known data.

In Hebrew, this is called a *Sevara*, meaning a logical assumption. The assumption is that if there are any two creatures "competing" for survival it will be the one who is more adept, due to change in his physique, that will be the "winner"/"survivor" of the competition.

Although the basic assertation is logical, in practice it is incredibly hard to bring actual proof to back it up, as it would require that we know, from the outset;

What the actual "competition" is about;

Which of the two species is the more "adept" in regard to said competition; and

We must be shown, conclusively, that it was because of the adaptation that the "winner" won.

All of these criteria must be present to be able to prove, conclusively, that this hypothesis is actually correct.

In addition to the above, the process must also be shown to be repeatable. Otherwise, it is impossible to prove conclusively that it wasn't because of a fluke that the "adept" "won". (More on this later).

However, for the hypotheses to work with the observable data, (archeology and anthropology), the following two postulates were theorized:

- All of the changes were small and incremental.
- All of the changes took a very long time[105].

Which leads us to the difficulties:

Problem A:

The archeological records show only evidence of complex forms, as if life arose instantly, out of nowhere.

Problem B:

The archeological records evidence only instant change as opposed to gradual changes, as postulated.

Indeed, problems A and B are intertwined in a way, as they both relate to the fact that the observable data, the archeological record, doesn't record anything leading up to what science refers to as life, (a single-celled organism[106]). It also doesn't actually contain any incremental life-forms either, a point that bothered Darwin himself in The Origin, and I quote:

---

[105] I am aware of the issue of "Punctuated Equilibrium", which refers to a sudden change within the genome; I am here bringing the postulations of Darwin. We will speak about punctuated equilibrium and the topic of epigenetics later on in the chapter.

[106] It should be noted that according to Jewish law a single-celled organism is not called life at all, unless we equate it to plant life.

But just in proportion as this process of extermination has acted on an enormous scale, so must the number of intermediate varieties, which have formerly existed on the earth, be truly enormous. Why then is not every geological formation and every stratum full of such intermediate links? Geology assuredly does not reveal any such finely graduated organic chain; and this, perhaps, is the most obvious and gravest objection which can be urged against my theory.

Darwin's conclusion?

The explanation lies, as I believe, in the extreme imperfection of the geological record.

"I'm not the problem," says Darwin, "the other guys must be wrong"! Is he correct? Concerning this dilemma, I found the following answer in the book Evolution for Dummies by Dr. Fred Kukonis Ph.D., (pg. 53)

In studying the fossil record, scientists in Darwin's day were limited in a couple of ways that scientists today aren't:

Their fossil record was even more incomplete than ours today. They didn't have any fossils older than 500 million years.

They lacked the technology to find microscopic fossils. What Darwin and others perceived as gaps in the fossil record actually weren't gaps at all. Today, scientists have the advantage of a much more thorough search of the planet for older fossils and, more important, far more sophisticated techniques for identifying microscopic fossils in rocks.

Essentially, he's telling us that Darwin was right, and the geological records of his day were imperfect, as Darwin postulated.

Well, if that's the case, then this issue should be an open and shut case, no? Yet, despite the previous assertion, Dr. Kukonis, on pg. 55, tells us:

> *Today, scientists know that life has existed continuously on Earth for about the past 3.5 billion to 4 billion years, and they see the same increase in complexity through time that scientists observed in Darwin's day. (i.e. we still haven't found any significant findings that have become the basis for better proof than Darwin did in his time).*

I thought that the "more sophisticated techniques" solved the issue of the gaps. Where are the "significant advances" that we were told about earlier?

In addition, why do you write (ibid.):

> *Darwin wondered where to find the transitional life forms (consider them the in-between-this-and-that forms). Although we've had more success in finding transitional life forms, today's scientists (still) feel his pain. They are better at knowing where to look, and they have more people looking, but they still struggle to find them.*

All of this is supposed to explain to us how we, today, are in possession of the "transitional life-forms", (also known as "the missing links"), those which demonstrate Darwin's assertion of "small incremental forms" that lead to macroevolution. However, it still begs the question of where did life come from in the first place?

Dr. Kukonis addresses this issue in his book, for Dummies, with the following answer (pg. 57)

> *This book concerns itself with the evolution of organisms that are already present, not with the question — fascinating as it is — of where organisms came from in the first place. The question of how life arose on Earth really isn't a question for*

evolutionary biology. It's a question for chemistry because in asking about the transition from nonliving to living systems, you must ask questions about the chemical environment that existed on Earth at the time when life appeared.

This is what is commonly referred to in intellectual circles as "the Ostrich Syndrome". Just as the ostrich is known to hide its head in the sand when faced with danger, so did Dr. Kukonis hide his face in the sand in regard to this question! He noted a serious problem with the underpinnings of his theory and avoided the issue entirely!

Chemistry does not have an answer to this question, as we will see in the chapter *"Abraham and Abiogenesis."* The reason that this is a fundamental issue is because you cannot claim that evolution using just plain old biology works just fine without G-d, if your only recourse to explain chemical evolution is G-d. Either the entire process is random, without direction or none of it is!

Evolution and the Gaps in the Fossil Record

Getting back to the previous point, the lack of apparent transitional forms and the recognition that, even today, there are clear and obvious gaps in the fossil record. How does evolutionary science address this? What solutions do they offer?

Dr. Kukonis gives us the following answer (pg. 55) which really encapsulates the modern position

Scientists hypothesize that evolution doesn't occur at a constant rate: It can occur in bursts separated by long periods when not much happens[107]. If the transitional period was brief, the

---

[107]   This is what we mentioned before in the footnotes.
     ↄhttp://en.wikipedia.org/wiki/Punctuated_equilibrium

chance that such forms would have been fossilized is even more dicey.

In the first part of his answer, Dr. Kukonis introduces us to the hypothesis known as "punctuated equilibrium", (an instant change in the relatively constant, (=equilibrium), of the species).

In addition, he tells us that the processes of fossilization and fossils, in general, are tough to find and that it's a miracle that we have any fossilized remains in the first place. Therefore, it's no wonder that we can't find any transitional forms.

What he means is that since "macro" evolution could, maybe, (contrary to all observable data, yet still possible, (Please G-d!)), be right, AND because it's just so difficult to make a fossil, so … what can we do? We just missed it! SO... no transitional fossils.

This is a classic case of circular logic[108]! The archeological records show immediate changes in species and yet according to modern dating techniques[109] they took A VERY LONG TIME to happen. The functional process of evolutionary theory is that changes in species, (macroevolution), are the result of many small, incremental changes that occur over a long time. Yet we are to believe that the actual "jump" from one species to another … was too quick to follow?

Also, I should point out that, to date, there have never been any examples of observed cases of "punctuated equilibrium". This is not to be confused with modern observations of "evolution in action," in which we find that changes of the "micro-evolutionary" type can – and do – happen very, very fast! (More on this later).

---

[108] My good friend and student, Dr. Carl Ashkenasi, told me that this is evasionary tactics, not circular logic. I left my original thinking as is, but it could be that his is the more correct assertion.

[109] I say this according to their thinking. I disagree with this entirely, as I will explain in chapter 9.

Richard Dawkins, noted Professor of Zoology at Oxford University and outspoken advocate of evolution, answers the problem like this[110]:

> *What do you mean there are no transitional forms? Go to the museum and take a look!*
>
> *Just don't expect to find a fronkey (frog-donkey) or a parrot-shark. Transitional forms don't work like that. Rather the "transition" is usually so small that it is not noticeable until after many generations have gone by.*

This, also, is a play on the previous statement as to the difficulty of the fossilization process. What he says is that because evolution occurs by small incremental steps … there are no transitional forms!

Well, in theory, that assumption sounds logical. However, it just skips over the issue by drawing a very long "family tree" spread out over, say, millions of years, (as we are familiar with), that basically avoids the question. It's as if he said "Well, OF COURSE, you won't see a transitional form right now! You must be patient and wait for it! So, while we are waiting, why don't we have some tea and... Oops! You *just* missed it!"

Why don't we see any transitional forms? Because they happen so slowly, you don't notice them. However, they have to happen at some point in time, don't they? Of course, they do! Yet, there should also be millions of such examples, as Darwin himself postulated! But since the fossilization process is so iffy, we are lucky to have any at all!

"So," says Dawkins, "go to the museum and see the, (very few), that we DO have, (just don't expect to see a fronkey)."

Well – is that a proven truth? Let's explore:

---

[110] The Greatest Show on Earth pg. 153

The Existing "Transitional Forms"

There are several types of "transitional forms" that have been paraded around for years as "clear proof" as to the lack of gaps in the evolutionary scale. The findings, mostly using anthropological study, but, more recently, via comparative DNA, have been espoused as being "living" proof as to the existence of transitional forms. But just how much proof do they pack?

The relevant types of anthropology are biological and archeological, both of which are based on the study of remains, whether they are fossilized or not. It uses comparative biology as the basis for the categorization of the various species. Based on the similarity, or the lack thereof, an anthropologist concludes where to place the remains on the familial and evolutionary scale.

However, despite the fact that it relies on some of the "exact" sciences, (meaning that the remains can be weighed, rigorously compared with similar artifacts, and, in many instances, can be even compared biologically), the conclusions of this science do not always fall into the category of OBSERVABLE, MEASURABLE or REPEATABLE science. Much of it is conjecture. Let's take some examples:

Of what, in your opinion, is the following picture?

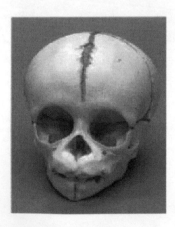

The answer:

These pictures were brought by Dawkins in his book The Greatest Show on Earth to demonstrate mistakes that could be made in deduction by the untrained eye. The trained eye would note the various differences between the skulls brought previously, as compared to a baby's skull and discern that it belonged to a monkey.

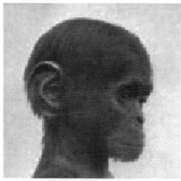

The implication is that the trained eye is not fooled by the generalities; it will focus on the nuances and arrive at the correct conclusion.

In other words, we are told, "I'm smart, you're not. If you were as smart as I am – then you would know that I am right".

The question is: Is that really true? If the thing that we are scrutinizing is alive and well today, then there really, truly, is a way of verifying the theory. Just take a look at the evidence in front of your eyes. However, what happens if the animal under discussion isn't alive anymore? Can the remains be trusted as evidence if there is no way of actually verifying the conclusions?

Well let's take a look at some of the prime examples of "missing links" that were discovered over the last 100 years or so:

The Coelacanth

The coelacanth is commonly referred to as a "living fossil". This is because it is one of many species that were presumed to be extinct as the most recent fossilized remains known were from about 70 million years ago[111]. These fossilized remains were discovered in the early 1800's and were seized upon by Darwin and his constituents as proof of the existence of the "missing link" of development between fish and amphibian life. The reason for this assumption was the build of bony projections that the fish has on its underside whose skeletal structures look similar to the feet of amphibians. "This was the fish that braved the land to make way for the creatures to come," they said... until in 1938 a living one was actually caught and dissected.

What was discovered was that the "foot" was not a foot and that the fish was incapable of living on land, thus shattering the coelacanth's status as the "missing link" between fish and amphibians.

Very recently, the coelacanth was put through the process of genome mapping. The following was discovered:

> *Ending one long-standing argument, analysis of the coelacanth genome clearly shows that it is not the closest living fishy relative to tetrapods, (the first 4 footed animals/reptiles) ...[112]*

Robert L. Carroll, a paleontologist from McGill University, concludes:

> *"We have no intermediate fossils between Rhipidistian fish [coelacanth] and early amphibians." "Unfortunately, not a single specimen of an appropriate reptilian ancestor is known prior to the appearance of true reptiles. The absence of such*

---

[111] http://www.scientificamerican.com/article.cfm?id=slow-evolving-lobe-finned-coelacanth-genome-unlocked

[112] http://www.scientificamerican.com/article.cfm?id=slow-evolving-lobe-finned-coelacanth-genome-unlocked

ancestral forms leaves many problems of the amphibian–reptile transition unanswered.[113]"

From this example, we see that as long as there are no living representatives of the remains under discussion, it is quite easy to arrive at conclusions that have no basis in reality. Only a live specimen is acceptable as a valid means of comparison.

In baseball, we would call this batting 0 for 1 or a batting average of 0.

Archaeopteryx

Another of the more famous of the "missing link" remains found is that of Archaeopteryx. The reason for its fame is its proposed status as the "missing link" between dinosaurs and birds.

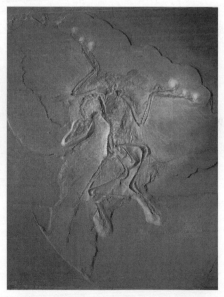

Nevertheless, upon scrutiny, we must ask ourselves: What, really, is the reason that it is considered more dinosaur than a bird in the first place?

Maybe it's the age of the finding, (measured as having lived roughly 150 million years ago, well into the timeline of the dinosaurs)? In other words: if it's OLD then it must be a dinosaur! Really?

NOPE! Can't be that because in 2008, during excavations in China Eoconfuciusornis Zheng was discovered, concerning whom there is absolutely no doubt that it was a bird! Measured as having lived 131 million years ago it was a contemporary of Archaeopteryx.

---

[113]   **Carroll, R. L.** *The Rise of Amphibians: 365 Million Years of Evolution.* The Johns Hopkins University Press 2009

In truth, the recent discovery of Protoavis, a modern-like bird that preceded[114] Archaeopteryx, destroys – utterly – this issue.

(In other words: OLD does NOT necessarily equal dinosaur)

Perhaps it's the fact that we can see that its mouth is lined with sharp teeth, something rather uncommon in beaked birds?

NOPE! Can't be that either! Meet Ichthyornidae (right) a BIRD that lived a very long time ago yet had a fanged maw!

Perhaps, one might think, it is because we find that Archaeopteryx had, on its wings, claws with 3 fingers?

This, too, cannot present irrefutable evidence as to archaeopteryx's having been a dinosaur as this is a trait that we find even in some modern birds today!

The HOATZIN, for example, is a modern bird that has claws on its wings as well!

> *Many birds have claws. These include adult flightless birds such as Emus, Cassowaries, Ostrich, and Kiwis. Also, many other birds sometimes exhibit vestigial claws, including Swifts, Falcons, and many others. In fact, it is quite common, but most lose them in adulthood. The Hoatzin appears to be one of the few, possibly the only one, where the claws are actually functional.*

---

[114] **http://www.ucmp.berkeley.edu/diapsids/birds/birdfr.html** *Protoavis:* A Revolution in Bird Evolution?

So perhaps it is the long bony tail, a trait that we don't generally find in birds?

Perhaps... but perhaps not as well! Granted, this may be a feature that is not found in modern birds, whereas it is common in lizards and their like, however, it is still not conclusive proof that the animal remains that we are looking at is more lizard than a bird!

What IS clear is that the FEATHERS of Archaeopteryx would NOT seem to place it with the dinosaurs, but rather with the birds! The reason for this is that this animal is in possession of clearly developed feathers, akin to those of modern birds.

The truth is that the existence of the feather is a tremendous difficulty in evolutionary thinking itself! Why is this? Simply because the feather has no known predecessors!

> *Originally hypothesized as having "developed" from scales. Almost all scientists disregard this hypothesis.*
>
> *The problem with that scenario is that scales are basically flat folds of the integument whereas feathers are tubular structures. A pennaceous feather becomes 'flat' only after emerging from a cylindrical (Prum and Brush 2002). In addition, the type and distribution of protein (keratin) in feathers and scales differ (Sawyer et al. 2000). The only feature shared by feathers and scales is that they both begin development as a morphologically distinct placode – an epidermal thickening above a condensation, or congregation, of dermal cells. Feathers, then, are not derived from scales, but, rather, are evolutionary novelties with numerous unique features, including the feather follicle, tubular feather germ (an elevated area of epidermal cells), and a complex branching structure (Prum and Brush 2002)[115].*

---

[115]   http://people.eku.edu/ritchisong/feather_evolution.htm

Although there has been much talk of finding "protofeathers", (predecessors to modern flight feathers), feathers just "spring up" on the fossil record with no plausible explanation as to what mutation could have caused these hollow, tubular and complex structures to evolve.

In an article in National Geographic magazine, Carl Zimmer[116] concludes that:

The origin of this wonderful mechanism is one of evolution's most durable mysteries.

One of the more common ways of bringing proof in the area of anthropology is to make a "structural line" based on varying species. A classic example of this is when assorted simian skeletal structures are lined up one after the other to form a "chain of progression" from monkey to man; or when various eye structures are lined up one after the other showing a "progression" from simple eyes to complex ones like our own. Although ingenious and interesting, there's only one problem with it: who says it's right?

While the comparative structures are fascinating, and it's really neat to match them up like this, unfortunately this isn't actual proof as to its truth. For just as much as it could be right, it could also be totally wrong. The problem is association. Aside from them all having similar structures, there is no actual proof that one has anything to do with the other, or that they have any common ancestry at all! This is classically referred to as "circumstantial evidence." It could be that the comparative structures are signs of a progression chain; however, it could also be that one has nothing whatsoever to do with the other. This is especially true in light of the issue of speciation, otherwise known as "micro-evolution" which we will look at specifically later in the chapter.

---

116   http://ngm.nationalgeographic.com/2011/02/feathers/zimmer-text/2

So, when it comes to comparative biology concerning the evolution of man from the apes or any such sort of supposition, we must realize that it must be "taken with an OCEAN of salt."

I don't know about you, but to me, this means that anthropology is batting 0 for 2, for an average of 0.

Let's take Australopithecus Afarensis for example:

Clearly, upon scrutiny, many features are similar in appearance to those of modern humans... but does that mean that this skull belonged to a human?

Maybe... but maybe not! The only way to really know would be to have MET him! Alas, that just isn't in the cards...

Reconstructive methods such as forensic facial reconstruction are not actually capable of showing conclusively that the skull belonged to a human as opposed to a simian (monkey)[117].

Depending on the type of reconstruction done it could be either something that looks like a gorilla or the anthropologist who classified it as pre-human species! The following are a list of know issues that apply to the use of facial reconstruction in modern man:

- *Insufficient tissue thickness data*

  The most pressing issue relates to the data used to average facial tissue thickness. The data available to forensic artists are still very limited in ranges of ages, sexes, and body builds. This disparity greatly affects the accuracy of reconstructions. Until

---

[117] There are multiple outstanding problems associated with forensic facial reconstruction.

this data is expanded, the likelihood of producing the most accurate reconstruction possible is largely limited.

- *Lack of methodological standardization*

  A second problem is the lack of a methodological standardization in approximating facial features. …. facial features like the eyes and nose and individuating characteristics like hairstyle – the features most likely to be recalled by witnesses – lack a standard way of being reconstructed.

- *Subjectivity*

  Reconstructions only reveal the type of face a person may have exhibited because of artistic subjectivity. The position and general shape of the main facial features are mostly accurate because they are greatly determined by the skull. (Wikipedia "Forensic facial reconstruction")

So, scientists today rely on DNA and genome comparison. But we will come back to talk about that later when we discuss the topic of DNA.

This becomes especially more challenging when we consider that most of the time anthropologists compile evidence when there isn't even a full skeleton, or a complete bone available, to adequately scrutinize. So how is it possible to come to a proper conclusion?

Live examples of "in-between" species are also discussed, such as the Duck-Billed Platypus and the Lungfish, for instance. These examples are no better than the non-living examples mentioned earlier, as the fact that they have qualities that are "neither here nor there" doesn't prove that they are transitional forms. Not only that, but recent findings seem to show conclusively that the platypus[118] and the lungfish[119] have undergone no change in their genome and were alive and well at the same time as the dinosaurs themselves! None of the observable data can prove, conclusively, that they are intermediate forms. The only way to do so would be to actively observe their "evolutionary tree," to watch them as they developed into what they are today. The completely wrong approach to "proof" is to bring a bunch of skeletons and say "Look! Don't you see that they have similarities? Why *in my imagination* I can picture this one coming from this one, coming from this one! It's a whole (imaginary) family tree"!

It might be good fiction, but it's not good proof!

In Summary of Part 1:

- The fossil record contains no conclusive evidence for evolution.
- There are no real "intermediate forms" that clearly show one species changing into another species; and
- There are no PRE-life examples (more on this next chapter); and
- The proofs from anthropology are inconclusive and based on CONJECTURE and CIRCUMSTANTIAL EVIDENCE.

Our sages, ob"m, summed this up by saying "Just because we can compare things doesn't mean that we should act based on it (the comparison)" (Tractate *Gittin* 19a). This is especially true if you are formulating life-changing theories based on such flimsy evidence.

---

[118] See, for example, *http://news.nationalgeographic.com/news/2013/11/131104-giant-platypus-evolution-science-animals-paleontology/* Giant Platypus Found, Shakes Up Evolutionary Tree and *http://news.nationalgeographic.com/news/2008/01/080122-platypus.html* Platypus Much Older Than Thought, Lived with Dinos.

[119] The oldest known examples of lungfish in archeology are 375-400 million years old (modern scientific scale).

Observable Biology and Its Related Sciences:
Micro-Evolution

The third type of evidence that Darwin relied upon was the tried-and-true results of selective breeding. Selective breeding was used to make faster racehorses, milkier cows, stinkier skunks, etc. any particular trait could be improved upon if we intervened to ensure that the animals with the strongest of the desired quality mated to produce offspring with the desired attributes.

Dogs are a fascinating example of how crossbreeding produces massive changes within the genome. All we have to do to see this is to look at all of the various breeds of dogs! Schnauzers, Bulldogs, Labradors, Chihuahuas and many, many others. Where did all of these different types of dogs come from?

Clearly, there is both a) massive genetic variation going on; and also b) the availability and clear reality of selective breeding that allows for us to produce animals in which a certain trait is stronger than in others of the same species. We are told that this proves that "natural selection" works. After all, many small incremental changes could also add up to a massive shift in the genome!

This area has been dubbed "micro-evolution" by the media, it is also commonly known as "speciation" and it is brought as incontestable proof that evolution works. Although, as we will see, this issue relies heavily on the topic of mutations, which we will discuss later in section 4. We will also see that an advanced understanding of mutations is not necessary to properly grasp the issues at hand.

The Definition of a Species

Before we can start, I would like to point out an intrinsic difference between the scientific definition of a species as opposed to the Torah's definition.

Science defines a species as any two creatures that can mate with one another. As a result of this definition, if they can develop, for example, two types of fruit fly that cannot mate with one another then we now have in front of us two distinct species. The Torah clearly disagrees with this, in that it holds that form and function defines a species.

The reason that I say this is because the Torah discusses species in many places. One such example is Leviticus 11, when listing the types of animals that are permissible for a Jew to eat. There the Torah clearly speaks about species of animals. When it talks about pigs, camels, and various types of birds, it is talking about species. By the birds, this is stated explicitly. This is because the features of the creatures define a species. All types of pigs, for example, are called "pig" and all types of eagles are called "eagles." It is the common features that they share that define them as a species. In the same light, all types of dogs are called "dogs" not because of their genetic makeup, but rather because of their shared features. It's not just an issue of breeding.

Because all of the examples without exception, to my knowledge, rely on the same model to supply the proof of evolution, therefore, I will bring several examples, explain them, and then scrutinize them.

Let's look at some of the classic examples that are touted as clear proof as to the truth of evolution:

Smart Bacteria

The following is from the book Evolution for Dummies pg. 34

Here's an example: Suppose that you collect a bunch of a particular kind of bacteria and measure the frequency of the gene that makes the bacteria resistant to a new type of antibiotic. In your initial count, you find that the frequency of this gene is extremely low: Less than 1 percent of the bacteria have the gene that makes them antibiotic resistant. You come back in a few years. Your original bacteria are gone, but in their place, are their great-great-great-great-etcetera grandkids, and you repeat the analysis. This time, you find that 30 percent of the bacteria have the antibiotic-resistant gene. Although you haven't actually witnessed evolution, you're looking at its result: the change in the frequency of particular genes over time. The antibiotic-resistant gene appeared in less than 1 percent of the original bacteria; it appears in 30 percent of the descendants.

Ibid pg. 49

Mutations don't occur in response to environmental change. Instead, the mutations already exist and are favored in the new environment. Beakers full of bacteria tend to contain mutants that are resistant to antibiotics even when no antibiotics are around. Toss an antibiotic into the mix, and the mutation gets its chance to shine by enabling the bacteria to survive in the presence of the antibiotic.

This is one of the most famous of all the microevolutionary examples "on the market". It states that:

Evolution doesn't happen as the result of a disaster; it precedes such phenomenon.

This means that "mutations" are constantly occurring and that there are always "mutants" within the mix of the biological community.

Something happens that causes the "mutants" to gain dominance within the community.

The "mutant" then becomes a dominant trait within the genome.

In regard to the antibiotic resistance of bacteria, this means 1) there always were bacteria resistant to antibiotics. 2) Antibiotics killed off much of, or all of, the bacteria without the resistance. 3) The resistant bacteria became dominant and, as a result, so did the genome.

Industrial Melanism in the Peppered Moth

This is probably THE most famous of all of the proofs for microevolution as it is one of the oldest.

The evolution of the peppered moth over the last two hundred years has been studied in detail. Originally, the vast majority of peppered moths had light coloration, which effectively camouflaged them against the light-colored trees and lichens, upon which they rested. However, because of widespread pollution during the Industrial Revolution in England, many of the lichens died out, and the trees that peppered moths rested on became blackened by soot, causing most of the light-colored moths, or Typica, to die off from predation. At the same time, the dark-colored, or melanic, moths, Carbonara, flourished because of their ability to hide on the darkened trees.

Since then, with improved environmental standards, light-colored peppered moths have again become common, but the dramatic change in the peppered moth's population has remained a subject of much interest and study and has led to the coining of the term "industrial melanism" to refer to the genetic darkening of species in response to pollutants[120].

Here, too, we find the same pattern: Before the industrial revolution, there always were both black and light-colored moths. Before the I.R. (Industrial Revolution), the light-colored moths were the predominant

---

[120] http://en.wikipedia.org/wiki/Peppered_moth_evolution

ones. After the I.R., the dark colored ones became dominant. What caused the change? Said Professor Bernard Kettlewell this was due to: a) change in the tree color from the soot produced by the factories; which led to b) increased predation of the light-colored moths, who now stood out on the tree trunks; and therefore c) the black moths now became predominant as they had "the better" camouflage.

Wild Guppy Coloration and Predation

Another example: the experimentation with predation of wild guppies and its effect on the natural colors of male guppies. (One of the examples quoted by Dawkins). The experiments seem to show conclusively that because of predation guppies tend to lose their colors, whereas in places where predation is not aggressive it is normal that the male guppies have beautiful colors.

We are told that this is because the females are more attracted to the colored males as opposed to the drab ones.

Once again. There have ALWAYS been both colorful and drab male guppies in the wild. In the presence of predators, the drab males become the dominant of the species. ERGO it's due to predation that the guppies change their "spots".

The Problem with These Proofs:

As mentioned earlier each of these examples is assumed to be a solid proof of evolution even though they have not actually brought any evidence to validate them.

For example: concerning the guppies, we are told that the reason for the change in coloration is the proximity and the presence of predators. The colorful ones just stick out so much that they are quickly gobbled up by the predators... or maybe there is a *different* reason?

Maybe it's because, around predators, a gene kicks in to lose the colors so as to better blend in with the surroundings? Have there been extensive studies of colored vs. drab predation that can show, conclusively, that the colors disappeared only because of predation? To the best of my knowledge: NO.

We are told that the reason for the colors is because female guppies will choose a colored mate over a drab one any day of the week... but is that really true? Have guppy females been extensively interviewed concerning their choice of partners? Have they been on "The Dating Game" and always chosen the more colorful male? How do we know that this is a truism?

Concerning industrial melanism: Who says that the color of trees has any effect whatsoever on the birds? Is there conclusive proof that the amount of predation changes based on the color of the moth? Perhaps neither of them is cause for a significant difference in predation, (if any at all[121])? Is there a difference whether moths alight on the trees in a manner that make them more visible, such as on the tree trunk or in a less visible manner, on the underside of branches, to their predators[122]? And even more so – the crux of the issue – is there any observable proof that predation, in fact, INCREASES AT ALL as a result of a change in coloration?![123]

---

[121] Modern studies seem to show, conclusively, that birds are not affected, in any way, by what WE perceive as camouflage. He (kettlewell) also records how well camouflaged the moths seemed to be by visual inspection. This might have seemed like a good idea at the time, but since his work it has become clear that birds see ultraviolet much better than we do, and therefore what seems well-camouflaged to the human eye may not be to a bird. http://www.millerandlevine.com/km/evol/Moths/moths.html

[122] This issue, and many others, were raised in the book *Evolution in Action* by Michael Majerus Oxford University Press, New York, 1998

[123] Although there have been those who claim that they have done video studies to try to decide this issue, I can imagine just how reliable such studies are. Students are paid in order to watch hundreds of hours of video during which they are told that if they see a bird eating a white moth (or colored guppy) - press the right button, and if it's a dark one - press the left button. It would be more interesting to find out what happens to the students during the study than the actual study itself.

However, all of the above aside, *these issues are not even the real problem here with all of the above proofs.*

The Real Problem - The Giant Hole in the Investigation

The real problem stems from the fact that every single example brought as evidence of "microevolution in action" lives or dies based on the issue of "mutations."

In all the above examples - *without exception* - we are told that mutants existed before X happened. Then X happened, and it kills off most/all of the non-mutants, and THEREFORE, mutants became the dominant genome of the species.

It would seem to me; therefore, that if we found problems with this first axiom – subsequently NONE OF THESE PROOFS, or any like them, are evidence of anything! If I cannot prove that the existence of "mutants" is due to what scientists call a "mutation" and that it was, in fact, random, then there is no proof of "evolution" whatsoever! (More on this later).

But ... maybe the problem is me. Perhaps I don't know enough about DNA and mutations to accurately judge this issue? After all, Darwin, himself, wasn't sure as to how his proposed theory was supposed to work! He assumed that (for example); the giraffe got its long neck because its mother stretched her neck so hard to reach the high leaves that her neck grew a bit... and mom passed her new neck on to her offspring.

But today we know that's not possible. Why? Because today we know conclusively that whatever is in the DNA... is what's going to come out!

Which brings us to the next issue:

Biology and Its Related Sciences: DNA

Dawkins tells us that even without the fossil records the case for evolution is so strong that it wouldn't, couldn't, and doesn't suffer, even if no fossil evidence existed. (As we already have demonstrated, there really is no conclusive fossil evidence at all). Those are very strong words, but are they true? Let's find out!

One of the most difficult issues I have found sifting through the scientific literature is that in most instances, the sheer volume of information presented is so great that there is a tendency to just take them at their word. I mean, if they are so knowledgeable – how could they be wrong?

However, upon scrutiny, I have found that once the actual claim being leveled is examined, (by just removing the voluminous amounts of redundant and unnecessary information), it becomes evident – that that was the whole point of the information-overload in the first place! As the saying goes "If ya can't convince 'em – confuse 'em"! It also relies on the dictum of our sages, ob"m, who tell us[124] *"any falsehood that has no truth in its beginning cannot stand at its end"*. I pray that the following distilled information helps to show this.

SO, if that which is in the DNA is what comes out – how can there EVER be any real evolution of any sort? If the DNA spells M.O.U.S.E., then the result will always be... Mickey! How, therefore, is genome change even remotely possible?

Well, clearly, there must have been extra information that was inserted into the genome, which allows for a new reading of the DNA. But how does this happen?

To this, we are given two possible answers. Either:

a) The DNA has a whole lot (around 97%) unnecessary, non-coding parts, also called "junk"; or

---

[124] Rashi on Bamidbar (Numbers) 13:27. Meaning that if you want to say a lie, start by saying something true first, then the lie will not be recognized as such. A lie with no truth to it within a short time will be revealed as such.

b) That somehow more information was added in which the change can, and will, occur.

Either way both of these tell us the same thing: either there always HAS been, or, as time goes on, there always WILL BE extra information within the genome. Let's explore this:

Junk DNA

Because evolutionary theory states that DNA is really an amalgam of genetic information that was accrued, (the "how" is not relevant to the claim), over the course of centuries and millennia; and because there was no guiding hand in its creation; therefore, there must be a ton of useless stuff in there. We are told that because of all the "junk" available, evolution has something to play with to allow for genetic evolution. At least, that's what we are led to believe.

But the truth of the matter is that we have no means, or capability, to verify this claim. That's all it is at the end of the day: just a claim. And a bad one at that!

The Law of Biological Conservation of Energy

As we will discuss in more detail in the next chapter, biology abhors waste. All cellular life has very limited supplies of energy and cannot "afford" to spend it on unnecessary things. Yet, for some unexplainable reason, the "junk" of DNA is consistently reproduced, despite the "fact" that it serves no function.

But let's ask a different question: is there any evidence to the contrary? Do we know of any existing scientific data that would lead us to believe that the *opposite* is true, that, in truth, the "junk" is not so junky? The answer: OH, YES!

Let's take a look at some of that, shall we?

Junk DNA – not as junky as we thought

'Junk' DNA Has Important Role, Researchers Find

ScienceDaily (May 21, 2009) — Scientists have called it "junk DNA." They have long been perplexed by these extensive strands of genetic material that dominate the genome but seem to lack specific functions. Why would nature force the genome to carry so much excess baggage? Now researchers from Princeton University and Indiana University who have been studying the genome of a pond organism have found that junk DNA may not be so junky after all. They have discovered that DNA sequences from regions of what had been viewed as the "dispensable genome" are actually performing functions that are central for the organism[125].

ScienceDaily (Jan. 31, 2011) –

Recently, however, it has become clear that junk DNA performs a wide range of important tasks. As a result, attention is shifting to asking why some organisms have so much of it and other organisms so little[126].

New Scientist 19 March 2010 in an article by Ewen Callaway entitled "Junk" DNA gets credit for making us who we are

In recent years, researchers have recognized that non-coding DNA, which makes up about 98 percent of the human genome, plays a critical role in determining whether genes are active or not and how much of a particular protein gets churned out.

---

[125]   http://www.sciencedaily.com/releases/2009/05/090520140408.htm
[126]   http://www.sciencedaily.com/releases/2011/01/110131133137.htm

SO, it would seem that the closer we look, the more we find that there is a lot less "junk" than we initially thought. How does evolutionary science deal with this issue? Let's take a look at another statement in New Scientist from June 19th, 2010

> *"Myth - "Junk DNA isn't junk after all". Once the vast majority of our DNA was dismissed as junk, but now we know it is important – or so you might have read recently. In fact, it still appears likely that 85 to 95 percent of our DNA is indeed useless. While many bits of DNA that do not code for proteins are turning out to have some function or other, this was predicted by some all along, and the overall proportion of our DNA with proven function remains tiny" (pg. 35)*

In a nutshell: the response is "So what if there is less junk than we originally thought? We never claimed to know definitively that there might be more important DNA beyond that which was previously known! So, there's less junk. So, what?"

Let's take a moment to consider the logic of this statement, and – at the same time – the issue in general:

We initially understood that there was a small percentage of information contained in the DNA that was ABSOLUTELY VITAL for the coding of protein synthesis (the making of your body's various parts).

Fact: The more that we explore the function of DNA coding the more we find that what we at first called "junk" is, in fact, NOT junk.

Lastly, and most importantly, WE NEVER CALLED THE 90 SOMETHING PERCENT "JUNK" BECAUSE WE KNEW THAT IT WAS JUNK. We did so because it fit with evolutionary theory.

In truth, we have no idea as to the purpose of the "junk" DNA or lack thereof. Therefore, it makes much more sense to conclude the following:

IF the more we study the stuff, the more we find that it *does* have a purpose; AND if biology continues to reproduce it despite the need for conservation of energy. ERGO we should conclude that there is no junk, it's just that we don't – as of yet – understand the purpose of the other 90 odd percent of the genome. (More on this later.)

A Growing Genome: Adding Information

The other option that is given to explain the change in the outcome of the gene sequencing, (i.e. the DNA spells "mouse" yet, somehow, it gives birth to a "lion"), is that there was information added to the genome that changed the biological "spelling".

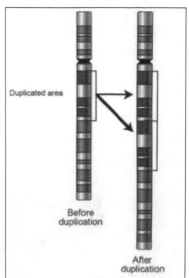

Duplicated area

Before duplication

After duplication

Remember: if all you have are vanilla and chocolate ice cream – you can never make strawberry! If all you have are the pieces to build a go-cart – you will never be able to build a jet engine. Therefore, most assuredly, this is even more true concerning something as complex as the creation of the Human genome.

So, just how does the genome gain information?

We are told that "gene duplication" is the way to go. So, what is that?

> *Gene duplication (or chromosomal duplication or gene amplification) is any duplication of a region of DNA that contains a gene; it may occur as an error in homologous recombination, a retrotransposition event, or duplication of an entire chromosome.*

What this means is that instead of the one gene coding for protein x, of which the organism needs only one … it now has two!

However, say scientists, maybe now, (stress on maybe, as there is no concrete evidence to this claim), there is room for mutation!??

Yes, maybe... and maybe not!

I have yet to see an article that brings testimony as to the existence of any observable, measurable and repeatable examples of this being the engine of evolution[127]. There certainly are no examples of this being a POSITIVE engine for evolution, whereas there ARE examples of it being a NEGATIVE engine.

Down syndrome is an example of how this is a bad driving force: Down syndrome is a chromosomal condition characterized by the presence of an extra copy of genetic material on the 21st chromosome. I'm sure that there are many other examples of how gene duplication is terrible for the organism – look them up and you'll surely find them!

In truth, the science behind this answer is a hypothesis at the very best, (and a bad one, as we have seen)! It also goes against almost all of the observable data!

Evolution's mutation mechanism does not explain how the growth of a genome is possible (more on mutation in the fourth topic). How can point mutations create new chromosomes or lengthen a strand of DNA?

It is interesting to note that, in all of the selective breeding of dogs, there has been no change to the basic dog genome. All breeds of dog can still mate with one another. People have not seen any increase in dog's DNA but have simply selected

---

127   If you have lots of patience and are willing to read through a very long article by the renown evolutionist, Richard Dawkins, then check out the following link http://www.skeptics.com.au/publications/articles/the-information-challenge/. There Dawkins relates his indignity at having accepted an interview with a certain reporter in his home, during the course of which the interviewer asked if he knew of any examples in which there was observation of the genome growing, (this question was followed by lots of "Umm"s and "Err"s, but otherwise – nothing). In rebuttal of, and in indignation of, the unprepared question – he wrote the above article. However, if we actually pay attention to what he did write in the article we find that the "if you can't convince 'em – confuse 'em" rule was used. Despite the long-windedness – the article still doesn't bring any observable examples at all!

different genes from the existing dog gene pool to create the different breeds[128].

What this means is that despite the frequency with which "micro-evolution"/"speciation" has been cited as a proof as to the validity of evolution – there really has never been, despite all of the years of trials and experimentation since the issue's inception, any real concrete proof of a significant change occurring within the genome as a result of speciation. There are no known cases of information having been added at all! SO, WHERE'S THE BEEF? WHERE are the examples of the promised additional information that changes the genome allowing a new genetic "spelling" to occur that leads to the arrival of a new species?

Horizontal Gene Transfer

This issue would not be complete without addressing the concept known as "horizontal gene transfer". This is a process which has been found occurring only in single cell life where one bacterium, (for example), "borrows" DNA from another type and adds its information to its own DNA.

However, it makes sense to say that this occurs only in single-cell organisms, where "reproduction" is achieved by copying the entirety of the "Mother" cell, (or is it "father" cell?), that this "gene transfer" is possible. This process works because the means of reproduction of single-celled life is via copying the entirety of the DNA and then splitting into two exact copies. Whereas in multicellular life, in which reproduction is done sexually, the process is different and therefore, wouldn't work by means of "transfer."[129]

---

[128] http://science.howstuffworks.com/environmental/life/evolution/evolution9.htm I must also point out that the author wrote this article as a pro-evolution article.

[129] I say this despite that much of the scientific literature nowadays does state that HGT does occur in multicellular creatures, such as animals and man. However, it should

THE EMPEROR'S NEW CLOTHING

Upon scrutiny of the literature, it appears that other than the fact that transference happens, it is not clear how or why it does! What does appear to be true, however, is that the process is selective, not random, in that the genes are chosen by the organism in order to "upgrade" preexisting abilities in a sort of plug-and-play fashion. Therefore, to call this an ability that arose through random mutation seems incredibly far-fetched.

Yet even the ability to transfer genes is still a far cry from showing an actual case of "evolution at work." Although this has been observed in the lab, never has there been a case of a new species arising as a result. Even among bacteria, after the transference has occurred and new genetic material acquired, the bacteria – remain bacteria! Also, as we will see soon in this chapter this mechanism is no different than all of the others that are brought as proofs.

Mitochondrial Eve and Y-chromosome Adam

There has been much "to-do" concerning the issue of mitochondrial DNA and the question of whether it involves any coding that affects the genome and how it might do so.

"Mitochondria" are the "power plants" of the cell and contain their own DNA. Since this DNA is inheritable solely from the egg, (i.e. the mother's DNA), the assumption, therefore, is that if a mutation occurred in the egg, it would be passed onto the offspring.

---

be clear that when scrutinized none of the articles and papers written actually attest to having witnessed this in the lab. Rather, they ascribe HGT as the cause for the mutation of various genes. That's nice. More science fiction to the rescue. {In more recent studies, it seems that then instances of transfer being referred to are from human/animal bacteria to other bacteria. It also occurs from single celled organisms to other like organisms, such as algae, for example. However, algae reproduce in a similar manner, it therefore makes sense that transference would occur by them as well. See https://elifesciences.org/articles/48999 for example.}

Page | 132

Similarly, as women don't have a Y-chromosome, (only men do); therefore, a mutation in the Y-chromosome would be transferable via the father's DNA.

Conversely, it is therefore, possible to "track" a person's lineage via the existence of either the mitochondria or the Y-chromosome. An excellent example of this is the test of the Cohanim's genetic makeup, (also referred to as "Y-chromosome Aaron")[130].

According to some opinions, there is a possibility of gene transfer within the mitochondria which would then be passed down to all of the offspring, (as we said, the mitochondria is almost exclusively[131] maternal), and voila! Instant gene-splicing!

However:

- Since the mitochondria's purpose is almost solely the production of ATP, (the cells fuel); and
- Since it's DNA does NOT code for the reproduction of anything except future mitochondria[132]; and
- Since almost all, (if not all), known damage and/or mutations in the mitochondrial DNA result in diseases and/or mutations that damage the organism's ability to survive[133], even though – hypothetically – it might convey some sort of genetic superiority. THEREFORE:

---

[130] http://en.wikipedia.org/wiki/Y-chromosomal_Aaron

[131] Mitochondrial DNA (mtDNA) is not transmitted through nuclear DNA (nDNA, the DNA that codes for you). In humans, as in most multicellular organisms, mitochondrial DNA is inherited only from the mother's ovum. There are theories, however, that paternal mtDNA transmission in humans can occur in certain circumstances. http://en.wikipedia.org/wiki/Human_mitochondrial_genetics

[132] http://en.wikipedia.org/wiki/Mitochondrion#Replication_and_inheritance. The process of mitochondrial DNA reproduction is an entirely separate replication process from the nuclear DNA (the DNA that codes for you). During the cell replication process "the cell" must be very careful to *shtup* at least one new mitochondrion into the daughter cell or else "she" is up the creek!

[133] See http://en.wikipedia.org/wiki/Mitochondrial_disease and http://en.wikipedia.org/wiki/Mitochondrion#Mitochondrial_diseases for more on this.

It makes much more sense to conclude that although helpful in establishing links back to "Adam" and "Eve" no one actually considers mutations to the x or y chromosomes of the mitochondria as the real source of genetic variation within the human genome.

Comparative Genetics: Just How Similar Are Humans and Chimps?

I'm sure that you have heard that we are genetically close cousins of the monkeys. That's it! Topic closed because of DNA sequencing. Or is it? We are told that 96% of a human's DNA is similar to that of a chimpanzee[134], but this still is not really a conclusive proof of anything!

First of all, it is because this number is an "optical illusion." It makes it sound as if they lined up the two strands of DNA, found them to be of equal length, and then, moving from the 0 of the line upwards, they found that from 0 up until point 96-98 (=96-98%) everything matched perfectly. It sounds like the only difference between them is in the last 2-4%. However, that isn't true. In truth, a much smaller amount of the genomes is actually similar. So how did they get to 96%? By explaining that the significant amount of DNA left, which point-for-point *isn't* actually similar, is really still one-and-the-same. There were "point mutations", fused genes, and other various odds-and-ends that "explain" how the rest is really comparable as well[135].

Second, even assuming that the percentage is small, what isn't small is the way in which the genes are expressed (more on this later[136]). Even

---

[134] http://www.sciencedaily.com/releases/2012/08/120823142735.htm

[135] For a brilliant short film on this, look at https://www.youtube.com/watch?time_continue=145&v=IbY122CSC5w also look at http://www.icr.org/article/human-chimp-dna-nearly-identical/. Really, we also share a significant amount of DNA with mice, chickens, bananas and many other types of creatures and things, yet for some reason, and despite the similarities, there is a tremendous amount of difference between man and them!

[136] I'll bring the sources there.

1% difference in genetic material could (and does) have far-reaching implications genetically.

Another reason for this is, as Dawkins himself is so fond of saying, DNA is not your classic blueprint[137]! All we have to do is look at the RESULT of the actual compilation of the DNA sequencing, something that requires us to use our eyes and nothing else, and we see conclusively that a chimpanzee is not a human! Despite some of the anatomical similarities – there is nothing else comparable at all!

Lastly, according to the scientific position that states that 97% of the human (and monkey) genome is junk, and doesn't code, then who cares? If the remaining 3% is the coding DNA, then guess what? They are 100% different scientifically!

Embryology

Another issue that is (there's not better way to say this) *touted* as being clear evidence for evolution is the topic of embryology. To be succinct, when we compare the embryonic development (how the fetus develops in the womb/egg) of various species to one another, we find that virtually all living creatures go through similar developmental stages. Even human embryos develop gills and a tail during gestation! The claim: if they didn't have similar genetic precursors, why do all things develop using similar stages of development?

This, too, isn't an example of the evidence proving evolution. It's the argument based on the observational data which is the "proof". Therefore, there are two basic questions that need to be asked on the interpretation of the data:

---

137   Dawkins is fond of saying that it's not a blueprint at all but even most of his colleagues disagree with him in this regard! He says this, however, because – as opposed to a blueprint – we cannot look at a printout of DNA and say, "Why this looks just like you"! As opposed to a house blueprint, where we can. More on this in section three concerning DNA and evolution.

1. Is that the only possible explanation? And
2. Is it proven beyond a shadow of a doubt that there is no need for the embryo to go through these stages of development?

Without getting into the further information in this chapter, all of which soundly rebuts this interpretation, even on a point basis this isn't a resounding difficulty.

First of all, let's take the "tail", for example. A human being, like all vertebrates, has a spine, which is an elongated chain of bones and more. The spine is the fulcrum for the creatures' future form, it therefore follows that before the form can be fully developed it must first build its basic superstructure, i.e. it's spine. After all, "form follows function". In addition, the spine is more than just bones, it is part and parcel of a person's/creature's neural pathways, connecting the brain to the heart, the lungs, the digestive system and more. Therefore, its development is absolutely crucial as a precursor to all of these other systems. The "tail" is a fully developed spine (for the embryo) that it then grows to fit (in humans, whereas in other creatures it remains a tail).

Secondly, as the genetic material of all creatures, great and small, is similar (in that, there is no argument), as we are all carbon-based life-forms, and our genetic material is similar, (which cannot be said about the end-product), therefore, it actually isn't at all surprising that their development is similar. In fact, this is actually dictated to them during their creation at Genesis on day six, as virtually all creatures are products of the *Adamah* (אדמה), whose root (either *damah*, or *dam*), say our sages, ob"m, is that they share similarities.

It is for the same reason that "molecular biology" cannot be used as a source of proof for evolution as well. It all is based on the same issues. Does the fact of *"the universality of DNA as the genetic material, in the near universality of the genetic code, and in the machinery of DNA replication and expression*[138]*"* really show that evolution is correct?

---

[138] https://bio.libretexts.org/Bookshelves/Microbiology/Book%3A_Microbiology_(Boundless)/8%3A_Microbial_Evolution%2C_Phylogeny%2C_and

This brings us back to the core issue: how do we interpret the data? Was it dictated this way from creation, and can be found in the genetic material as a result of Divine "programming", or is our genetics a slap-together patchwork of happenstance? Let's continue, and find out!

In Summary of Part 3:

DNA itself presents a fundamental difficulty with the concept of evolution, as whatever is coded in the DNA – is what is made into the offspring!

- There is no conclusive proof as to the existence of "junk" DNA, despite all advertisement to the contrary.
- It has never been proven that gene duplication is a means allowing for growth of the genome. All of the cases that we do know are in no way beneficial to the "mutant".
- All observation of microevolution has shown the opposite to be true. We don't find any real changes of DNA in an animal's genome despite all of the selective breeding that has been done.

Yet despite all of the above, there remain many evolutionary scientists who tell us that evolution works and that it's the greatest thing since sliced bread. They also say that – all of the above aside – they have no problems whatsoever with the biology involved in evolution. How is that? It's because of the magic biological "pill", called "mutations."

They also say that they have a fantastic used car to sell you. You can trust them. They are scientists after all! Would you trust them, so far, to sell you a car?

This brings us to part 4

Diversity/8.01%3A Origins of Life/8.1A%3A Evidence of Evolution

Biology and its Related Sciences: Mutations

The "saving grace" of evolution: random mutation.

If not for the existence of "mutations" evolution would have gone the way of the dinosaurs a long time ago. ("Thank G-d!" say the Evo's). We are told that all you need to recognize the truth of evolution is to understand mutations. If you understand this, then all of your questions about evolution will just... slip away... at least, that's what we are told.

However, it must be random, for only random mutations can allow the entire paradigm to work without G-d in the picture. If it's not random, if it follows a program then it's clearly designed, so that must be wrong!

Having said that, we now need to ask the following questions:

- Do mutations actually fit the bill? And more importantly:
- Is there any proof that they are random?

Let's start at the beginning, shall we?

How Do Mutations Occur?

Mutations in DNA sequences generally occur through one of two processes:

DNA damage from environmental agents such as ultraviolet light (sunshine), nuclear radiation or certain chemicals

Mistakes that occur when a cell copies its DNA in preparation for cell division[139].

---

[139] http://learn.genetics.utah.edu/archive/sloozeworm/mutationbg.html

SO, for mutations to work, we require that one of two things happen: A> That there be a significant amount of extraneous information within the DNA, either due to "junk" or gene duplication, as mentioned above; and the damage to the DNA occurs. OR B> that during the gene duplication process a mistake is made that leads to a new "reading" of the genetic information.

According to evolutionary thinking, this works as follows:

SINCE life evolved RANDOMLY;

AND each successive "stage" was due to the addition of new, YET RANDOM, information;

AND since the DNA chain is – essentially – only 4 "letters", (adenine (abbreviated A), cytosine (C), guanine (G) and thymine (T));

AND since the DNA reader, (polymerase), is stupid, it's programmed (for example) to read 2 base pairs and then skip 2;

Therefore, now that the DNA is missing a few base pairs the polymerase will read the DNA in a whole new way!

M.O.U.S.E. say "Hello!" to L.I.O.N.!

Gene Damage Via Radiation (and the like)

In my opinion, saying that damage to the genome is the source for the creation of a new breed of animal is like saying that the way to develop the next generation iPhone... is by throwing the last generation on the floor several times! Or randomly deleting lines of code from a computer program.

How often have we seen any improvement coming from such an action? Never. Yet we are led to believe that this is not only a source for change in the genome, (it is, but not in a good way), but it actually improves upon it in significant ways! Does that make any sense at all? No.

Yet despite this issue, we are told that because we are talking about biology, this makes it another matter entirely! Why? Because all the evolutionary biologist is looking for is VARIATION, and now, due to the new mutation caused by "dropping the gene on the floor" – we have some.

In addition, we are told that although MOST of the time that variation constitutes no more than a dropped iPhone on the floor, biologically it's enough that it works SOME of the time properly, even if the odds against it are 1 in a gazillion.

But is this true? Let's stop for a moment and ask ourselves a very fundamental question:

What Is Needed for A Mutation to Work as The Source of Evolutionary Theory?

As noted earlier, we all agree that speciation occurs within a genome, (there are, after all, many types of dogs and birds)[140]. However, the theory of evolution postulates that it is random mutation and variation that occurred, is this an actual fact?

By my calculations according to evolutionary theory, there are at least 10 things that must happen to allow an inheritable mutation to become part of the genome:

#1

A mutation must occur

DNA replication is a truly amazing biological phenomenon. Consider the countless number of times that your cells divide to make you who you are... Then consider that every time a human cell divides and its DNA replicates, it has to copy and

---

[140] The Torah is not oblivious to this fact as well, as anyone can plainly read in, for example, Leviticus 11 in the lists given of the animals that are permissible or forbidden to be eaten! There, it states clearly that we are not talking about specific animals, but rather about species. However, it should be noted that the Torah's definition of a species is totally different than that of science. Look back at part 2, the topic of microevolution for more on this.

transmit the exact same sequence of 3 billion nucleotides to its daughter cells. ... While most DNA replicates with fairly high fidelity, mistakes do happen...[141]

Just how "high fidelity" is this process?

Our data suggest an overall mutation rate of 2.14x10⁻⁸ per base per generation, or 128 mutations per human zygote (that's an embryo)[142].

#2

The mutation must be "free from selective pressure" or in the "junk".

The duplication of a gene results in an additional copy that is free from selective pressure[143]. One kind of view is that this allows the new copy of the gene to mutate without deleterious consequence to the organism. This freedom from consequences allows for the mutation of novel genes that could potentially increase the fitness of the organism or code for a new function[144].

#3

The mutation must occur in a way that is
transferable to the next generation,
i.e. To the sperm or egg cells

Most of the cells in the human body, for example (as relating to the animal kingdom), don't contribute directly to the next generation. Only

---

[141] http://www.nature.com/scitable/topicpage/dna-replication-and-causes-of-mutation-409

[142] http://www.ncbi.nlm.nih.gov/pubmed/10577911?dopt=Abstract

[143] This refers to a segment of the DNA that has no known function or isn't required to create a protein and/or limb necessary for biological functioning.

[144] http://en.wikipedia.org/wiki/Gene_duplication

the germ line (eggs and sperm) does so, and therefore, only mutations to those tissues will be passed to offspring[145].

However, if the mutation occurs using mistakes made during the copying process of the zygote (embryo's) development, it could then be passed on to future generations as well. Even if we accept this; however, all the successive stages are still required.

#4

The DNA must not immediately fix the mutation

DNA is tough, but it's not indestructible. It can be damaged, and although your cells try to repair the damage, they don't always get it right, resulting in mutations[146].

Mutations tend to be bad, so (not surprisingly) mechanisms exist within cells to reduce the probability of mutation. Biochemical mechanisms repair damaged DNA; proofreading mechanisms catch errors that occur during DNA replication. (Yes, each and every one of us has spell check built in!)[147].

#5

That the mutation affects the genome in some way, and that it should not negatively affect the DNA.

---

[145]   Evolution for Dummies pg. 84

[146]   Ibid. pg. 83

[147]   Ibid. pg. 87. In truth, this is one of the most nonsensical statements that Dr. Kukonis makes. "Spell Check" is NOT a simple program whatsoever! It is ASTOUNDING that we possess a "spell check" that corrects mistakes in gene duplication. Make no mistake about this. To find out about the complexity of spell check look at, for example, https://norvig.com/spell-correct.html

Despite the fact that most of the specific mutations aren't good for any organisms, mutations, in general, are absolutely necessary[148].

Even when a mutation occurs, it could have absolutely no effect whatsoever on the genome. In most (=almost all) cases, however, the mutation negatively affects the genome.

#6

That the child should

inherit the mutation

Not all of your genes are passed on to your offspring! It's roughly a 50-50 split (variable). Out of the 46 chromosomes that we have, 23 are taken from the egg cell and 23 from the sperm cell[149].

#7

That "Bambi", the mutated pig, should not meet "Godzilla."

This, I feel, requires no explanation. I could not resist using the name, though[150]! In the scientific literature, this is referred to as "genetic drift. "[151]

---

[148] Evolution for Dummies pg. 79

[149] http://www.genesandhealth.org/genes-your-health/genes-made-easy

[150] Based on a spoof movie that I saw in my youth called "Bambi meets Godzilla" - look it up on YouTube!

[151] **Genetic drift** is change in allele frequencies in a population from generation to generation that occurs due to chance events. For more information on this see: https://www.khanacademy.org/science/biology/her/heredity-and-genetics/a/genetic-drift-founder-bottleneck

#8

That something then happens to the rest of the genome so that this one has the opportunity to "shine" and become dominant.

As we mentioned earlier, without this step, the mutation will almost certainly disappear within the genome.

All of this is necessary to allow for one generation of mutations to proliferate.

#9

The entire process must be repeated to create a new level of genome growth.

Example: proto-feathers becoming modern feathers, as discussed earlier. Otherwise, we are left with a meaningless mutation.

AND #10

The new mutation must COMPLIMENT the old one

Otherwise, the animal will possess two random mutations that cause no growth whatsoever. More likely than not in this case the second mutation would be cause for a less favorable result rather than a positive one.

If all of the above is true AND mutation is an entirely RANDOM process – what is the likelihood that the process above happens? If we give an arbitrary 10% chance[152] to each of the 10 stages that gives us $0.1 \times 0.1 \times 0.1 \times 0.1 \times 0.1 \times 0.1 \times 0.1 \times 0.1 \times 0.1 \times 0.1 = 0.00000000001$ or $1/10,000,000,000$. In other words: it really should not happen EVER. (Especially if we work out the real statistics involved).

Yet, despite all of the above, it happens ALL OF THE TIME... and extremely fast[153]!

---

[152]   In this, I am being EXTREMELY liberal in the percentage rates.

[153]   This, of course, being contrary to Darwin's original proofs that showed the progression and mutations as being a very slow process.

Oceanic stickleback fish – within the space of only three years –
adapted to lower temperatures than that in which they should
be able to survive. For freshwater sticklebacks, this temperature
is not a problem[154].

If mutations are random – how likely are they to go through a reversal of evolution?

In an article in National Geographic from 2008, the issue of reverse evolution and the re-reverse evolution of the sticklebacks of Lake Washington is discussed. The article states that the sticklebacks metamorphosed into a prehistoric version of themselves because of the immense pollution of the lake in the 1950's. Once cleaned, they almost immediately re-metamorphosed back to the pre-pollutant version[155].

The article concluded by saying

…there aren't many documented examples of reverse evolution
in nature, Peichel said, "But perhaps that's just because people
haven't really looked."

Although this is a known phenomenon to the evolutionists, they refer to it as a "genetic switch"; however, this does not mean that this concept presents no problem for them. The fact that a gene or a set of genes can be turned on or off does not imply that the action is random. A switch is anything BUT random.

Let me make a quantifying statement: I am not claiming that there is no such thing as mutations. There clearly are. What I am saying is that mutations, as used by evolutionists, is NOT the what causes speciation/genetic variation to occur.

As we mentioned earlier concerning "micro-evolution" there is no proof brought that the existence of different types (black or white moths, colorful or drab guppies, etc.) within a genome is the result of a random

---

[154] **http://www.sciencedaily.com/releases/2010/08/100804133446.html**
[155] http://news.nationalgeographic.com/news/2008/05/080520-fish-evolution.html

mutation in the first place. We are told this as a "given" that we swallow hook, line, and sinker. However, in addition, the more exploration that is done, the more it seems that it's the environment that causes the changes in the genome.

Evolution and Epigenetics

All of which brings us to the the topic known as "epigenetics," which is defined as

> ...a *"stably heritable phenotype resulting from changes in a chromosome without alterations in the DNA sequence"* (Wikipedia *"Epigenetics"*)

Meaning that it is possible for variation to occur within a species which has nothing whatsoever to do with mutation or a change in the genome. The more that is learned about this, the more questionable the issue of evolution based on random mutation becomes. This is because it is quite possible for variation to happen without ever changing the genome, and therefore the fact that variation happens has nothing whatsoever to do with "evolution" as it is classically understood.

Colorful guppies could be the result of a lack of, or conversely as a result of the presence of genetic markers in the water in which predators reside, (which implies a genetic sub-routine, and not the emergence of dominance due to predation), that causes the offspring to be born colorful or drab.

Similarly, the presence of genetic markers, or lack thereof, could be the source of industrial melanism in the peppered moth – not predation. The same holds true for virtually, if not actually, all of the examples that are cited as proof for evolution.

In fact, in New Science magazine from April 11, 2011, in an article titled *"Evolution in the Fast Lane"* we find that the only real thing that is apparent, (and the lowest common denominator of all of the cases above), is that

> *"It now appears that whenever the environment changes in any way, life evolves. Fast"*

This statement, based on modern observations, is troubling for evolution. I, therefore, find it strange that Dawkins in his book *The Greatest Show on Earth*, in the chapter entitled *Before Our Very Eyes*, goes on to compile a list of cases in which mutations are occurring rapidly, yet fails to note that this happens despite the odds against it happening! "Mutations are happening all around us!" says Dawkins, "Clearly evolution in action!" he says. Really? How do you know?

Adaptation In the Talmud

That the environment is the source of life's adaptation is something that we find explicitly in the words of our sages, ob"m. The Gemara (Tractate Shabbos 30b-31a) relates the story of two Jewish men living in the times of the second temple who made a bet. One guy bets his friend that he could be the one to get the great sage Hillel the Elder (who lived around 30 BCE) angry. A large sum of money was on the line. The guy thought about everything! The worst time of the week, the worst time of the day, and the most annoying type of questions --- he had it down to a science! So, on that Friday afternoon, at the time of the day when everyone is rushing around to get ready for the Sabbath (Shabbos), this guy bursts into the area where Hillel lives yelling "Who here is Hillel? Who is this Hillel guy"? Hillel is in the midst of washing himself in honor of the Shabbos day, but when he hears someone calling him – ignoring the disrespectful way in which it is being done – he wraps himself up and goes out to meet the man. "Yes, my son," said Hillel, "what is it you need help with?" he said. The man responded, "I need to ask you a question". "Please ask it, my son", said Hillel. "Why are the heads of the Babylonians oval?" he asked. Hillel responded "That's a great question that you have asked! It is because the midwives of Babylon are not well trained [resulting in the child's head not forming properly after coming out of the birth canal]". The guy leaves for a while (without thanking Hillel for his answer) and comes back ten minutes later. "Who here is Hillel?" he shouts, "Who is this Hillel guy?" Hillel, again, wraps himself up (in his rabbinic garments) and comes out to greet him. "What is your need?" asked Hillel of the (really annoying) man. "I have a question to ask", he responded. "Please, ask your question, my son," said Hillel. "Why are the eyes of the Tarmudians (I have no idea who this is) terutot (which Rashi translates as either "soft" or as referring to the shape of their eyes)"? To which Hillel responded "That's a great question that you asked, my son! It is because they live among the sands (and the winds blow sand in their eyes... that place (where they live) caused a change so that their eye openings should not be open like ours in order that the sand shouldn't enter their eyes [Rashi])". So, the guy, once again, goes away, waits another five minutes and then comes back again yelling "Where is Hillel? Where is this Hillel guy"? Once again Hillel dons his rabbinical garments and comes out to greet the (really disrespectful and annoying) guy and calmly asks him "Yes, my son. How can I help you"? "I have a question to ask," he says. "Please ask, my son," said Hillel. "Why are the feet of the Africans so wide"? "That's a great question that you have asked" responded Hillel. "It is because they live among the swamps and wetlands (allowing for greater stability over loose ground)". "I have many questions that I want to ask you", said the man to Hillel "but I'm afraid that they will anger you". Hillel then wraps himself up (in his tallis, his outer garment), sits down calmly in front of the guy and says, "Ask all of the questions that you want to". So, the guy says to him "Are you Hillel, who is also called the Prince of Israel"? To which Hillel responded "Yes". "If it's you – there should be no more like you in Israel"! Hillel then asked, "Why is that, my son"? "As it is because of you that I lost 400 zuz (a significant amount of money, equal to about two years of the average salary in those times)"! To which Hillel responded "You must be very careful with your spirit. Hillel's worth is so great that it would be preferable for you to lose even twice that amount in order so that Hillel should not get angry".

Aside from the great lesson of the importance of humility and tranquility that the Gemara is teaching us, it is clear that the opinion of Hillel (he does state this outright, and Rashi elucidates it even more) is that it is the environment that is the direct cause of adaptation. It has nothing to do with "survival of the fittest" nor any other nonsense that is given in lieu of a real observation. It is also the only explanation that fits the observable data.

What science has discovered is that there are so many possible adaptations "waiting" to be called upon inside of the genetic coding, in the "*non*-junk", that any thinking person can see that *it was all pre-programmed in and was only waiting for the necessary environmental trigger to make it happen*. It is for this reason, and this reason only that the "junk" is always reproduced. It plays a part in the life of the species, as it is preprogrammed for adaptation/speciation. That is not random, nor is it chance. That is design.

Genome Complexity and In-Depth Knowledge of DNA

The really fundamental problem is that the scientific community of today still knows next to nothing about the genome and the microbiology of DNA.

Only relatively recently, mainly due to advances in computer science, was it possible to process the genome of various species. Up until that point, it was assumed that the more complex the creature – the more genes will be found in its genome.

WRONG!

The most surprising result of the human genome project was that it revealed that assumption to be entirely false! There is absolutely no correlation between the complexity of the organism and a greater number of genes. Amazingly enough, (unless you are a fan of Douglas Adams, who holds that the mice and dolphins are smarter than we are), humans possess fewer genes than many species. In volume, we are running neck and neck with the Nematode worm[156].

> *So, since we are so much more complex than these organisms, everyone thought that our genome would hold many more genes. Looks like this isn't the case[157].*

So, we find that the real problem remains. Why are humans so different and more advanced than all other creatures, (assuming, of course, that they are not G-d's creations)?

The answer, astoundingly, is that QUALITATIVELY our genome is radically different!

> *For starters, rather than each gene coding for one protein, they often code for many... a single (human) gene can potentially code for tens of thousands of different proteins, although the average is about 5. ... Even more astonishingly, in at least one case in humans, RNA copies of different genes are spliced together. If this is commonplace, it would vastly multiply the potential number of proteins[158].*

The question that we now have is WHY? If, essentially, we have the same genes as any other animal on the planet – why do our genes, (and it sounds like it's ONLY our genes), differ from that of all other life on the planet?

"No! No!" we are told, "the chimpanzee, our "closest cousin," also has the same number of genes. Our DNA is 96 (or 97 or 98) percentage the same. A statistical impossibility. (Amazingly, only here the statistics

---

[156] *New* Scientist June 19, 2011 in an article called "RNA rules, ok?"

[157] http://www.thetech.org/genetics/news.php?id=14

[158] New Scientist ibid

"work" in their favor and are cited as being infallible). So, this proves nothing as it's impossible for our genomes to be so similar by chance."

Really?

As we have already mentioned earlier in this chapter, the above is a fiction that was made popular by the media. The truth is that if we would stack up the human and chimpanzee genomes and compare them point for point, they are, in fact, incredibly DISsimilar. The above percentages were arrived at by ignoring large different parts of the genome, and by lots of good-old imagination in comparing the rest[159]. After all, the reason they are different is due to mutation, which is clearly a fact…right? Oh. You didn't actually *observe* the mutation, but you can imagine it? Good for you… in your fantasy world.

However, that is not the whole issue! It's only the most recent.

The REAL Scope of In-Depth Knowledge of DNA and Genetics

The above aside we have to ask one very stark and very real question. How much – truly – does anyone, molecular biologist or otherwise, know about the workings of DNA?

As we mentioned earlier the reasons why it was assumed that there is "junk" DNA is because of a> evolutionary theory, and b> because we didn't have the ability to note how it was used in genetic processing until recently.

---

[159]   Chimpanzee Sequencing; Analysis Consortium (2005). "Initial sequence of the chimpanzee genome and comparison with the human genome". Nature. **437** (7055): 69–87. "The alignable sequences within genomes of humans and chimpanzees differ by about 35 million single-nucleotide substitutions. Additionally, about 3% of the complete genomes differ by deletions, insertions and duplications." (Wikipedia Human evolutionary genetics) Since the authors sequenced a total of 2.7 billion DNA letters, this implies that only 2.4 billion of the letters matched well between humans and chimps leaving 0.3 billion (2.7–2.4) letters unmatched. A 0.3 billion letter difference is 11% of 2.7 billion. See also https://creation.com/greater-than-98-chimp-human-dna-similarity-not-any-more

What this really means is that the reason that evolutionists are so self-assured that there is "junk" DNA … is sheer ignorance.

How CAN we know if there is "junk" DNA or not? There is really only one way: if we understand the WHOLE "program/genome."

If we COMPREHEND the ENTIRE program, i.e. how the entire genome performs its sequencing; if we had a deep understanding as to what the whole thing was saying, then we can surely say "Yep! There's a ton of junk here!" and be correct. But until that time, the only reason to claim this is out of ignorance. (Illogical ignorance too, as we explained earlier)!

"But," you might say, "Maybe there IS someone out there who's in-the-know"? Let's think about that for just a minute:

> *To get an idea of the size of the human genome present in each of our cells, consider the following analogy: If the DNA sequence of the human genome were compiled in books, the equivalent of 200 volumes the size of a book series, (at 1000 pages each), would be needed to hold it all. It would take about 9.5 years to read out loud (without stopping) the 3 billion bases in a person's genome sequence. This is calculated on a reading rate of 10 bases per second, equaling 315,360,000 bases/year[160].*

In the above statement, we are not even talking about understanding any of the material, just reading it.

When we then take into account the fact that we are ignorant concerning 97% of the genome which is termed "junk"; AND

(If we are being really frankly honest, and admit that our knowledge of the other 3% isn't all that deep; AND)

When we consider that our understanding of the human genome only recently underwent an overhaul (via genome mapping) to work in ways that boggle the mind the following becomes apparent:

---

[160]   http://www.iitk.ac.in/infocell/Archive/dirnov3/science.html

That even the most learned scientists on the planet today understand only a fraction of a fraction of a fraction of the workings and infrastructure of the human genome.

> *The picture that has emerged since 2000 is that the classical understanding of how life's core cellular machinery functions is rather shallow. ... Sequencing revealed that genes only constituted a diminutive, fractional percentage of the human genome. ... But a deep understanding of how that transformation progresses, and how a protein's specific conformal configuration will influence cellular function, is still nascent[161].*

So, I ask why we should believe these knowledgeable people who claim to know that mutations are random, unguided processes?

Would you still like to buy that car from them?

Let's ask a further question:

Is it possible to prove what causes a mutation? In other words: is it possible to show that mutations are random?

> *Mutations appear to be spontaneous in most instances. That does not mean that they occur without cause but, rather, that the specific cause is almost always unknown. Subsequently, it is usually very difficult for lawyers to prove in a court of law that a particular mutagen is responsible for causing a specific mutation in people. With the aid of expert scientific testimony, they can often demonstrate that the mutagen can cause a particular kind of mutation. However, that is not the*

---

[161] http://seedmagazine.com/content/article/the_once_and_future_genome/. For those of you who, like me, never heard of seed magazine, I will point out that I was referred to this article from the home site of the Human Genome project.

same thing as proving that a plaintiff's mutation was caused
by that mutagen instead of some others[162].

What the above article states, (although not outright), is that we have NO IDEA WHATSOEVER what causes mutations! Moreover, to actually prove what the cause of a certain mutation is, is impossible!

In light of the above, how can someone utilize mutation as the redeeming quality of evolution when, clearly, there isn't, (and never will be), a person who can claim to actually understand genetic, biological processes, their causes, and their effects?

In a nutshell: we don't know *bupkis*, (Yiddish for "nothing"), about the real workings of DNA, let alone the entire genome.

Yet despite all of the above, for some reason...

...there is no area of observable phenomena where evolutionary scientists are as quick to point out the wonders of RANDOM mutations! HOW IN THE WORLD CAN YOU CLAIM, BASED ON IGNORANCE, THAT SOMETHING IS RANDOM OR EVEN THAT SOMETHING IS A (NATURAL) MUTATION?

Due to evolutionary theory, the medical profession is convinced that there are unnecessary limbs within the human body. Why is that? Because we "grew" out of types of animals, for which these limbs WERE useful, whereas we, having evolved, no longer have a need for them. OR, because we have, via the machinations of evolution, developed limbs/organs which, as of yet, have no function but one day might. Either way, we are told that the human body has within it "vestibular (unnecessary) organs." Really? Well, how do we know this? We are aware of it because evolutionary theory tells us so, but do we really know that this is true? No. However, this hasn't prevented the medical profession from making decisions based on this premise. Let's have some examples.

---

[162]   http://anthro.palomar.edu/synthetic/synth_3.html. Palomar College of San Marcos, California is a well-respected, accredited college. This is an excerpt from a published article about mutations.

I remember growing up, and several of my friends had the enjoyable experience of eating ice cream for about a week. Why? Because their tonsils became infected and they, therefore, had them removed. Why? "Well," said the doctor, "since they serve no purpose ANYWAY, so why not"? However, since that time it has been discovered that the tonsils are part of the human immune system and that they DO serve a purpose.

The same was thought about the appendix and about the pituitary gland as well until it was discovered that they also serve a purpose in the human system.

OOH! Batting average of 0!

Today the medical profession still holds a list of organs that they consider vestibular. Why? No new reasons. Just the same old ones: we don't see that it has a purpose and evolutionary theory!

Last Thoughts

Finally, let's consider this: Evolution is supposed to, at the very least, explain to us how a simple organism can evolve into a complex one. However, what it cannot do is explain the following two things:

Intelligence, (why humans have a greater use of their intellectual capacity as opposed to all other organisms); and

Morality, (why humans have an innate definition as to the "right" versus the "wrong").

Much ink has been spilled, pens broken, and keyboards pounded to try to fill in the "gaps" that evolutionary theory leaves behind. However, no matter how you slice it – it still remains baloney!

Neuroscience and intelligence concern the various neurological factors that may be responsible for the variation of intelligence within a species or between different species. Much of the work in this field is concerned with the variation in human intelligence, but other intelligent species such as the non-human primates, cetaceans, and rodents are also of interest. The basic mechanisms by which the brain produces complex phenomena such as consciousness and intelligence are still poorly understood[163].

What possibilities would allow for the advanced intelligence and rational thinking of humans as opposed to the comparatively low-functioning intelligence of all of the other creatures in the world?

Perhaps, one might think, it is the sheer SIZE of the brain that allows for this?

Nope.

The largest brains are those of blue whales, weighing about 8 kg (18 lb.). An elephant's brain weighs just over 5 kg (11lb), a bottlenose dolphin's 1.5 to 1.7 kg (3.3 to 3.7 lb.), whereas a human brain is around 1.3 to 1.5 kg (2.9 to 3.3 lb.)[164].

Yet neither the blue whale nor the elephant, despite the massive size of their craniums, are capable of feats of intelligence on par with, or even remotely close to, those of the average human being!

Not only that, but Neanderthal man also had a measured cranial size greater than that of modern man[165], yet the "tools" and all other remains that have been found indicate no great feats of intelligence when compared with those of modern man.

There is some evidence that a humans' brain size can be a factor pertaining to IQ. However, in terms of species, we have not found that differences exist in intelligence due to brain size. For example, blue whales display no more intelligence than, say, a hummingbird.

---

[163]   http://en.wikipedia.org/wiki/Neuroscience_and_intelligence
[164]   http://en.wikipedia.org/wiki/Brain_size
[165]   http://en.wikipedia.org/wiki/Cranial_capacity

So maybe, one might say, it's a matter of brain to body size ratio. Maybe. But maybe not!

Speaking in terms of mass and in proportion to body size, it is common knowledge that the human has the biggest brain in such proportions. A human's brain has a brain-to-body ratio of 1/49. This means that your entire body weighs 49 times more than your brain does. However, in terms of proportion to body size, the human is not the candidate for the biggest brain. Here are some known brain-to-body mass ratios of common animals in descending order:

Hummingbird: 1/25

Squirrel monkeys: 1/32 to 1/20

Mice: 1/40

Humans: 1/49[166]

According to that logic, the hummingbird and the Squirrel Monkeys should show their intelligence plainly, but they don't. Douglas Adams aside, we all know is that there is no animal that displays the intelligence that we humans have.

Despite the apparent ramifications of brain size to IQ quotient among humans, (which may-or-may-not have anything to do with one another, circumstantial evidence aside), it seems clear that sheer brain size has nothing whatsoever to do with sheer intelligence.

> *Not all investigators are happy with the amount of attention that has been paid to brain size. Roth and Dicke, for example, have argued that factors other than size are more highly correlated with intelligence, such as the number of cortical neurons and the speed of their connections. Moreover, they point out that intelligence depends not just on the amount of brain tissue, but on the details of how it is structured. It is also well known that crows, ravens, and African Grey Parrots are quite intelligent even though they have small brains[167].*

---

[166] http://wiki.answers.com/Q/Which_animal_has_the_biggest_brain

[167] http://en.wikipedia.org/wiki/Brain_size

If that is the case, then the question becomes why DO humans have such a qualitatively and quantitatively different brain than all other animals? Does it really make sense to say that it's just a fluke? Why is it that we find, only concerning human beings, the following?

A discovery in recent years is that the structure of the adult human brain changes when a new cognitive or motor skill, including vocabulary, is learned. Structural neuroplasticity (increased gray matter volume) has been demonstrated in adults after three months of training in a visual-motor skill, with the qualitative change (i.e. learning of a new task) appearing more critical for the brain to change its structure than continued training of an already-learned task. Such changes (e.g. revising for medical exams) have been shown to last for at least 3 months without further practicing; other examples include learning novel speech sounds, musical ability, navigation skills and learning to read mirror-reflected words[168].

Another aspect concerning human brains and intellect is the following:

The human brain is big, and it's powerful, able to dream up innovative solutions to complex problems. Yet our brains don't age well: As we grow older, they tend to shrink and become increasingly vulnerable to cognitive dysfunctions such as memory loss and dementia. A new magnetic resonance imaging (MRI) study comparing humans and chimpanzees finds that chimp brains maintain their size as they age. Slowly losing our minds, it turns out, may be the evolutionary price we pay for having bigger brains and longer life spans.

As far as researchers can tell, humans are the only animals subject to specific brain maladies such as Alzheimer's disease

---

[168] http://en.wikipedia.org/wiki/Brain_size

... and previous studies of human brains have suggested that these brain regions, which include the frontal lobe and the hippocampus, are especially prone to shrinkage with age.

Although few similar studies of other primates have been conducted, recent research with rhesus monkeys has shown only very limited shrinkage with age. Nevertheless, the evolutionary lineages leading to humans and rhesus monkeys diverged about 30 million years ago, leaving scientists in the dark about when the human pattern of brain aging might have begun[169].

Clearly, there is something that sets apart human beings from all other creations in regard to his intellect.

What about the importance of morality to mankind? Why are there so many people who, for the sake of an ideal, will even go to the extreme of giving away their only real possession, (their lives), to do the "right thing"? What happened to "survival of the fittest"? How do they overcome the "fight-or-flight" response when science totes man as being only the "fittest" among the world's creatures, an animal at his core?

If the ancient world was a "dog eat dog world", (or "fish eat fish", take your pick), then when – exactly – would it have changed?

Did Oog, son of Bork, wake up one morning and start teaching the philosophy of the sanctity of life? Who would have listened to him? What would Oog say to his son, Goo? How would he inculcate his philosophy?

One day Goo is sitting at his table, and he turns to his father, Oog, and says "Dad. If killing is so wrong, why is grandpa Bork out there killing the possums for dinner"? To which Oog would say, "Well son, grandpa Bork is a primitive." "Well dad, if that's true," Goo would say, "then why are we the only ones not doing it? I mean all of my friends and their families had roast Megalodon for dinner while we had a few berries and a handful

---

169 http://news.sciencemag.org/sciencenow/2011/07/the-incredible-shrinking-human-b.html take a look there as they elaborate on the issue

of grains! WHERE'S THE BEEF"? What is he going to say? That it's society that inculcated him that way? What a joke!

Yet we find that the traditional view of social scientists has been that morality is a construct, and is thus culturally relative, although others argue that there is a science of morality[170].

> *Evolutionary scientists believe that our social structure evolved from within the animal kingdom. Since we find that animals, wolves, for example, live in a social hierarchy, which is imposed to allow them to function better as a group. Also, since the pack is an all-important need in animal society, therefore the individual learned to act according to the rules of the group to benefit from the advantages of the group.*

Sounds good, no? Umm... NO! This assumption, although based on the observable phenomenon, (that animals' function with a social hierarchy), rests on the preconceived notion that the individual animals sit and weigh the pros and the cons of living in a social group vs. not doing so and therefore straightens himself out to follow the pack. The truth is that this is great science fiction. Animals, even social animals, tend not to have the ability to learn from their mistakes (although some do) or to weigh the outcome of their actions to come to a rational decision. They do, however, act on instinct. Their instinct binds them to act by the group social norms. Where did that instinct come from? Is it learned? No. Is it inbred? You betcha!

Do animals ever consider what the "right/good" thing is before doing or not doing something? NO! (Only in the movies). They have no concept of "good" or "bad" or the capacity to weigh the difference between them or their eventual outcome. Only humans have this ability, and only humans do this.

Why is it that in all of recorded ancient human history we never find an instance in which man assumed he was just another animal (until recent

---

[170] http://en.wikipedia.org/wiki/Evolution_of_morality

history)? All recorded human history in the ancient world expresses the same thing: the world was divinely created, and there is another plane of existence: the world to come.

Are these constructs that we find among the animal kingdom as well? Well, we don't know for sure, but I think it's safe to say that ... NOT!

Do animals have a drive, as Viktor Frankl teaches in Logotherapy, that their lives have meaning and purpose? Do animals in the wild experience depression? Do they have dog psychologists? Do they think that they should leave behind something that lasts beyond them? NO. It's all just instinct for them, nothing more.

But COULD IT BE...? Maybe. But would you bet your life on it? Does it enrich your life if it is true? Are you intrinsically a better person for it? Would it be meaningful to you that someone states this at your eulogy?

Does biology have a real answer for any of this in physical terms? NO. Will it? Certainly not. Why is this? It's because of the principle that I have mentioned before Science is the study of observable, measurable phenomenon. It, therefore, cannot explain the "WHY" of anything unless it is the result of something that is observable, (sickness due to bacteria, for example). Unless the actual evolution of brainpower can be reproduced in the lab – there is no way, outside of science fiction, to know why only humans stand alone in the world.

No one has observed a cause-and-effect relationship that can explain the complexity of human intelligence. Has anyone observed a cause-and-effect relationship to explain how social norms in animals have led to a human constructed morality? No. Will someone one day? Absolutely not!

Would you bet your life on this rickety, unstable construct of wet paper cards?

Would you trust such a person to sell you their used car?

How about to trust him with your most prized possession, your life?

In Summary

There is no obvious mechanism for making a simple genome into a more complex one.

Statistically, RANDOM "mutations" (i.e. variation within the genome) should never happen, yet variation happens all of the time!

RANDOM "mutations" should not be reversible, let alone re-reversible! Genome variation is NOT a proof for evolution via mutation.

The issue of epigenetics allows for variation within the genome without changing it by turning on or off genes that are already there. Ergo no mutation or evolution is required to make speciation happen.

The "proofs" of microevolution are all based on the aforementioned preconceived notions concerning mutation.

The explanations into WHY these creatures evolved the way that they did are based, purely, on unadulterated SCIENCE FICTION. And:

The human genome is RADICALLY MORE COMPLEX than those of all other life.

Human intelligence and morality logically defy the theory of evolution.

SO, if an evolutionary theory makes NO sense – then should you really live your life based on it? (Please review the lesson "Darwinism in the Twilight Zone"). Think about it.

For a complete summary of the difficulties with the theory of evolution – please look in the appendix, (Appendix II).

7

A-braham and A-bio-genesis:

Abraham's Quest for Truth and The Theory Of A-Bio-Genesis

NE OF THE NAMES given to the Jewish people is עבריים, (*Ivri'im*), which is (poorly) translated as "Hebrews". In truth, this name goes back to Noah's grandson, the son of Shem, whose name was EVER, (עבר). All of the descendants of Ever were called *Ivri'im*, meaning "sons of Ever." Our Sages tell us, however, that this name was appended to Avram in a derogatory fashion, due to his "heretical" thoughts and attitudes. He was called "*THE* Ivri," meaning "the one who is on the other side."

This name – like many other derogatory jabs of non-Jews throughout the centuries – was a nickname given to our great forefather AVRAHAM for the simple reason that ideologically and theologically he was on one side of the world and the rest of the world on the other side! Since the time of Avraham our Father, it is a name that we "wear" with the utmost of pride!

Let me tell you all a bit of a story. It's the story of AVRAHAM AVINU and what earned him his name, "Ha Ivri".

Avram, as he was called at birth, was born in the area of Mesopotamia known as UR CASDIM (Ur of Chaldees). At the time of his birth, our legends tell us that soothsayers said to the king, a man by the name of NIMROD, that today a boy was born in the city who will grow to become his destroyer. (Esau, Avraham's grandson eventually killed him). Nimrod immediately dispatched his soldiers to search for the boy to have him killed.

Avram's father, *Terach*, fearing for his son's life, took him away to the mountains where he hid him in a cave. Avram lived in this cave for the first 43 years of his life. There is a bit of a difference of opinion as to how old he was exactly when the following event took place, but he was somewhere between the ages of 3 and 43.

One-day Avram was out thinking, (I mean all alone in the mountains, in a cave, what else is there for someone to do?), "This world, this grand and complex world, there's just no way that it came to be on its own! It's as if I'm looking at a castle with its lights on! Who could have built this fantastic Castle (world)"!

So, Avram decides that he just has to meet The Architect and The Contractor..., and he goes out of the cave. At this point, the powerful rays and heat of the sun greet him, and he says to himself, "What power! What majesty! This must be the Creator"! He immediately begins to pray and prostrate to the sun. All day long, there is Avram, thanking the sun! Praising the sun! Beseeching the sun! Until... the sun set... and in its place, came the darkness. "Nope," said Avram to himself, "it can't be the sun! That thing runs out of juice after about twelve hours". Just then the moon came out in its entire splendor, (middle of the lunar month), and Avram thought, "That must be IT! That must be the Creator!", and immediately set about thanking, praising and beseeching the moon. Well, you might have guessed that about 12 hours later the moon disappeared, and the sun came up, and Avram understood that the moon was not it, it was not the Creator.

It was at this time that Avram turned his eyes to the heavens, and he said, "It must be that the real Creator is here, but I just can't see or smell or touch Him! Master of the universe", he shouted, "help me to know your truth"!

Well, we all know that as a direct result of this conclusion Avram started down the path that was less traveled, belief in the One True G-D.

Well, it's certainly tough to have the whole world against you ideologically, but that was where Avram's strength was: to go against the flow. It was not long, therefore, before Avram had a confrontation of note concerning the matter of theology.

The Midrash Rabba on Genesis chapter 38, section 13, tells us the (famous) story of how one day, after the threat against Avram's life had passed, *Terach*, Avram's father, calls him into the family store, and says to him "Son, I need to go out on a little business for a while. Please mind the store while I'm gone". Well normally that might not be a bad thing, but when you consider what *Terach's* business was, (he was the local Idol merchant), then that's really just setting yourself up for failure! It's like asking a sworn pacifist to guard the local weapons cache, or asking a Vegan to guard the local butcher shop, or asking an animal rights activist to watch the laboratories that perform studies on rats! What in the world WAS he thinking?

In any case, here's Avram minding the store when a woman walks in with an amount of flour and says to Avram "Please offer this to that idol, over there." At which point Avram says to her, "do you think THAT's what you offer this? That's not what you offer it! THIS is what you offer it!" and he picks up his Louisville Slugger bat and starts smashing the idol to whom she wanted to bring the offering. After thoroughly enjoying breaking the first idol, he continues to destroy all of the rest of the idols in the store. However, Avram is smart; he knows that he can't get away with it unless he has an alibi, so he destroys all of the idols in the store except for one, the biggest one in the shop. Immediately he takes the bat and puts it into the hand of the last remaining idol.

Just then, his father comes back and... lo, and behold! (I always wanted to say that!) What does he find? (It's a rhetorical question, don't bother answering it!) All of his idols that he worked so hard to build were smashed to smithereens!

Well, he DID leave a competent adult in charge when he left, (even though we still don't know WHAT he was thinking), so he turns to Avram and asks him the obvious question, "What's up doc"?

"I couldn't believe it," Avram said, "this woman came to give an offering to one of the idols, and I was bringing it to the one she told me when all of a sudden the idols started a whole argument! This one said, "Give ME the offering!" this one said, "No, give ME the offering!" They started to fight amongst themselves. Just then, the biggest idol got up and said, "I have the solution! No problem!" he then took my Louisville slugger and proceeded to slug the stuffing out of all of the other idols, grabbed the offering and ate it"!

Well, *Terach*, after listening to Avram's explanation responded "Oh come... ON! Whom do you think you are fooling here? You and I both know that these idols they don't breathe, they don't see, hear, feel or smell; and they most certainly do not eat"!

At this point Avram interjected "Abba, are you listening to what you have to say about idols and their worship"?

Apparently, like most people, *Terach* did not take well to his son's reprimand concerning his cherished beliefs. So, he took him to none other than Nimrod, the person from whom he saved Avram when he was a baby, to straighten his son out theologically.

Avram was brought into the throne room and stood in front of Nimrod. Immediately a theological debate ensued:

Nimrod says to Avram, "Boy! Do you know who the god I worship is?" to which Avram responded, "No, your highness! No clue"!

"I worship the god of FIRE, boy!" said Nimrod and immediately went off into some diatribe. Ranting and raving about how great the god of fire is, pointing to the fire symbol on his shirt and the multitude of priests in the throne room. "Why," said Avram, "don't you worship the god of water? Isn't he great?" asked Avram. "Isn't he even greater than the god of fire? After all," said Avram, "water DOES put out fires"! "Good point!" said

Nimrod, tearing the fire symbol off his shirt while waving to a servant to get him a water symbol with which to replace it and motioning to his soldiers to kill off the fire priests. "Good point! You know what? I was on my way – just today – to begin worshiping the god of Water!" yelled Nimrod. "The Great and Mighty God of water, that's who I worship!" said Nimrod.

"Well, your highness," said Avram, "don't clouds CARRY water in them? Aren't clouds, therefore, even MIGHTIER than water?" said Avram. "An excellent observation!" said Nimrod once again tearing the newly sewn water symbol off his shirt, motioning for the cloud symbol to be sewn on and signaling for the water priests to be executed. "I worship the god of CLOUDS!" he roared. "The Great and Mighty cloud god!" said Nimrod, "Better than fire! Stronger than water! CLOUDS! That's the way to go!" he yelled.

"And yet," said Avram, "WINDS blow the clouds around ALL DAY," he said. "Isn't wind therefore STRONGER than clouds? I mean if clouds are so wimpy that they can get pushed around by the wind all the time, (I mean did you ever see a cloud push back?), then wind must be even stronger than clouds"!

At this point Nimrod shot Avram this "Oh, come ON!" type look, (he was, after all, quickly running out of priests and clothing), tore the cloud off his chest and sewed on a wind symbol and snapped to Avram "OK! Wind it is! Let's go wind! Prepare a sacrifice for the wind god!" he yelled, beckoning the wind priests forward.

"HMMM!" said Avram, "But you know, your majesty, that most of the time when a good wind is blowing, it doesn't seem to affect most men! They appear to be able to stand up to the wind! Therefore, it makes sense that a MAN is stronger than the wind! Maybe we should worship man"! (Please note that he did not intend to say anything about monkeys being stronger than the wind. After all, it was CLEAR in those days that man was intrinsically better than animals).

Well finally, Nimrod catches on to the game of hoops that Avram has been making him run through, and he interjects, "Do you know what

Avram? I'm back to the fire god!" (Pretty indecisive, no?), "let's just see how you, a man, fare against him"!

Well, this is the point in Avram's life where G-D truly first appears to him. Nimrod prepared a furnace especially for the occasion that he filled to the brim with firewood, lit it, and let it heat up. Our sages tell us that the heat was so intense that if you were in proximity of the furnace, your eyebrows would get singed! Avram was then THROWN into the furnace and the door was sealed behind him so that he would roast nicely. Then a funny thing happened. Nimrod was kind of expecting that he would hear screaming coming from the furnace, but he heard nothing. He commanded that the door should be opened so that they could see what was happening to Avram. They slowly opened the door and – lo and behold – (there! I said it again!) What did they see? Avram sitting in the midst of the fire just as relaxed as if he were seated in an air-conditioned room! Apparently, a miracle was performed on his behalf.

This was one of the first theological debates in history.

Nimrod, being a product of his time, worshiped the elements and considered them to have been the progenitors of all life. It was Avram, who was well on his way, at this point in his life, to becoming AVRAHAM, our Forefather, who showed him – to the best of his ability – the fallacy behind that notion.

It's so amazing: the more things change, the more they stay the same!

Modern science, as we discussed in the previous lesson, also believes that all life on the planet emanates from the elements. It's just that as opposed to Nimrod, who thought that they were the "essential elements" of Earth, Wind, and Fire, science today postulates that all living life is the product of chemical evolution: from base elements to complex chemical chains and eventually, gradually, to simple life forms.

As I stated in the previous lesson, from the work of Dr. Kukonis, in his aptly named book "Evolution (is) for Dummies", most evolutionary scientists say, "listen I know a lot about the biomechanics of evolution, but what transpired before the first living cell, (i.e. "simple" life), is not evolutions problem! It's the problem of the chemists and biochemists"!

This is a classic example of "the Ostrich Syndrome". After all, we know that when an ostrich is in danger, it will – many times – stick its head in the sand as an evasive tactic instead of fight or flight. Well, that, my friends, is exactly what Dr. Kukonis did. He noted a tough issue, which directly affects evolutionary theory, (i.e. unassisted, undirected cellular mutation and development, without the aid of a supernatural agent. Which implies that the same occurred in the development, etc. of the first cell as well), and instead of noting a real answer, (and instead of what he actually did: making up a false answer by adding imaginary data to one of the experiments in abiogenesis, which we will touch on later), he says to us "Listen! I don't know the answer to that question, and it really is a toughie! However, there is an answer, it's just that my field of expertise is not in chemistry, and therefore I don't happen to know what the answer is. However, I'm sure that if you asked a chemist or a biochemist, they would know how to answer"!

Classic "Ostrich Syndrome", stuck his head right into the sand!

Considering that the purpose of "evolution" is to show that complex life came about from simple life without any supernatural aid by means of evolution and "natural processes," you then have to continue that train of thought and say that simple life came about from chemical life by some mechanism of similar means.

So, if that's the case and, as Dr. Kukonis would have us believe, that the chemists can find the answer to this dilemma, then it makes sense that that's where we will have to go next!

A-biogenesis

This area of evolutionary science is called "Abiogenesis," meaning the beginnings (Genesis) of life (bio) from non-life (prefix A).

When looking into this area of science we have to consider several things:

Problem A: The time-frame chemical evolution had in which to take place.

Problem B: The second law of thermodynamics.

Problem C: The environment in which simple life systems could propagate.

Problem D: The complexity of biological systems.

Problem E: The interconnectedness of biological systems.

Problem F: The Shortcomings of the Scientific method in this regard.

Problem A: The Time-Frame Chemical Evolution Had in Which To Take Place

Before we begin to explore the issues that scientists of the evolutionary persuasion must deal with, first let us ask ourselves: Just how much time did "Nature" have at "it's" disposal in which to synthesize simple life from chemical life?

To know that, let's estimate science's findings concerning the early earth: when did it first became an "Earth" vs. when the first simple, (and yet so complex!), life was first found on the planet:

The following is an excerpt from Wikipedia[171], which includes in it some of the theories of scientists today as to where life came from.

---

[171] http://en.wikipedia.org/wiki/Timeline_of_evolution#cite_note-0

Date (Ma=million years)	Event
4600 Ma	The planet Earth forms from the accretion disk, revolving around the young Sun.
100,000,000 years go by and…	
4500 Ma	According to one plausible theory, the planet Earth and the planet Theia[172] collide, sending a vast number of moonlets into orbit around the young Earth. These moonlets eventually coalesce to form the Moon. The gravitational pull of the new Moon stabilizes the Earth's fluctuating axis of rotation and sets up the conditions in which life formed.
4100 Ma	The surface of the Earth cools enough for the crust to solidify. The atmosphere and the oceans form. PAH infall and iron sulfide synthesis along deep ocean platelet boundaries may have led to the RNA world of competing for organic compounds.
Between 4500 and 3500 Ma	The earliest life appears, possibly derived from self-reproducing RNA molecules. The replication of these organisms requires resources like energy, space, and smaller building blocks, which soon become limited, resulting in competition, with natural selection favoring those molecules that are more efficient at replication. DNA molecules then take over as the primary replicators and these archaic genomes soon develop inside enclosing membranes, which provide a stable physical and chemical environment conducive to their replication: proto-cells.

---

[172] For lack of a better term, "Theia" is only a Theory, and a bad one at that. In the Wikipedia article on Theia called the *"Giant Impact Hypothesis"*, it states: *Indirect evidence for this impact scenario comes from rocks collected during the Apollo Moon landings, which show oxygen isotope ratios identical to those of Earth. The highly anorthositic composition of the lunar crust, as well as the existence of KREEP-rich samples, gave rise*

In other words, at sometime around 4300 Ma, the earth became somewhat hospitable towards the synthesis of chemical compounds, (but let's assume, for argument's sake, that this occurred at the time of the forming of Earth's crust, at 4100 Ma). Well, the oldest known life, meaning simple organisms known as prokaryotes, was, in the words of Science Daily[173]:

> *Microbes and Bacteria were the first living organisms on*
> *Earth, and they can be preserved in Archean silica-rich rocks.*
> *One such outcrop from Western Australia, dated to 3.5 billion*
> *years ago, may hold the oldest "micro-fossils."*

There have been findings dating even earlier than that, at 3.8 billion years old, although there has been severe debate concerning this finding.

Accordingly, if it truly is a sign of organic life, it turns out that the Earth had – roughly – a period of only 300-600,000,000 years[174] in which to synthesize organic life from inorganic life. Evolutionarily speaking that is not a lot of time!

When you consider that the "evolution" of the eukaryotes, a more advanced form of single-celled bacteria, took until roughly 1.85 billion years to occur that means that it took 3.5 (age of the oldest prokaryotes) -1.85 (age of oldest eukaryotes) =1.65 billion additional years for the evolution of prokaryotes into eukaryotes! However, evolutionarily speaking, just the opposite should be true! Because the quantitative change from

---

to the idea that a large portion of the Moon was once molten, and a giant impact scenario could easily have supplied the energy needed to form such a magma ocean.

Interestingly enough our holy Torah tells us that on the fourth day of creation *TWO* great lights were created in the sky: the sun *and the moon*. It really was molten, just like the sun is. HMM. How did that ancient committee know that? Must be G-D...

[173] July 2 2009

[174] Concerning the issue of scientific dating of millions/billions of years – I disagree, and we'll talk about that in a later chapter (*chapter nine*). I am quoting the dates of modern science for the sake of argument alone.

non-life to life was much greater than a qualitative change that occurred, comparatively, between prokaryotes and eukaryotes! If life from non-life was like going from 1-1000, then single-celled life to single-celled life is like 1000-1200! So why then did the smaller change take – at the very least – two times longer?

This issue, the short span of time available to synthesize organic life from inorganic compounds, leads evolutionary scientists to say the following. Either life is a "once in a lifetime" fluke, (in a seemingly never-ending series of once-in-a-lifetime flukes), it's just that we are not sure WHERE this fluke occurred, (on earth or in space or some by mixture of the two. We'll explore this soon enough); or we must say that life is a "natural imperative", which – in you-and-me language – means that the cards were stacked, and the dice were loaded and therefore the outcome of this lotto to end all lottos was fixed from the beginning. Life has to come about; it is the certain consequence of chemical and biological recombination[175].

---

[175]   This course focuses exclusively on the scientific approach to the question of life's origins. In this lecture series, I make an assumption that life emerged from basic raw materials through a sequence of events that was completely consistent with the natural laws of chemistry and physics. Even with this scientific approach, there is a possibility that we'll never know how life originated. It is possible that life emerged by an almost infinitely improbable sequence of difficult chemical reactions. If that's true, then living planets must be rare in the cosmos. It is even possible that Earth is the only living planet. If life is the result of an infinitely improbable succession of chemical steps, then any scientific attempt to understand life's origin is doomed to failure; such a succession could not be duplicated in a program of lab experiments. The other possibility is that the universe is pregnant with life. Perhaps nature is organized in such a way that life emerges inevitably as a consequence of chemistry— what chemistry Nobel-ist Christian de Duve calls a "cosmic imperative." If that's true, then scientists can fruitfully study life's origins in the lab. Not surprisingly, virtually all origins-of-life researchers adopt the philosophical view that life is indeed a cosmic imperative. However, we cannot prove that idea until we find a second, independent origin of life, either on another world or in the lab" Professor Robert Hazen in the Teaching Company's series on the origins of life.

Either way, it seems quite logical that one of the places that we have to look at as a possible source for life is the stars!

More on this later on, G-D willing.

Problem B: The Second Law of Thermodynamics

"In the Beginning..."

One of the most important issues that we have to contend with in looking at these systems is known as the second law of thermodynamics, the law of "entropy". It states:

> *The Second Law of Thermodynamics is primarily concerned with whether or not a given process is possible. The Second Law states that no natural process can occur unless it is accompanied by an increase in the entropy of the universe*[176].

Stated differently, an isolated system will always tend to disorder.

> *The second law of thermodynamics applied on the origin of life is a far more complicated issue than the further development of life* (=the second law seems to fly in the face of abiogenesis, whereas for biological evolution it supposedly does not) *since there is no "standard model" model of how the first biological life forms emerged; only a number of competing hypotheses. The problem is discussed within the area of Abiogenesis, implying gradual pre-Darwinian chemical evolution*[177].

---

[176]   http://en.wikipedia.org/wiki/Biological_thermodynamics
[177]   http://en.wikipedia.org/wiki/Entropy_and_life

Living organisms are often mistakenly believed to defy the Second Law because they are able to increase their level of organization.

To correct this misinterpretation, only must simply refer to the definition of systems and boundaries"[178].

Ahh! The wonderful world of "If only you were smart enough to understand"! Of course! All along, I was misinterpreting the issue as a closed system (=doesn't interact with its surroundings) as opposed to an open system. Now everything is absolutely clear! Isn't that right? Well, let's continue a little bit more in this frame of reason...

"A living organism is an open system, able to exchange both matter and energy with its environment. Take, for example, the assembly of a virus molecule from its subunits, which clearly involves an increase of order. (In this, we are all in agreement!) *If the virus is considered an isolated system, this process would be in defiance of the Second Law. However, a virus molecule interacts directly with its environment.*

The assembly of a virus molecule, (i.e. an increase in the order from a purely chemical system to become a biological system of the magnitude of "only" a virus molecule), *results in an increase of entropy in the system as a whole due to the liberation of water [by means] of solvation,* (i.e. "the process of attraction and association of molecules of a solvent, (the stuff that causes a substance to break down into its base components)), *with molecules or ions of a solute,* (the thing that dissolves/breaks down"), *from the components and the resulting increase in rotational and translational entropy of the solvent".*

---

[178] http://en.wikipedia.org/wiki/Biological_thermodynamics

Professor Robert Hazen in the Teaching Company's lecture series "The Origins of Life", lecture number 2, quotes one Ilya Promazine who explained it this way:

Complex emergence systems arise when energy flows through a collection of many interacting particles, such as sand dunes.

This analogy, given instead of an explanation, is that sand dunes – for example – which are created using random forces, (the wind, and various other factors), display an increase in the magnitude of their complexity seemingly in conflict with the second law of thermodynamics. The reason, he postulates, is because this increase in complexity is done in order to facilitate better energy dispersal through the system and therefore, although they display an increase in complexity since that is just an elaborate means of achieving a higher order of entropy – it does not constitute a conflict with the second law of thermodynamics.

Well, that's all nice and good, Professor Hazen, (assuming that it is even correct. Hello? Does anyone actually have any evidence to back this claim up?), if the dispersal process is the facilitation of LOSS OF ENERGY and the order of complexity – even though it exists – is really not a quantum leap from what it would be under the rule of chaos alone.

However, if the order of complexity that we note constitutes a quantum leap in magnitude, such as from a complex chemical chain to an ordered multifaceted, complex biological system, well, that just does not jive with the thermodynamic law of entropy no matter how you slice it.

Let me explain the fallacy of this reasoning with the following parable. According to the logic of the above statement when water forms complex crystals as it freezes, it does so to allow for a greater loss of thermal energy and therefore is an example of the second law of thermodynamics, entropy. If that is the case, then it should also be possible for the water to form a Pentium chip, which would allow for an even greater facilitation of energy dispersal.

To quote Mr. Spock "It's not logical, Captain".

I call this technique the "pull the wool over your eyes" method. See with wool over your eyes you can see... a little bit, but not any real details. As long as you can't/don't scrutinize what you see, it "looks" good! So too here: the claim sounds logical so long as no one really inspects it carefully, but upon scrutiny, it just "doesn't cut the muster".

However, to actually understand the complexity of these systems and how they constitute a quantum leap in complexity, we must get into the next issue.

Problem C: The Environment in Which Simple Life Systems Could Propagate

One of my good yeshiva friends is also a teacher of computer sciences at a well-known institution in Jerusalem. I remember in his first year of teaching he related to me the dilemma in which he found himself upon making his first grading test. He just didn't know what to do! Should he make it a difficult test, to actually test his students and the knowledge that he had imparted to them; or should he make it an easy test so that more people would make the grade? He just couldn't make up his mind. So, he decided he was going to ask his father, a tenured professor at a respected institution, what he should do. "Make it an easy one," his father said, "they'll love you for it"! "But Abba, (daddy)," my friend said, "If I make it easy, no one will fail!" my friend protested. To which his father responded, "Don't worry son! Someone will find the tenacity within himself to rise to the challenge and fail anyway"!

This... is a truism. Because there are so many people who rose to the challenge when it came to trying to "set the table" for evolution!

Just what do they tell us?

That since the world is "billions of years old" if we are to assume that there was the possibility of myriad possible chemical reactions due to either massive amounts of chemicals or tremendous amounts of catalyzing elements then the "possibility" of life becomes more feasible.

Towards this end, many HYPOTHESES have been forwarded. However, we must always remember what the issues are that we have to keep in mind.

Issue #1: The Water Dilemma

Whenever scientists attempt to determine whether there is life on Mars or other planets, they first seek to establish whether or not water is present there for the simple reason that life on earth totally depends on water. Not only a high percentage of living things, both plants and animals are found in water, all life on earth is thought to have arisen from water, and the bodies of all living organisms are composed largely of water. About 70 to 90 percent of all organic matter is water. The chemical reactions in all plants and animals that support life take place in a water medium. Water not only provides the medium to make these life-sustaining reactions possible, but water itself is often an important reactant or product of these reactions. In short, the chemistry of life is water chemistry[179].

However, one of the core difficulties with the origin of life theories is the following. Everyone agrees that water is the very basic ingredient necessary for organic life and that carbon is the basic molecule of life. The problem is, however, that water and carbon are not catalysts that react well with each other!

"Most of the key chemical steps in assembling carbon-based bio-molecules don't work in water. For example, you just can't

---

[179] http://www.articlesbase.com/college-and-university-articles/why-water-is-called-the-universal-solvent-662091.html

link amino acids together to make peptide bonds to form a protein in any obvious water-rich environment"[180]. Not only that, but water is itself considered to be the greatest solvent in existence today. Water is a good solvent and is referred to as "the universal solvent" [as it dissolves many, although not all, acids and bases]. ... All the major components in cells (proteins, DNA, and polysaccharides) are also dissolved in water. All of which doesn't bode well for explaining how life can evolve chemically from a watery origin, and yet it must be that life has its watery origins because, and I quote NASA on this, "Water is key because almost everywhere we find water on Earth, we find life."

"But," say the scientists, "the fact that I can't explain it – be damned! We see that life is here today despite its watery origin, so it must be that evolution can even do it in the water"!

Therefore, it could truly be that LIFE requires water to be present for it to flourish. However, PRE-life has real problems with the stuff!

Another interesting thing about water is that for all extents and purposes – nothing about this substance makes any sense! In an article entitled "Quantum weirdness makes life possible" in the Oct. 11, 2011, issue of New Scientist the following statement was made:

Waters life-giving properties exist on a knife's edge. It turns out that life, as we know it relies on a fortuitous, but incredibly delicate, balance of quantum forces. ... How water continues to exist, as a network of Hydrogen bonds, in the face of these destabilizing quantum effects, was a mystery. ... What was discovered is that Water, fortuitously, has two quantum uncertainty effects, which cancel each other out! ... Therefore, the conclusion of the article is *that we are used to the idea*

---

[180] Robert Hazen in the Teaching Company lecture series number 12 *"Experiments at High Pressure"*.

that the cosmos' physical constants are fine-tuned for life. Now it seems water's quantum forces can be added to this "just right" list.

For something so incredibly necessary for the existence of life, too – by some miracle – have "just the right" forces necessary to exist is quite the coincidence don't you think? But do you want to know something? The incredible properties of water don't stop there!

Pradeep Kumar and H. Eugene Stanley[181] explain that water is one weird substance, exhibiting more than 80 unusual properties, by one count, including some that scientists still struggle to understand. For example, water can exist in all three states of matter (solid, liquid, gas) at the same time. And the forces at its surface enable insects to walk on water and water to rise up from the roots into the leaves of trees and other plants.

That's one incredible substance, that water. The source of life... yet it seems unviable as the source of abiogenesis.

Issue #2: The Carbon Dilemma What's in a Cell?

Another one on the interesting conundrums of cellular life in abiogenesis is this:

Since all cellular life is made up of ORGANIC MOLECULES; and

Since all Organic molecules are made from CARBON (as the definition of an "organic molecule" is a carbon-based chemical chain)

SO

Where did all of the CARBON and CARBON-BASED MOLECULES come from?

---

[181] The following is from an article at the site ScienceDaily.com from November 9, 2011

Carbon, apparently, is a tough molecule to make. A whole lot has to go into making a carbon molecule and, indeed, it is a highly unlikely thing that we should have so much of it in the first place[182].

Carbon-based molecules, especially Organic Molecules, which are the building blocks of all life, are difficult to come by. Earth, itself, is a lousy candidate for many reasons. It is for this reason that the planet Mars, Earth's closest cousin, has such a limited quantity of organic molecules if, indeed, it has any at all.

More on this in a moment.

Issue #3: The Oxygen Dilemma

As early as the 1930s, Alexander I. Oparin in Russia and J.B.S. Haldane in England had pointed out that the organic compounds needed for life could not have formed on the Earth if the atmosphere was as rich in oxygen (oxidizing) as it is today. Oxygen, which takes hydrogen atoms from other compounds, interferes with the reactions that transform simple organic molecules into complex ones[183].

Well: make up your mind already! On the one hand, all cellular life REQUIRES the presence of oxygen to allow for their vital processes... yet chemical bonding cannot take place in the presence of oxygen! Well... what will it be? Do we have it, or do we not?

It is due to all of the problems mentioned above that lead scientists to the formulation of the main hypotheses concerning abiogenesis today:

---

[182] See **http://www.wired.com/2011/05/where-does-the-carbon-come-from/**
[183] http://www.indiana.edu/~geol105b/1425chap10.html

Space: The Origin of Life?

Many are the hypotheses as to where the optimal "breeding ground" for chemical life could have been. One of those hypotheses is that the origin lies in space. This is a wonderfully fertile theory as it "solves" the problems above of water and oxygen, (as in space – there are none).

In fact, this one possibility has been a spawning ground upon which many different hypotheses have been posited. The "Primitive Extraterrestrial Life" hypothesis, the "Extraterrestrial Amino acid" hypothesis and the "PAH world" hypothesis all agree that the origin of "organic compounds" on earth must be from space.

The thinking is that we also "know" that there must have been a time, and very early at that, during which organic molecules were synthesized. Now, in this chapter I am not going to get into the question of how the earth's crust, atmosphere, and water formed, we'll just have to save those issues for a later chapter! However, it is imperative that we understand what is required to make organic molecules and what is problematic in the creation of organic molecules.

As mentioned before, the first thing you need to create an "organic molecule/compound" is CARBON. The very definition of an "organic" molecule is that it is a carbon-based molecular chain.

It, therefore, follows that if Earth – by whatever means – has attained the ability to produce such an abundance of organic compounds, then other places in the galaxy and in the universe should have produced them as well. Carbon is, after all, the fourth most common element in existence in the universe[184]. We certainly don't have a monopoly on the stuff! So, scientists of the Evo persuasion have to ask, have we found any such organic compounds on other planets? If no, then they should ask "Why not"? Why is it that Earth has developed these incredible carbon-based compounds, but nowhere else has? However, even if we DO find other planets have

---

[184] http://en.wikipedia.org/wiki/Carbon

organic compounds – so what? It's still not the discovery of actual life! If we don't find life (and we haven't) on other planets, then we are back to square one. For why, then, is the Earth different?

In this, the proving ground of all hypotheses will be the planet Mars. Why? Because it has – roughly – all of the same basic qualities and qualifications that Earth does. So, what do we know about Mars?

> *Among our discoveries about Mars, one stands out above all others: the possible[185] presence of liquid water on Mars, either in its ancient past or preserved in the subsurface today. Water is key because almost everywhere we find water on Earth, we find life. If Mars once had liquid water or still does today, it's compelling to ask whether any microscopic life forms could have developed on its surface. Is there any evidence of life in the planet's past? If so, could any of these tiny living creatures still exist today? Imagine how exciting it would be to answer, "Yes!"[186]*

In the Teaching Company's "Origins of life w/ prof. Hazen" lesson number 4, Professor Hazen speaks about the Viking lander's mission to Mars and its experiments to try to find life there. Yet in its analysis of the soil of Mars, the Viking lander found no traces of organic molecules, which is, as previously stated, the foundation of all known life. To this day, there still are virtually no known organic molecules to be found on Mars[187].

As of 2008, when NASA landed the Phoenix lander, the following was discovered:

---

[185] I find that this is one of many words used commonly in describing many discoveries. One wonders why there is so little that is sure in these matters? Interestingly enough it seems that NASA has yet to update this part of their site because of the more recent discoveries of the mar's lander was – apparently – ice patches somewhere underneath the soil of mars.

[186] **http://mars.jpl.nasa.gov/programmissions/science/**

[187] **http://www.space.com/16873-how-curiosity-will-unravel-mars-organic-molecules-mystery-video.html**

Phoenix's preliminary data revealed that Mars soil contains perchlorate, and thus may not be as life-friendly as thought earlier. The pH (acidity) and salinity (amounts of salt) level were viewed as benign from the standpoint of biology. The analyzers also indicated the presence of bound water and CO_2[188].

The above is true even though Mars has roughly the same exposure to space debris that Earth does, which would seem to imply that space isn't the source of life that scientists are hoping.

Even if we were to find empirical proof as to the existence of amino acids and whatnot on other planets,[189] this would not represent a proof of anything in any way because, as we will elaborate on later, the existence of amino acids is a galaxy away from showing DNA synthesis[190]. However, the apparent lack of organic molecules and the inherently inhospitable environment of Mars would seem to be indicative of just the opposite: the apparent absence of life anywhere else in the universe. If life doesn't arise under the best of conditions, (i.e. those similar to Earth, where clearly life has "arisen"), then how likely is it to emerge under the worst?

For many years now, (at the expense of billions, if not trillions, of tax-funded research dollars), one of the primary focuses of the NASA space program has been the search for life and for pre-life on other planets: The Moon, Mars, Jupiter and many comets and asteroids. Every couple of years there is a new article published relating the most recent finds... but to my knowledge, they have yet to find the necessary signs pointing to the existence of life anywhere else in the universe.

---

[188] **http://en.wikipedia.org/wiki/Life_on_Mars**

[189] In 2009 it was announced by NASA that scientists have identified one of the fundamental chemical building blocks of life in a comet. Glycine, an amino acid, was detected in the material ejected from Comet Wild-2 in 2004 and grabbed by NASA's Stardust probe.

[190] Concerning which there is no argument that it is the basis of all life.

This disturbs the scientific community greatly. So much, in fact, that every couple of months they will create a front-page sensation about new discoveries. They are full of pomp and circumstance. "We found something which might possibly be a remote sign of something not quite resembling, but it's still kind of interesting, type of thingamajig which "hails life" or "is indicative of life" or some other such thing!" the article will say. It's just that about a week later, or even a few months later it will be retracted in a little-known footnote of someone's article about the cellular growth rate of foot fungus.

The Primordial Soup Hypotheses

As I was educated in an institution with institutionalized cuisine, (commonly referred to as "cafeteria lunch"), it is easy for me to imagine how one could arrive at the conclusion that the environment of evolution could have occurred in a chemical soup. It's certainly liquidy, (unless mass amounts of potatoes and overcooking are added!) if left overnight it undoubtedly goes through chemical changes and it certainly is a hotbed of microbial activity! Many times, you can even see stuff swimming in it!

All kidding aside, what was the thinking that led to the "primordial soup" hypothesis?

In truth, it was no other than Darwin himself who first suggested it! In a letter to Joseph Dalton Hooker on February 1, 1871, Darwin addressed the question of where life synthesized. He suggested that the original spark of life might have begun in a "warm little pond, with all sorts of ammonia and phosphoric salts, lights, heat, electricity, etc. present, so that a protein compound was chemically formed ready to undergo still more complex changes".

It is based on the following observation[191]. Since the building blocks of life are cells, the building blocks of cells are amino acids, the building

---

[191]   Clearly, this explanation is not Darwin's. Most of the chemical and biological information was not available in his time.

blocks of amino acids are organic compounds, and the components of organic compounds are base chemicals. It, therefore, stands to reason that there must have been a primordial chemical goo, (that being a mixture of base chemicals), from which the whole process must have started. That, coupled with the statement that we saw earlier from NASA, "wherever we find water – we find life," led him to believe that the pond was the classic example of early life-synthesis.

Later on, in 1924, Alexander Oparin, a Soviet biochemist known for his contributions to the theory of the origin of life, reasoned that atmospheric oxygen (O_2) would prevent the synthesis of certain organic compounds that are necessary to make the building blocks for the evolution of life. In his book The Origin of Life, he put forward the theory that life on Earth developed through the gradual chemical evolution of carbon-based molecules in... Primordial soup.

Just what is primordial soup, you ask? Well, it's basically a mixture of base chemicals. Oparin suggested that the infant Earth had possessed a strongly reducing atmosphere, (i.e. no, or at least substantially reduced, levels of oxygen), which was comprised of methane, ammonia, hydrogen, and water vapor. In his opinion, these were the raw materials for the evolution of life. But Oparin never tested his theory. It was only in 1954 that a science graduate student, Stanley Miller, and his professor, Harold Urey, concocted an experiment to simulate the "soup".

The Miller-Urey Experiment and Similar Discoveries

One of the most famous – and misunderstood – experiments in the synthesis of life from un-living chemicals is the Miller-Urey experiment of 1954.

It is one of the most widely cited studies used to support the hypothesis of abiogenesis. Most certainly, the major (if not only) research cited to prove abiogenesis.

The experiment used water (H_2O), methane (CH_4), ammonia (NH_3), and hydrogen (H_2). The chemicals were all sealed inside a sterile array of glass tubes and flasks connected in a loop, with one flask half-full of liquid water and another flask containing a pair of electrodes. The liquid water was heated to induce evaporation, sparks were fired between the electrodes to simulate lightning through the atmosphere and water vapor, and then the atmosphere was cooled again so that the water could condense and trickle back into the first flask in a continuous cycle.

At the end of one week of continuous operation, Miller and Urey observed that as much as 10–15% of the carbon within the system was now in the form of organic compounds. Two percent of the carbon had formed amino acids that are used to make proteins in living cells, with glycine as the most abundant. Sugars, liquids, were also formed. Nucleic acids were not formed within the reaction. But the common 20 amino acids were formed but in various concentrations.

In an interview, Stanley Miller stated, "Just turning on the spark in a basic pre-biotic experiment will yield 11 out of 20 amino acids."

As observed in all subsequent experiments, both left-handed (L) and right-handed (D) optical isomers (i.e. chiral (mirror image) molecules) *were created in a racemic mixture*[192] (a combination that has equal amounts of left and right-handed molecules that differ only in the three-dimensional orientations of their atoms in space. They are referred to as "chiral molecules" (more on this later)).

---

[192]   http://en.wikipedia.org/wiki/Miller%E2%80%93Urey_experiment

The assumption that was leaped upon by the scientific community based on the results of this experiment is that if complex carbon-based compounds could be made "so easily", resulting in the synthesis of chemical compounds found commonly in life then actual cellular life cannot be far behind.

There are two basic problems with this:

Concerning the validity of the experiment and its parameters

See, for example, (as there are very many who agree to this), the site http://www.answersingenesis.org/tj/v18/i2/abiogenesis.asp for rebuttal of the context of the Miller-Urey experiment.

However, scientists have discovered organic carbon compounds, like those found in the Miller-Urey experiment, around deep-sea geothermal vents where the pressure is tremendous (around 2000 atmospheres) and the heat is great. They have also been found in debris from space, meteorites that crashed to earth enduring tremendous re-entry heat and the vacuum of space.

So, let's assume we can answer this problem of parameters and that the most appropriate parameters for the synthesis of carbon compounds can be found. Now does it make sense? No.

Even more challenging than 1>

Let's assume the existence of compound "organic molecules" in a broad array, assuming that it would comprise only those complex compounds found in life and no others. If I would then swirl them around in a test-tube and apply "electricity" (or whatever, geothermal heat, undersea lava vents, re-entry heat of meteorites) what then is the likelihood that said, "organic compounds" would join together to create cellular life?

Let me give you a hint: in the hundreds, if not thousands, of controlled experiments that have been attempted in laboratories around the world it has yet to ever happen. So, what do you think is the likelihood that it would ever happen it the face of uncontrolled circumstances? Not very likely!

For this reason, this experiment is so misunderstood. When people speak about this research and talk about the synthesis of "Organic

Compounds" the public and the average layman understands it thusly: that after putting some chemicals into a test tube and applying electricity something crawled out of the test-tube and said "Hi"! As I pointed out in the quote from the (appropriately named) book *"Evolution for Dummies"* there was no synthesis here of DNA or RNA, only the synthesis of many of the amino acids which are utilized by DNA and RNA. However, that's still not life. Even more so, even all 20 amino acids in a test tube are still not DNA. ORGANIC COMPOUNDS DOES NOT EQUAL LIFE.

There could be nothing further from the truth.

In fact, "ORGANIC MOLECULES" or "ORGANIC COMPOUNDS" which are – albeit – found in living organisms are not indicative of life in any shape way or form. They are complex chemical chains based on carbon molecules. That's it!

Problem D: The Complexity of Biological Systems

Concerning this issue, I would like to look at two systems (out of the possible hundreds (thousands?)): DNA itself and the bacterial flagellum.

DNA

To understand the real complexity of the DNA molecule, we need to consider a few facts as to what, exactly, is contained in this teeny-tiny speck, which can only be seen by the most powerful of today's microscopes, the electron microscope.

Issue #1: Just how BIG is DNA?

Despite its immensely minuscule nature, scientific observation has measured that the DNA molecule contained in a one-celled organism, when straightened out, is about 6 feet long[193]!

Considering that I have, on estimation, about 100 trillion cells in my body, therefore if I stacked all of my DNA strands end to end, that would make for 600,000,000,000,000 feet. As 3.3 feet are equal to 1 meter, (for simplicity we'll call 1 meter 3 feet), that's 200,000,000,000,000 meters, or 200,000,000,000 kilometers!

Let's put this in perspective. Considering that the distance from the earth to the sun is roughly 150,000,000 kilometers, then stacked back-to-back there is enough DNA in my body to make the trip to the sun and back 6.666666665 times[194]!

How is that for "random" Nano-technology?

Issue #2: Just how MUCH information is contained in DNA?

Well, let's keep going on this subject! Just how much information is, (or at least, could), be contained in a DNA molecule? I mean, after all, the information from which we are all made is contained within the DNA, and the human body is incredibly complex, so that would seem to indicate that there is a tremendous amount of information that they contain! Just how much ARE we talking about?

Let's start with something that we can relate to modern experimentation. Did you know that the US Government has authorized a grant to research teams who are trying to utilize the DNA molecule for the storage of

---

[193]   See **http://hypertextbook.com/facts/1998/StevenChen.shtml** for example

[194]   That's the aforementioned amount divided by 150,000,000 divided by 2.

information? Why would they do that? Very simple: because the DNA molecule is – almost assuredly – the most effective thing in existence when it comes to the compact storage of information! Take a close look at the quote from the following site[195]:

Why are roughly 100 to 150 researchers in the world establishing the field of DNA computing at all? What's the lure? Most important, what's in it for us, the impatient computing public?

The most pressing reason to search for alternative methods of processing information is the sheer volume of the information we're processing. "Humans produce about 1018 bytes of information every year, which completely boggles my mind," said Deaton. "That includes books, newspapers, magazines, Web sites, blogs... you name it. We have to find better ways to deal with this information avalanche to store it, search it and retrieve it."

And DNA computing promises the potential of much better ways to do exactly that. ... ["... you might use DNA as a device to store an enormous amount of data. For example, you might be able to carry around the entire IRS database."]

I'm not sure about you, but to me: that sounds like quite a lot of capacity! But even so: still give us an idea of what we are talking about! Still more great quotes from the site above:

Adelman puts it another way when he writes, "One gram of DNA, which when dry would occupy a volume of approximately one cubic centimeter, can store as much information as approximately one trillion CDs." (Or 250,000,000,000

---

[195] **http://researchfrontiers.uark.edu/6284.php**

DVDs) ... Indeed, the entire contents of the Internet actually could be stored in a drop of water.

But it doesn't end there! Oh, no! NO! NO! NO! NO!

Issue #3: Just how EFFICIENT is DNA at storing and processing data?

Because not only is DNA's CAPACITY for storing information incredible, but it's EFFICIENCY at storing that data and other amazing "tricks" is, in my opinion, (and I choose my wording very carefully), BEYOND BELIEF! (i.e. faith, meaning to assume something to be true without basis, as it is explained in the world-at-large).

THIS IS SCIENCE AT ITS BEST! QUANTIFICATION.

(More on that later!)

Let's continue to read the article there!

With great technological marvels have come great demands on the electrical supply. DNA computing offers the hope of a remarkably energy efficient machine, more than a million times more efficient than a PC. ... Because most electronic computers operate on a sequential basis, they essentially perform tasks one at a time, albeit very quickly. DNA computers, however, offer a much more intriguing reality: massively parallel processing. ... Which means DNA strands can produce billions of potential answers simultaneously, making DNA computers incredibly well suited for solving problems that require searching for solutions among a massive number of possibilities. ...

Yet to actually comprehend the meaning of DNA's efficiency we have to compare it to something. So, let's see how DNA stacks up to the world's speediest computer: the IBM Blue Gene.

Blue Gene is an IBM Research project dedicated to exploring the frontiers in supercomputing. The goal is to produce several supercomputers, designed to reach operating speeds in the PFLOPS (petaFLOPS (FLoating point OPerations per Second)) range (one petaFLOP = one quadrillion calculations per second (that's a one followed by 15 zeroes)), and currently reaching sustained speeds of nearly 500 TFLOPS (teraFLOPS (That's 500 trillion operations per second!)). Wikipedia "Blue Gene".

One of the first "Jobs" that one undertook was to model "gene folding". To create this simulation one of the simpler proteins of the body was used (one with only 300 amino acids). In 2001, the assumption was that it would take up to three full years working at almost one petaFLOPS speed to achieve this. In reality, it took one full year (365 days 24 hours a day) at such rates to reach the simulation.

Consider this:

It takes your cells a little less than a minute to achieve the same result! All things considered:

365 (days) X 24 (hrs.) X 60 (min) = 525,600 minutes in a year.

This means that our tiny cells work over 500,000 times faster than today's fastest, most sophisticated computers! Also, speed factors aside; there is also the SIZE difference to take into account. After all, there is a tremendous size difference to consider when we are comparing similar capabilities (Blue Gene takes up an entire office floor).

Issue #4: Just how STABLE and powerful is DNA?

As amazing as the concept of DNA computing is, Kim remains most amazed by the elegance of DNA itself. "Here is the basis for our bodies, the basis for everything, the source of life itself," said Kim. "Yet the material is so simple. And there is so much potential and so many more mysteries."

"Scientists like to say that DNA is robust," said Tung, assistant professor of mechanical engineering. "You can extract it from old bones, (say 1,000,000 years old?), and still test it. That toughness makes it very appealing from a materials standpoint."

How can any thinking person read this and still go on thinking that this is all based on a random sequence of accidents being led by, if you pardon the expression, a cheap dime-a-dozen assumption referred to as "natural selection"?

Yet even beyond the incredible DNA molecule is the fact that – in essence – all it is... is a "hard-drive". For no matter what its capacity is, it is utterly useless if there is nothing to READ the information! Moreover, even if there is something to read it, if there is nothing which then TAKES THAT INFORMATION AND "ACT"s ON IT then of what value is the information? In addition to the DNA molecule, we also have to consider ALL OF THE VARIOUS ENZYMES which take the information "encoded" in DNA and utilize it for biological processes! If you think about it, the sheer amount of work that is performed by the enzymes is staggering!

Issue #5: Just how EFFICIENT are ENZYMES?

Enzymes are a class of proteins that greatly increase the rate of chemical reactions in an organism. Nearly every chemical process that takes place in living things is facilitated by an enzyme[196]. Most enzyme reaction rates are millions of times faster than those of comparable un-catalyzed reactions. As with all catalysts, enzymes are not consumed by the reactions that they catalyze, nor do they alter the equilibrium of these reactions.

Issue #6: Just how PRECISE is the configuration of ENZYMES?

However, enzymes do differ from most other catalysts by being much more specific. Enzymes are known to catalyze about 4,000 biochemical reactions. ... Some of the enzymes showing the highest specificity and accuracy are involved in the copying and expression of the genome. These enzymes have "proof-reading" mechanisms. Here, an enzyme such as DNA polymerase catalyzes a reaction in a first step and then checks that the product is correct in a second step. This two-step process results in average error rates of less than 1 error in 100 million reactions in high-fidelity mammalian polymerases ...

---

[196] http://wps.prenhall.com/esm_krogh_biology_3/0,8750,1135751-,00.html

Issue #7: Just how FAST are the reaction rates of ENZYMES?

Enzymes can catalyze up to several million reactions per second. ... Some enzymes operate with kinetics, which are faster than diffusion rates, which would seem to be impossible.[197]

Well, it seems that these enzymes thingies are quite good and well suited to do their jobs. If you ask me, they are even a little too well-suited to do their job for us to assume that "chance," "fate" and the blind eye of "natural selection" to have had a hand in their construction.

However, do you know what? Let's put that theory to the test! Let's look at an article written by proponents of evolution[198] concerning the intentional construction of enzymes:

Early attempts to design proteins from scratch resulted in fairly crude enzymes that were outperformed by nature's more elegant and finely tuned efforts. Scientists have since developed more efficient (than their first attempts at) artificial enzymes using the same evolutionary principles that generated naturally occurring ones. ... This (i.e. the culling of designer enzymes), is laborious and time-consuming work, and it requires the attention of experimenters at every step of the way. It's also not quite as elegant as a biologist might like. If designing proteins from scratch seems a bit like the work of a creator, then checking and steering the development of evolving proteins is rather like the work of an intelligent designer. A more Darwinian system would apply a set of rules to some starting ingredients and let events unfold without tampering.

---

[197] http://en.wikipedia.org/wiki/Enzyme

[198] http://blogs.discovermagazine.com/notrocketscience/2008/04/07/ automatic-evolution-machine-creates-more-efficient-enzymes-on-a-microchip/

Wow! Here they are, setting out to make, intentionally, "designer" enzymes, and they tell us the following two things:

First> In their attempts to make an enzyme out of scratch they failed miserably, despite the intention and intelligence that went into their construction.

Second> That even utilizing more advanced methods it still wouldn't work if they weren't constantly "tweaking" and monitoring the whole way!

Lastly> Even with the more advanced methods the created enzymes still aren't as efficient as those occurring "naturally"[199].

So once again, the question must be asked: What is more likely to create a more advanced, more capable substance? Blind chance or Concentrated Intelligence, (C.I.)? I would venture to say C.I.! So why is it that every time that we try to create something using our intelligence, for some reason, we never succeed in rivaling that which is achieved "blindly" by "nature", (or should I say "Nature", G-D's mask)?

Enzymes are guided into their correct 3D configuration by other enzyme complexes known as chaperones (part of the heat-shock protein family). What happens if the configurations are not right? Scientists determined that some enzymes, as in the case of ketosteroid isomerase, are so precisely folded for their particular ligand/substrate that if it the 3d conformation was off by even 10 picometers (10^{12} meters) it would lose its efficiency. Firstly, the conformation has to be just right to tightly bind the ligand into the pocket of the protein, then another mechanism (built-in property of the enzyme) is responsible the transfer of electrons in order to catalyze and complete the enzymatic reaction. Our current best efforts at designing artificial enzymes are

---

[199] See **http://www.sciencedaily.com/releases/2007/08/070815135116.htm**, the source for the above article which says: "We hope, [read "pray", "amen!"], our work on optimizing this enzyme will demonstrate that we can evolve catalysts with activity as good as that of naturally occurring enzymes".

(from the article) *"still tens of billions of times smaller than those of many enzymes[200]."*

Well, just how efficient are these enzyme doohickeys? Apparently, a lot more sophisticated and effective than we think!

The Bacterial Flagellum

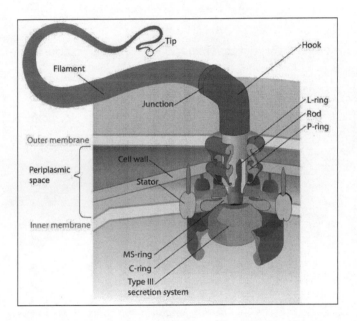

One more FEATURE that becomes quite necessary due to the mass replication of the organism is the issue of locomotion. If there were no locomotion, then all of the possible "food" required by the cell would quickly be used up, thus killing any future for the cell. In bacteria, locomotion is achieved using an appendage on the cell, embedded in the cell wall, which scientists call the FLAGELLUM.

---

[200] [Quoted from **http://www.nature.com/nature/journal/v456/n7218/full/456045a. html** at the site **http://biomolecularmachines.blogspot.com/2008/11/efficiency-of-enzymes.html**

A flagellum is a tail–like projection that protrudes from the cell body of certain prokaryotic and eukaryotic cells and functions in locomotion. There are some notable differences between prokaryotic and eukaryotic flagella, such as protein composition, structure, and mechanism of propulsion[201]. …

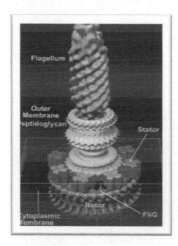 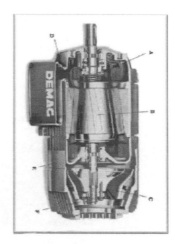

Issue #1: The flagellum both looks and acts like a motor

Bacterial flagella are helical filaments that rotate like screws. They provide two of several kinds of bacterial motility. … The bacterial flagellum is driven by a rotary engine, (the Mot complex), made up of protein, [which is] located at the flagellum's anchor point on the inner cell membrane. The engine is powered by proton motive force, i.e., by the flow of protons (hydrogen ions) across the bacterial cell membrane due to a concentration gradient set up by the cell's metabolism, (in Vibrio species … some are driven by a sodium ion pump

---

[201]   Almost all of the following quotes were taken from **http://en.wikipedia.org/wiki/Flagellum**

rather than a proton pump). The rotor transports protons across the membrane and is turned in the process. The rotor alone can operate at 6,000 to 17,000 rpm, but with the flagellar filament attached usually only reaches 200 to 1000 rpm.

When we consider that the average maximum speed of a jet engine is estimated at about 15,000 RPM,[202] it boggles the mind that this Nano-engine should have capabilities greater than those that we find in an intentional, designed piece of machinery!

Issue #2: The flagellum exhibits capabilities beyond that of a motor

The direction of rotation can be switched almost instantaneously, caused by a slight change in the position of a protein, FliG, in the rotor. ...

Try doing that with your car engine and see what happens!

Flagella do not rotate at a constant speed but instead can increase or decrease their rotational speed in relation to the strength of the proton motive force. Flagellar rotation can move bacteria through liquid media at speeds of up to 60-cell lengths/ second. ... By comparison, the cheetah, the fastest land animal, can sprint at 110 km/h (68 mph), which is approximately 25-body lengths/sec[203]. ...

---

[202] See **http://answers.yahoo.com/question/index?qid=20081213182519AAZKJjB.** However, there are engines that revolve much faster than that, as stated in the article here https://en.wikipedia.org/wiki/Gas_turbine, even so, the point is a powerful one.

[203] Let's do the math. If the cheetah at 68 MPH=25 body-lengths, then traveling at that speed for an hour the cheetah would travel 90,000 body lengths (=25 bl/s*60 seconds in a minute*60 minute in an hour). Comparatively then 60 body-lengths per second *60*60= 216,000 body lengths per hour!

[The Irreducible complexity argument]

In his 1996 book Darwin's Black Box, intelligent design proponent Michael Behe ... cited the bacterial flagellum as an example of an irreducibly complex structure that could not have evolved through naturalistic means. Behe argued that the flagellum becomes useless if any one of its constituent parts is removed, and thus could not have arisen through numerous, successive, slight modifications; therefore, it is hopelessly improbable that the proteins making up the flagellar motor could have come together all at once, by chance"[204].

[The counter argument]

"The most powerful rebuttals to the flagellum story ... emerged from the steady progress of scientific work on the genes and proteins associated with the flagellum and other cellular structures. Such studies have now established that the... premise by which this molecular machine has been advanced as an argument against evolution is wrong ... (i.e. the claim that "any precursor to an irreducibly complex system that is missing a part is by definition nonfunctional). .... As the evidence has shown, nature is filled with examples of "precursors" to the flagellum that are indeed "missing a part," and yet are fully functional. Functional enough, in some cases, to pose a serious threat to human life".

[A proof of this statement, the fulcrum of the argument:] The Type -III Secretory Apparatus

In the popular imagination, bacteria are "germs" – tiny microscopic bugs that make us sick. Microbiologists smile at

---

[204] http://en.wikipedia.org/wiki/Flagellum

that generalization ... Pathogenic or disease–causing, bacteria threaten the organisms they infect in a variety of ways, one of which is to produce poisons and inject them directly into the cells of the body. ... In order to carry out this diabolical work, bacteria must not only produce the protein toxins that bring about the demise of their hosts, but they must efficiently inject them across the cell membranes and into the cells of their hosts. They do this by means of any number of specialized protein secretory systems. One, known as the type III secretory system (TTSS)...

At first glance, the existence of the TTSS ... would seem to have little to do with the flagellum. However, molecular studies of proteins in the TTSS have revealed ... (that) ... the proteins of the TTSS are directly homologous to the proteins in the basal portion of the bacterial flagellum. As figure 2 (Heuck 1998) shows, these homologies extend to a cluster of closely associated proteins found in both of these molecular "machines." On the basis of these homologies, McNab (McNab 1999) has argued that the flagellum itself should be regarded as a type III secretory system. ...

Stated directly, the TTSS does its dirty work using a handful of proteins from the base of the flagellum. From the evolutionary point of view, this relationship is hardly surprising. In fact, it's to be expected that the opportunism of evolutionary processes would mix and match proteins to produce new and novel functions. According to the doctrine of irreducible complexity, however, this should not be possible. If the flagellum is indeed irreducibly complex, then removing just one part, let alone 10 or 15, should render what remains "by definition nonfunctional." Yet the TTSS is indeed fully functional, even though it is missing most of the parts of the flagellum. The TTSS may be bad news for us, but for the bacteria that possess it, it is a truly valuable biochemical machine[205].

What comes out of both sides of the argument is that everyone agrees that there is simply no way that the entirety of the compound system of either the flagella or the TTSS is the result of a random mixing of chemicals.

They had to – in the best plausible situation – have been the result of a chain of unrelated events which eventually lead up to the entirety of the TTSS and then, in evolutionary theory, (unless we want to further stretch the issue and call it "convergent evolution"), on to the flagellum which is a more sophisticated apparatus than the TTSS.

Therefore, if the argument made is that no part of the flagellum's system would work, as Behe postulated in his 1996 book, without any one of its components, then the counterarguments make lots of sense. However, upon scrutiny, this is a case of "mistaken identity". This is not only a question of how the flagellar motor happened but also a question as to WHY it occurred in the first place[206].

The counterargument poised here, the existence of a less developed, yet complex, piece of biological machinery in comparison to the flagellum, although touted as a rebuttal of the claim of irreducible complexity (as it was explained), in reality, is not a rebuttal at all! Because instead of having one complex biological machine to contend with – you now have two! A logical argument can only be disproven in one of two ways: either by showing that it is – in actuality – illogical; or by exposing a flaw in the argument.

If we scrutinize the counter-argument, we find that it does neither of the above. It does not re-interpret the complexity of the bacterial flagellum,

---

[205] **http://www.millerandlevine.com/km/evol/design2/article.html**
[206] Even though we like to say that "necessity is the mother of invention" that only works when there is wisdom and understanding that drive the invention, but not when the driving force is chance.

nor does it provide a framework to explain where it may have come from. It also utilizes faulty logic.

The underlying principle here is where the cell/bacterium got this complex motor/injection system in the first place. What freak of nature, what natural process, would – or could – cause the synthesis of such a structure? What type of time frame would be required to do so? (Also, would the organism live long enough for this to happen?)

Furthermore, the claim of irreducible complexity never was that components utilized by cells, for one thing, cannot be used for another. That's like saying that a motor used to drive a car could not be used to power a drill, which is inherently incorrect. The issue is that if the flagellum would not have, say, the rod, (see above illustration), then it would not be able to perform its function of locomotion. If it were missing the filament, it would not carry out the function of locomotion. Certainly not with the efficiency that it does. This is the train of thought.

If we take a look at the motor component on its own, there is no doubt that it could be used to power multiple functions, not just locomotion. But to be utilized for the sake of locomotion it has to have all of the assembled parts!

Not only that, but both the flagellar and the TTSS motor, on their own, are incredible examples of great feats of engineering. And one wonders, because of this, does science have some means of giving a description, not based on flights of fancy, which sheds light on this issue? Does science claim that it possesses the knowledge to explain how the TTSS injection system "developed" based on evolutionary principals?

I haven't found any yet. What I did find is that although recent studies have expanded our knowledge of the structure and function of many type III translocated effectors, *the precise mechanisms of type III protein secretion and translocation, and the detailed structural characteristics of the secretion apparatus, remain poorly understood*[207]. This means that scientists today... really have no clue.

---

[207]   This is from the article at the site **http://142.103.64.1/pdf/55.pdf** entitled "*Structural Characterization of a Type III Secretion System Filament Protein in a Complex Chaperone*"

Yet if I were to find one – I can assure you that it will be based on hypotheses and other types of assumptions only. Is there truly any reason why they are a better explanation than that ever-so-simple one, called G-D?

So, in reality, the TTSS is not a rebuttal of the argument of Intelligent Design, but the marking of another instance of Complexity on the cellular level without any real reason which is "scientific", (i.e. observable, measurable and reproducible), capable of explaining both WHY and HOW these structures came to be. I categorize this with all of the other things that we humans give a name to, so that other people will assume that we actually know something about it, even though we, ourselves, haven't the faintest clue. So too the TTSS argument is one which says, "That's not difficult! Look, I found one similar to it that's also complex! So now I don't have to answer your question".

Welcome to second-grade debate!

Therefore, it would seem that the complexity of both structure and function of the biological world on a microscopic level is clearly beyond both the structural and functional capability of most designed, intentional and purposeful structures.

It follows, therefore, that what we find on a microscopic level is also:

DESIGNED
INTENTIONAL
And
PURPOSEFUL

It's just that the extent of the design and the intelligence is so great that we are stumbling along in our vain attempts to try and fathom its greatness!

But the above examples, despite their elegance and function, are only small pieces of the whole. Let's take a step back and see how the amazing parts of a cell work as an integral whole.

---

from 2005.

Problem E: The Interconnectedness of Biological Systems

The issue of "What constitutes life?" is a matter of which science has yet to make head or tails[208].

To simplify this issue, so that all sorts of irrelevant details and definitions do not sidetrack us, let's assume that "Life" equals the simplest of cells. Having said that, there is one thing that everyone agrees on: an entire cell is way too complex to have "occurred" all by itself. If it happened by circumstance/abiogenesis, it happened piecemeal (each part developed individually) and then was synthesized into a whole.

So, if we are going to look at the cell as a "whole", we first have to consider what is needed for the cell to be. In other words, what are the most essential systems inherent in a cell?

To the best of my knowledge that would be at the very least the following five life systems:

An AUTOIMMUNE system, (otherwise it will be killed – literally – by all of the neighboring chemicals and solvents, (especially water, one of the greatest solvents of them all))

A gastronomic, (DIGESTIVE), system, (otherwise there are no means of powering and/or maintaining the organism's own systems).

A RESPIRATORY system, (which is, effectively, a transference system of said nutrients to the system, like the respiratory + circulatory system in humans and animals)

A SKELETAL system, which provides the basic structure of the cell, which would otherwise collapse on itself.

Lastly, a REPRODUCTIVE system, otherwise this life just isn't going anywhere!

---

[208] For a detailed account of this conundrum listen to Prof. Hazen in the Teaching Company's lecture series *"Origins of Life"* number 3 *"What is life?"*.

To understand fully what is involved in these systems we have to know what these terms mean. In particular what they mean to a simple one-celled organism.

To this end, we will look at the oldest known one-celled organism: prokaryotes. "The oldest known fossilized prokaryotes were laid down approximately 3.5 billion years ago, (and there are those who claim even earlier findings than this as we mentioned earlier in this chapter), only about 1 billion years after the formation of the Earth's crust." We will, therefore, look upon the prokaryotes as the first form of "life".

Science teaches us that these simple cells are made up of many parts, but we will focus only on the corresponding parts of what we previously mentioned:

The IMMUNE system: In primitive/simple life, the IMMUNE system is the cell wall and membrane that allows certain things to get through and keeps other things out. This is the simplest form of an autoimmune system.

The DIGESTIVE and RESPIRATORY system: In cell "anatomy", the digestive system is – effectively – the ribosomes, which take the nutrients in the cytoplasm and synthesize them into proteins. The respiratory system is what is known as cytoplasm, which is the gelatinous medium through which all nutrients and all waste products travel until expelled from the cell wall and membrane.

The SKELETAL system: In cell "anatomy", this is called the cytoskeleton. Only recently, it was discovered that prokaryotes possess a cytoskeleton. The "prokaryote cytoskeleton" is the collective name for all structural filaments in prokaryotes.

The REPRODUCTIVE system: In cell "anatomy", the reproductive system is the gene and the DNA, which can be found in the prokaryotes in what is called the nucleoid. This is the repository of the DNA, which holds the "blueprint" to reproduce the entirety of the "mother" cell.

Now if we were to get into the science involved in the actual processes of these four/five systems, I would have to write an entire encyclopedia of my own and even then, I probably wouldn't understand most of what I was writing anyway.

What is important here is to understand the underlying function that is necessary to fulfill the ultimate goal of each of these systems.

Now I would like to look at the aforementioned systems purely on an individual level:

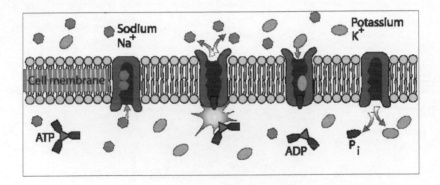

The Cellular Immune System:

The cell membrane is a biological membrane that separates the interior of all cells from the outside environment. The cell membrane is selectively permeable to ions and organic molecules and controls the movement of substances in and out of cells.

Embedded within this membrane is a variety of protein molecules that act as channels and pumps that move different molecules into and out of the cell. The membrane is said to be 'semi-permeable,' in that it can either let a substance, (molecule or ion), pass through freely, pass through to a limited extent or not pass through at all.

Cell surface membranes also contain receptor proteins that allow cells to detect external signaling molecules such as hormones. ...It also prevents the cell from expanding and finally bursting (cytolysis) from osmotic pressure against a hypotonic environment[209].

Because the cellular immune system is made up of between two to four components and because of my desire to keep matters as simple as possible without getting into confusing names and details, I will, therefore, refer to the cellular immune system simply as the "cell wall". Also, I will not cite all of the components that comprise the cell wall, because the actual chemical makeup of the cell wall is irrelevant. I will, therefore, refer to it simply as a "protein chain" or "protein molecule chain", (whichever I feel like using!).

What we are looking at here is a "smart" protein molecule chain. It is:
Selectively permeable, meaning that it chooses which molecules it lets in and those it doesn't. And even those that are let through the outer part of the cell wall then meet up with:
The inner cell wall which is also "smart" and then makes a "decision" as to whether or not this substance will make it into the inner "sanctum" of the cell.
Also, some of the proteins in the molecule chain are even smarter than the others in that they:

- sense signals from outside molecules
- sense and regulate the internal pressure of the cell.

Now, leaving aside the issue of the relation of the cell membrane to the rest of the cell system, scientists today are at a loss as to how in the

---

[209] http://en.wikipedia.org/wiki/Cell_membrane

world the cell membrane could have developed on its own. Remember, even evolutionarily science agrees that due to the quantum complexity of a biological cell it is purely impossible that all of its components developed together. (It's impossible that even two of them did)!

Many theories have been postulated. In fact, in the Teaching Company's lecture series "the Origins of Life", Professor Hazen spends about three lectures specifically on this subject to try to find a way of chemically synthesizing the cell wall. However, none of the experiments or hypotheses have been able to synthesize a multi-protein chain of even simple complexity, let alone a "smart" wall like the one just described!

The difficulty with this issue is the fact that the cell wall has to multitask. It cannot have randomly evolved into an "air-tight" wall around the cell, as that would have – quite literally – suffocated the inner workings of the cell itself. This in addition to the fact that we are looking at a way to chemically synthesize the cell wall on its own in order to be "introduced" at a later time to the various other components which eventually form the complete cell. SO, if the cell wall was entirely airtight, impermeable, then how in the world did the other "ingredients" find their way inside?

On the other hand, you can't say that the cell wall was permeable because if that were true the cells "guts" would spill out or the cell would be invaded by foreign substances, which could and would destroy the cell from the inside out! Not a very effective immune system!

In addition, we have to remember that the cell wall cannot be semi-permeable in only one direction, (i.e. to let in other substances from the outside only in order to "feed" the inside); it had to be doubly permeable to allow the jettison of waste products and the regulation of internal fluid pressures.

Are we done yet, Rabbi Shlomo?

Oh no! We're not quite done yet! Because the cell wall itself is an integral component of the reproductive cycle as well!

For how does a cell reproduce?

With a process that scientists call the "cell cycle."

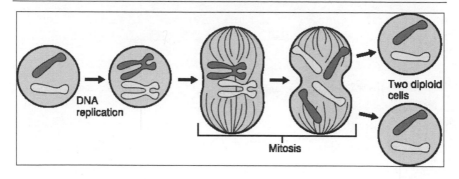

Researchers divide this into four stages, of which only the last one, M phase, is of any interest to us at this point. M phase is described as consisting:

> "...of nuclear division, (karyokinesis), and cytoplasmic division, (cytokinesis), accompanied by the formation of a new cell membrane to close off the cell wall to complete the process of cell division. This is the physical division of "mother" and "daughter" cells. The M phase has been broken down into several distinct phases, sequentially known as prophase, prometaphase, metaphase, anaphase, and telophase leading to cytokinesis"[210]. (The process can be more easily understood by looking at the above graphic displaying the cell cycle.)

As we see clearly, a basic part of cell reproduction not only requires that there be a cell wall present but the cell wall is actually part of the reproduction process! If there were no cell wall, reproduction would be impossible unless we find that the genetic information can survive on its own in a random chemical bath without its IMMUNE system to support it. (It doesn't). More on this later on, WG"H (With G-D's Help) when we discuss the REPRODUCTIVE system.

---

[210] http://en.wikipedia.org/wiki/Cell_reproduction

The Cellular Digestive System:

In biochemistry, metabolic pathways are a series of chemical reactions occurring within a cell[211].

> *A metabolic pathway involves the systematic modification of an initial molecule to form another product. The resulting product can be used in one of three ways:*
>
> *Immediately, as the end-product of a metabolic pathway*
>
> *To initiate another metabolic pathway, called a flux generating step*
>
> *To be stored in the cell.*
>
> *Pathways are important to the maintenance of homeostasis, (i.e. the regulation of the cell's own internal environment, allowing it to maintain a stable, constant condition within an organism). Catabolic (breakdown) and Anabolic (synthesis) pathways often work interdependently to create new biomolecules as the final end products.*

This means that a cell has two requirements, (minimum, it is very likely that there are more than these two. But let's keep it simple!), for having a metabolic process: in order to get the ENERGY that it requires to function (catabolic) and to allow for BIOLOGICAL CONSTRUCTION to take place (anabolic, think "steroids"). "Biological construction" is further broken down into "replacement parts", (cell components), and to make additional building blocks which are then utilized in the

---

[211]   http://en.wikipedia.org/wiki/Metabolic_pathway. Not quoted verbatim. I reordered and added here and there for – in my opinion – greater understanding and efficiency.

REPRODUCTIVE PROCESS. (Oh! So, this means that it is linked to the reproductive process as well! Hmm…)

Now, this is just what the DIGESTIVE system does, now let's move on to understand just how a cell goes about doing that!

> *In each pathway, a principal chemical is modified by a series of chemical reactions. Enzymes catalyze these reactions and often require dietary minerals, vitamins, and other cofactors to function properly. Because of the many chemicals (a.k.a. "metabolites") that may be involved, metabolic pathways can be quite elaborate. Also, numerous distinct pathways co-exist within a cell. This collection of pathways is called the metabolic network.*

Meaning:

The purpose of the metabolic pathways is to create any and all components required by the cell. This is achieved by utilizing "principal chemicals", basic building blocks, and transforming them.

These processes are controlled/synthesized by ENZYMES.

Each pathway has its own – distinct – enzyme.

ENZYMES require their own base substances, (food/fuel), to allow them to function.

There are multitudes of different pathways required by the cell.

All of these processes are elaborate and require many different chemicals to be involved.

SO:

If the cell processes need replacement parts;

And the replacement parts can only be made using complex chemical processes;

And the complex chemical processes cannot be performed without specific enzymes;

And the specific enzymes cannot exist without specific "foods";

And the specific foods cannot get to the enzymes without penetrating the cell wall;

And the cell wall doesn't let just anything through that is not needed by the cell for its own functioning...

SO, WHAT CAME FIRST?

The cell wall or the enzymes? The enzymes or the cell processes? The cell processes or the cell wall? Just where – evolutionarily speaking – can we even think of beginning?

Let's continue with the processes, as it doesn't stop there!

Several distinct – but linked – metabolic pathways are used by cells to transfer the energy released by the breakdown of fuel molecules into ATP and other small molecules used for energy (e.g. GTP, NADPH, and FADH).

These pathways occur within all living organisms in some form:

Glycolysis

Aerobic respiration and/or Anaerobic respiration

Citric acid cycle / Krebs cycle

Oxidative phosphorylation

Other pathways occurring in (most or) all living organisms include (but are not limited to):

Fatty acid oxidation (β-oxidation)

Gluconeogenesis

Amino acid metabolism

Urea cycle / Nitrogen metabolism

Nucleotide metabolism

Glycogen synthesis / Glycogen storage

Pentose phosphate pathway (hexose monophosphate shunt)

Porphyrin synthesis (or heme synthesis) pathway

Lipogenesis

HMG-CoA reductase pathway (isoprene prenylation chains, see cholesterol)

Because there is no way for us to look at all of these processes in depth let's just pick one to study: Glycolysis.

The process involved in actually doing the CATABOLIC work is called "Glycolysis", the "Catabolic Metabolism" and "Cellular Respiration".

Glycolysis is a definite sequence of ten reactions involving ten intermediate compounds (one of the steps involves two intermediates) ... Glycolysis is thought to be the archetype of a universal metabolic pathway. It occurs, with variations, in nearly all organisms... The wide occurrence of glycolysis indicates that it is one of the most ancient known metabolic pathways.

...The first five steps (of glycolysis) are regarded as the preparatory (or investment) phase since they consume energy to convert the glucose into two three-carbon sugar phosphates (G3P). ... The second half of glycolysis is known as the pay-off phase, characterized by a net gain of the energy-rich molecules ATP and NADH. ...

Glycolysis is regulated by slowing down or speeding up certain steps in the glycolysis pathway. This is accomplished by inhibiting or activating the enzymes that are involved. The steps that are regulated may be determined by calculating the change in free energy, ΔG, for each step. ...

This article concentrates on the catabolic role of glycolysis with regard to converting potential chemical energy to usable chemical energy during the oxidation of glucose to pyruvate. However, many of the metabolites in the glycolytic pathway are also used by anabolic pathways, and, as a consequence, flux through the pathway is critical to maintaining a supply of carbon skeletons for biosynthesis[212].

"Cellular respiration is the [title given to the] set of the metabolic reactions and processes that take place in the cells of organisms to convert biochemical energy from nutrients into adenosine triphosphate (ATP, an energy source for the cell), and then release waste products.

… Respiration is one of the key ways a cell gains useful energy to fuel cellular reformations. … The energy stored in ATP can then be used to drive processes requiring energy, including biosynthesis, locomotion [of the cell itself using the flagella] or transportation of [base and waste] molecules across cell membranes".

According to this definition, the cellular respiratory process is the primary source of all power production required by the cell. In other words: without the respiratory/catabolic metabolism system, there would be no cell, as the functioning of the cell requires power which it does not have without this vital system.

This definition states clearly that respiration is a substrate of the digestive system.

The "you and me" explanation of the quoted information is that "glycolysis" or "Cellular Respiration" or "Catabolic Metabolism", (converting to energy), is a very complicated process. It's:

Selective: As the core components that are brought into the cell – in their present form – are of no or of little use to the cell. However, those "ingredients" that do permeate the cell wall are only the ones needed in the actual digestive process, (remember what we said about the cell wall being selectively permeable?).

---

[212]   http://en.wikipedia.org/wiki/Glycolysis

This issue becomes extremely complicated when looked at through the evolutionist's looking glass, as in evolutionary theory each of the systems developed independently, (and then somehow, magically, discovered each other and synthesized correctly)!

Goal oriented: To achieve a product which is useful to the cell, it proceeds to go through a successive 10-stage conversion process. During this process an immediately useable substance, (ATP), is created and then reinvested in the successive processes to achieve an end-result, which is a higher-order yield!

How in the world does something unintelligent like a cell, recognize that it's "worth its while" to use up the ATP created in the middle stages of glycolysis, to achieve an end-result of a higher yield?

Furthermore, this flies in the face of the second law of thermodynamics, the law of entropy, as we learned earlier, as this is clearly a system which has made a significant *gain* in complexity for the sake of even greater PRODUCTION of energy, not – as evolutionists claim – to allow for superior energy LOSS, (entropy).

Specific: The cell must then utilize 10 separate enzymes successively to achieve the end-result. How in the world were these, very specific and precise, enzymes "drafted" into the cellular metabolic process in the first place?

Smart: A regulatory system oversees the production of the end-product and makes fine-tuned adjustments to the process as is required for the proper result!

Now all of the above is true concerning the manufacture of energy. In "biological construction", the process is even more complicated as it not only has to power the metabolism that is doing the building, but it also has to synthesize the components themselves!

Anabolic processes produce peptides, proteins, polysaccharides, lipids, and nucleic acids. These molecules comprise all the materials of living cells, such as membranes and chromosomes, as well as the specialized products of specific types of cells, such as enzymes, antibodies, hormones, and neurotransmitters[213].

...anabolism requires the input of energy and is, therefore, an energetically "uphill" process. At certain points in the anabolic pathway, the cell must put more energy into a reaction than is released during catabolism. Such anabolic steps require a different series of reactions that are used at this point during catabolism.

In you-and-me, this means the anabolic process is an energy hog: it doesn't produce energy, it only uses it. It is, therefore, impossible for the anabolic process to have developed without a catabolic process as well! If one does not have the energy to produce, then production = zero. Think of your car and how far it could get without gas.

However, it seems to me from the literature that the anabolic process should be considered more a part and parcel of the REPRODUCTIVE system. This is because the actual CONSTRUCTION of the molecules required for the cell, no matter what the need is, needs access to the DNA molecules which hold the blueprints needed to assemble the components.

So, we arrive at the next difficulty in the list:

If the assembly of the cell matter requires DNA; and the assembly process requires energy, which is produced by the catabolic processes of the metabolism; SO... It seems that these two systems cannot exist independently!

Even though one could object, that in the Urey-Miller experiment in which amino acids were produced by the application of electricity (energy) from an external source, (electrical stimulation). This is very different from proving that an amino acid produced at random in a chemical bath will then proceed to organize itself into a living cell system! Especially when we consider that the cell system under discussion is a self-sustaining system so long as there is an availability of necessary "fuel" components.

---

[213]   http://science.jrank.org/pages/319/Anabolism.html

This becomes even more challenging when we consider that when a cell produces an amino acid using the anabolic processes, it is done intentionally – not randomly – to fulfill a particular need within the cell's system.

If the cell were to produce factors at random then:

It would use up the valuable and limited energy resources that it has for naught; and

The cell would be filled with useless junk cutting off the cell's functionality and most likely kill it through "malnutrition" and "asphyxiation".

There is a vast difference between the production of specific amino acids vs. random amino acid production.

To state that utilizing an external energy source the anabolic processes of the metabolic system were developed only to, later on, develop the catabolic processes and to do so randomly is … extremely … far-fetched.

SO, if the cell systems cannot have been assembled randomly without an extended period of development, and yet the systems are interdependent... what should we conclude?

The Cellular Skeletal System:

The prokaryotic cytoskeleton is the collective name for all structural filaments in prokaryotes. It was once thought that prokaryotic cells did not possess cytoskeletons, but recent advances in visualization technology and structure determination have shown that filaments indeed exist in these cells. … Cytoskeletal elements play essential roles in cell division, protection, shape determination, and polarity determination in various prokaryotes[214].

---

[214]   http://en.wikipedia.org/wiki/Prokaryotic_cytoskeleton

Effectively 5 different types of systems comprise the cytoskeleton: 1. FtsZ, 2. MreB, 3. Crescentin, 4.ParM and SopA and 5. MinCDE system. We will look, shortly, at 3 out of the 5. I will address only a few of them: FtsZ, MreB and – briefly – Crescentin.

> *FtsZ is a protein encoded by the ftsZ gene that assembles into a ring at the future site of the septum, (the point at which the division of the cell takes place which is, subsequentially, sealed off by the formation of a new cell wall), of bacterial cell division. ... FtsZ has been named after "Filamenting temperature-sensitive mutant Z". ... During cell division, FtsZ is the first protein to move to the division site and is essential for recruiting other proteins that produce a new cell wall between the dividing cells. ... FtsZ has no known motor protein associated with it. The origin of the cytokinetic force, thus, remains unclear, but it is believed that the localized synthesis of new cell wall produces at least part of this force[215].*

In you-and-me language, this means that the FtsZ protein is pre-programmed to do the essential job of cell division: the separation of the one enlarged cell into two daughter cells. This job is performed by constricting the cell at a certain point and then separating and closing off the cell wall.

Cell division of the prokaryotes cannot be done without this protein.

In other words, this factor of the cytoskeleton plays an integral role in the REPRODUCTIVE system.

It, therefore, makes sense that the FtsZ cytoskeletal ring could not have developed independently of the reproductive system.

> *MreB assembles into a helical network of filamentous structures just under the cytoplasmic membrane, covering the whole length of the cell. MreB determines cell shape by mediating the*

---

215 http://en.wikipedia.org/wiki/FtsZ

position and activity of enzymes that synthesize peptidoglycan, (a polymer consisting of sugars and amino acids that forms a mesh-like layer outside the plasma membrane of bacteria forming the cell wall), and by acting as a rigid filament under the cell membrane that exerts outward pressure to sculpt and bolster the cell.

MreB condenses from its normal helical network and forms a tight ring at the septum (the point of cell division) in Caulobacter crescentus right before cell division, a mechanism that is believed to help locate its off-center septum. MreB is also important for polarity determination in polar bacteria, as it is responsible for the correct positioning of at least four different polar proteins in C. crescentus[216].

In you-and-me language, this means that MreB is the real "skeleton" of the cell. Think of it as the Ribcage of the prokaryotes. In addition to this "formative" role due to the style of reproduction, i.e. cell division, where the existence of a rigid skeleton would hinder the reproductive cycle, an adaptation "just had to be made" in order to facilitate this process.

However, in addition to this, each part of the MreB had to be fully functional, as at the point of cell division the MreB of the "mother" cell is now divided up into two parts. Each part then becomes the full skeleton for the new "daughter" cells, once again preparing itself to recreate and separate when called upon.

SO, when was MreB synthesized? Was it before the creation of the reproductive system or after? Was it before the creation of the cell wall or after?

Remember: prokaryotes are the earliest-known cells and therefore the cytoskeleton was already fully functional by then! So, which came first? The cytoskeleton or the cell wall? The reproductive system or the cytoskeleton?

---

[216]   http://en.wikipedia.org/wiki/Prokaryotic_cytoskeleton

Crescentin forms a continuous filament from pole to pole alongside the inner, concave side of the crescent-shaped bacterium Caulobacter crescentus. Both MreB and crescentin are necessary for C. crescentus to exist in its characteristic shape; it is believed that MreB molds the cell into a rod shape and crescentin bends this shape into a crescent.

However, as to why this type of cytoskeleton is important or necessary – is not known. I like to think of it as the spine of the prokaryotes.

I will not bring details as to the other aspects of the cytoskeleton as it would make the scope of this chapter even more lengthy than it already is.

The Cellular Reproduction System:

For a cell to divide, (i.e. reproduction), it must first replicate its DNA. In prokaryotic cells, such as bacterial cells, reproduction is achieved by means of binary fission. This is a process that includes DNA replication, chromosome segregation, (splitting of the two strands of DNA into 2 distinct pairs), and cytokinesis (i.e. cell division)[217].

Seeing as chromosomal segregation is straightforward and that we discussed cytokinesis within the framework of the cell wall, here we will deal with the heart of the matter: DNA and the process of replication. However, more background information is still required before we can actually understand what we are talking about.

Two different kinds of genetic material exist deoxyribonucleic acid (DNA (illustration left)) and ribonucleic acid (RNA (ibid)).

---

217 http://en.wikipedia.org/wiki/Cell_reproduction

All of the biological information contained in an organism is encoded in its DNA or RNA sequence[218].

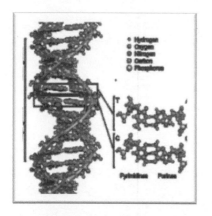 

RNA is also used for data transport (e.g., mRNA) and enzymatic functions (e.g., ribosomal RNA) in organisms that use DNA for the genetic code itself. Transfer RNA (tRNA) molecules are used to add amino acids during protein translation.

The reason for all of these components is that CELLULAR REPRODUCTION is a multifaceted, complicated process. There are two basic things that are "produced" by the cell: offspring, (i.e. "daughter" cells) and replacement parts.

To "produce" offspring the entire DNA sequence needs to be copied precisely. This is achieved using the process called DNA replication. To produce "spare/replacement parts", or even an entirely new cell, a two-step procedure is needed: transcription and translation.

First, let's look at DNA replication, (as it pertains to prokaryotes). But before we can do that, we have to know a few basic things about DNA.

The following information was culled from several articles[219]

---

[218] http://en.wikipedia.org/wiki/Cell_(biology)#Growth_and_metabolism
[219] See Wikipedia or any other encyclopedia on "DNA", "DNA replication", "Binary Fission", "Chromosome" and the "Replication Bubble"

DeoxyriboNucleic Acid, or DNA, is a nucleic acid that is built for long-term storage of massive amounts of information (we expanded this issue earlier). This genetic information is read from like a set of blueprints and then used to construct all of the components found in all known living organisms. The information in DNA is held in the sequence of the repeating units along the DNA chain. These units are four types of nucleotides, (A, T, G, and C), and the sequence of nucleotides stores the information in an alphabet called the genetic code.

[Nucleotides are molecules that, when joined together: a> Make up the structural units of RNA and DNA, and b> Play central roles in metabolism. In that capacity, they serve as sources of chemical energy (ATP and GTP), participate in cellular signaling and are incorporated into important cofactors of enzymatic reactions.] The DNA segments that carry this genetic information are called genes.

[Genes refers to a region of the DNA strand that influences a particular characteristic in an organism. For example, eye color. The function of genes is to provide the information needed to make molecules called proteins in cells].

DNA usually occurs as ... circular chromosomes in prokaryotes.

[A chromosome (see picture) is an organized structure of DNA and protein that is found in cells. [The chromosome] is a single piece of coiled DNA containing many genes, regulatory elements, and other nucleotide sequences].

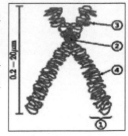

> Additional background information
>
> The set of chromosomes in a cell makes up its genome...
>
> [The genome is the entirety of an organism's hereditary information, (i.e. its means of reproduction). It is encoded either in DNA or, for many types of viruses, in RNA. The genome includes both the genes and the non-coding sequences of the DNA/RNA)[220]]. [The complete set of this information in an organism is called its genotype].

Now, back to the reproductive process... Binary fission begins with DNA replication.

> *Prokaryotic chromosomes and plasmids are generally supercoiled. The DNA must first be released into its relaxed state (i.e. uncoiled) for access for transcription, regulation, and replication.*
>
> *The initiation of DNA replication is mediated by DnaA, a protein that binds to a region of the origin known as the DnaA box. Binding of DnaA to this region causes it to become negatively supercoiled. Following this, a region of OriC upstream of the DnaA boxes, (known as DnaB boxes), become melted. Following melting, DnaA then recruits a hexameric helicase to opposite ends of the melted DNA. This enzyme, helicase, then proceeds to pull apart the single DNA strand to form two single strands of DNA. This is referred to as the "Replication fork".*

(See illustration below of the whole process)

---

[220] http://en.wikipedia.org/wiki/Genome

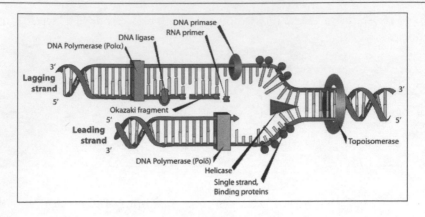

As helicase unwinds DNA at the replication fork, the DNA ahead is forced to rotate. This process results in a build-up of twists in the DNA ahead. This build-up would form a resistance that would eventually halt the progress of the replication fork. DNA topoisomerases are enzymes that solve these physical problems in the coiling of DNA. Topoisomerase I cut a single backbone on the DNA, enabling the strands to swivel around each other to remove the build-up of twists. Topoisomerase II cuts both backbones, enabling one double-stranded DNA to pass through another, thereby removing knots and entanglements that can form within and between DNA molecules.

Each strand's complementary DNA sequence is then recreated by a family of enzymes called DNA polymerase that carries out all types of DNA replication. These enzymes make the complementary strand by finding the correct base through complementary base pairing and bonding it onto the original strand.

["Base Pairs" refers to two nucleotides on opposite complementary DNA or RNA strands that are connected via hydrogen bonds].

This segment of the replication process is referred to as a "replication bubble".

However, a DNA polymerase can only extend an existing DNA strand paired with a template strand; it cannot begin the synthesis of a new strand. To begin synthesis, a short fragment of DNA or RNA, called a primer, must be created and paired with the template DNA strand.

The process of replication ends by means of another enzyme, (DNA ligase), which then zips the strands closed. This procedure produces two new pieces of DNA, each containing one strand from the old DNA and one newly made strand.

[End of DNA synthesis in the binary fission process]

Each circular DNA strand then attaches to the cell membrane. The cell elongates, causing the DNA to separate. [End of chromosomal segregation. Lastly, the cell splits in two and seals, which is the cytokinesis]

From here, we see that DNA replication is a three-step process: finding the origin of replication on the DNA strand, opening up a replication bubble and then the copying process of the DNA strand.

What is so interesting about this process is the fact that it is self-perpetuating. This means that the reproduction of DNA is a perpetual cycle: the one DNA strand is divided and then a new strand is attached to create two strands, both identical to the first. But that's not all! Each new strand that is formed contains – literally – a piece of the original! What I find fascinating about that is that this means that the DNA of, say, all of the prokaryotes in existence today came from one strand of original DNA.

So, the question is: where did the first DNA strand come from? If every successive DNA strand has in it a piece of the original, then where did the original one come from?

Also, we see that the process of DNA replication requires the existence of several other complex factors that work in unison to achieve the end result: the doubling of the genetic information contained in the DNA strand.

So, the question is: what came first? The DNA strands? The Helicase enzyme? DnaA? What is the likelihood that a DNA strand which – by some miracle – came into existence without all of these factors would survive long enough to ensure the transmission of its vital, (yet somehow, "random"), information on to the "next generation"?

Well, these questions are just the tip of the iceberg! Let's continue to look at the reproductive process, shall we?

For the cell to survive and function, it has to have proteins. *"Proteins are essential parts of organisms and participate in virtually every process within cells"*[221]. This means no proteins – no function. So how are proteins made?

One of the central tenets of biology often referred to as the "central dogma of molecular biology", is that DNA is used to make RNA, which is used to make protein.

Please note that this "Central Dogma" is one of the most problematic issues which abiogenesis has to deal with. Especially with regard to the theory called the "RNA world", which hypothesizes that the "original genetic material" was a strand of RNA. This flies in the face of the central dogma in which we find that DNA creates RNA. Furthermore, if RNA (as we see it in the scientific methodology, i.e. observable, measurable, repeatable), was the progenitor of the DNA strand, then it makes more sense to say that it should be the opposite! RNA to DNA to Everything else!

Onwards with protein synthesis:

Protein synthesis generally consists of two major steps: transcription and translation.

---

[221] http://en.wikipedia.org/wiki/Protein

Transcription is the process of creating a complementary RNA copy of a sequence of DNA. Transcription is controlled by other DNA sequences, (such as promoters), which show a cell where genes are, and monitor how often they are copied.

Transcription can be explained as containing 4 simple steps, (just... how... simple... are they?), each moving like a wave along the DNA.

RNA polymerase unwinds/"unzips" the DNA by breaking the hydrogen bonds between complementary nucleotides.

RNA nucleotides are paired with complementary DNA bases.

RNA sugar-phosphate backbone forms with assistance from RNA polymerase.

Hydrogen bonds of the untwisted RNA+DNA helix break, freeing the newly synthesized RNA (single) strand.

The portion of DNA transcribed into an RNA molecule is called a transcription unit and encodes at least one gene. If the gene transcribed encodes a protein, the result of transcription is messenger RNA (mRNA), which will then be used to create that protein via the process of translation. Alternatively, the transcribed gene may encode for either ribosomal RNA (rRNA) or transfer RNA (tRNA), other components of the protein-assembly process, or other ribozymes.

The process of moving information from the language of DNA into the language of amino acids is called "translation".

Translation is achieved when the RNA copy made from a gene is then fed through a structure called a ribosome. The ribosome then translates the sequence of nucleotides in the RNA into the correct sequence of amino acids and joins these amino acids together to make a complete protein chain. The new protein then folds up into its active form[222].

So... it turns out that for the cell to function it has to have proteins. Proteins are created using RNA translation inside of the ribosome. However, there is nothing to "translate" so long as there is no DNA to encode the RNA in the first place with the proper "program" to be utilized by the ribosome! (See earlier when we mentioned the "central dogma" of biology). Remember: without the ribosome, there is no real production of the necessary proteins required by the cell!

So here we are, back at the classic question: which came first? The chicken or the egg? The DNA or the RNA? The RNA or the ribosome, (let's not forget that it, itself, is a very complex molecule!)?

What is it that subjugates/dominated all of these seemingly random functions, (and according to evolutionary science is all random synthesis of biological parts), and makes them into a seamless biochemical machine? We are not looking at a slapstick routine here! This is a phenomenally organized, self-sustaining and self-perpetuating system!

Now the antagonists of Intelligent Design call this type of argument the "G-D of the gaps" argument, meaning that we utilize G-D to fill in all of the "small, unexplained phenomena" that exist in evolutionary theory.

Let me bring a quote to this effect from the book "God, the Failed Hypothesis" by Victor J. Stenger: (in the Preface, pg. 13-14)

Existing scientific models contain no place, where God is included as an ingredient in order to describe observations. Thus, if God exists, he must appear somewhere within the gaps or errors of scientific models.

---

[222] http://en.wikipedia.org/wiki/Introduction_to_genetics

Indeed, the "God of the gaps" has long been a common argument for God. Science does not explain everything, so there is always room for other explanations, and the believer is easily convinced that the explanation is God. However, the God of the gaps argument by itself fails, at least as a scientific argument, unless the phenomenon in question is not only currently scientifically inexplicable but can be shown to forever defy natural description. God can only show up by proving to be necessary, with science equally proven to be incapable of providing a plausible account of the phenomenon based on natural or material processes alone.

I hope that I have made it clear here that we are not looking at "gaps". We are not even looking at "chasms" here! We are looking at galactic million light year leaps of sheer complexity and interconnectedness. Furthermore, the sheer audacity of scientists such as Stenger in claiming that science can even begin to give a realistic explanation of the processes above is nothing but a leap of pure unadulterated "faith" a' la' dictionary. (See Chapter 2 "Emunah vs. Faith" for more depth on this subject). Not only can modern science not account for the sheer complexity of a biological cell, but in all likelihood neither will the grandchildren or great-great-great-great-grandchildren of these scientists.

Stated otherwise: this isn't the "G-D of the gaps" argument, this is the "Science of Grasping at Straws" argument.

G-d willing we will discuss this issue further in the chapter entitled "In the Beginning".

In any case, in summary of this problem, we find that all of the systems of even the most basic life forms cannot exist without one another. When we compare this to the fundamental problem with which we began this issue, that a whole cell – even in evolutionary thinking – is way too complex to have happened all at once, this becomes a conundrum of galactic proportions. There can be no doubt that all of the systems came to be all together, which is the only reason why they all work together so seamlessly. Yes, Dr. Stenger, science will never, ever be able to explain this. It's not a "gap", it's a universe.

Problem F: The Shortcomings of The Scientific Method

One of the great arguments against the "no G-D in creation" theory of existence was, and always will be, the issue of the intricate, organized biological, natural systems inherent in all life and in the world and its Eco-system. Our Sages of blessed memory tell a story of Rabbi Meir who, in response to the argument of an agnostic, came and presented said agnostic with a scroll filled with beautiful writing and prose. After looking at the artistry and the genius of what was written he commended R' Meir, whereupon R' Meir told him "I didn't write it! I was just sitting there one day, and a bottle of ink spilled on the parchment, and that was the result!"

We all recognize that the likelihood of that being true is zero, and that is the argument: if there is organized wisdom inherent it cannot be the result of blind chance!

Well in my research on this topic, I saw a clever response to this on Youtube.com, of all places! The basic premise of this person, who put up videos of several computer-simulated models, is this: the chemical reality is different from that of prose on a parchment in that there is something called chemical bonding affinities. This means that biological systems differ from this in one regard. As opposed to ink on a parchment, or any other such example, which is 100% by chance, when we are looking at chemical and biological systems there is a twist: not everything is random. For some reason, (which we don't know), it is clearly observable and reproducible that certain chemicals have an affinity to bond with other chemicals. That being the case it is much more likely that certain chemicals will bond with each other as opposed to certain drops of ink forming letters, let alone coherent words, on a piece of parchment.

This fellow even went so far as to write several computer simulations to "prove" how chemical and biological affinity can be a sort of "catalyst" in evolution. Even though he says it has no relevance for abiogenesis, this statement is inherently false. If the claim holds true for evolution, then the same principals must be equally applicable to abiogenesis. It would be ridiculous for a person to say that G-D is not a factor in evolution, but He is in abiogenesis! If there is a G-D, He helped the whole way through; and if there isn't, He never helped even at the outset!

The problem is that in noting this fact and in proving it using a program, he shoots himself in the foot. This is true for one simple reason: Only when there is a program will this logic hold.

The basic premise of this is that "Nature", (whatever it is, but surely... it's not G-D! Heaven Forbid!), made a program for chemical interaction. I don't have a clue as to how or why it is so, but as it is observable, measurable and reproducible it, therefore, fits the dogma of scientific method. Also, since I didn't see G-D at work here, just the presence of a program, it's certainly not G-D.

Well, Mr. Smart, if there is a program at work – there is a Programmer. Think about it.

While we are at it, let's consider a few more things concerning the scientific method:

Science does not explain. It quantifies.

"Empirical evidence" is only as good as the observer.

Complexity is a sign of intelligence.

Let's explain these points one at a time:

1) Science Does Not Explain. It Quantifies.

Let me give a concrete example of this issue: "The peculiar handedness of life"

In the Teaching Company's lecture, "The Origins of Life with Robert Hazen", number 18 Professor Hazen states quite clearly that:

> *"The selection of 'just the right mix (of compounds and circumstances required to make life) remains a central puzzle in origins of life research. ...the most confounding problem in the pre-biotic selection of molecules is the origin of the curious handedness of life. ... Many of life's molecules occur in mirror image pairs, like left and right hands. ... Handedness turns out to be a pervasive feature of life. From simple amino acids... to the DNA double helix, ... each of these molecules has a mirror image and these mirror image pairs are known as "chiral molecules". ... Yet at the molecular level life is curiously 'one-handed' even though non-life shows no preference. ... there is just no obvious reason as to why left or right should be preferred, and yet living cells are highly selective, they almost invariably choose right-handed sugars over left, left-handed amino acids over right. ... The origin of this biochemical one handedness known as "homo-chirality" is still one of the great mysteries of life's emergence" (Robert Hazen, ibid.)*

I have to commend Professor Hazen because he is completely open and clear about the fact that science has no explanations at all which can account for the immense complexity that we noted above. In his opening lecture (number 1), he states this clearly. What confounds me is that he goes on to give another 27 speeches that are all needed to explain the tremendous difficulties that are inherent to abiogenesis. From an outsider's perspective, it sounded like that if they pray really hard that one day the proponents of evolution might be able to convince themselves, (in my opinion using sheer obfuscation), that maybe one day their great-great-great-great-(to the nth degree)-grandchildren may find something which might be plausible.

That day is certainly not today!

This area is a classic case of how "scientific method" has gone to many a professional's heads! There are – to the best of my knowledge – very few cases, if any, of observable, measurable and repeatable WHYs in the entire scientific world. Rather all scientific experimentation is geared to see how those forces of "Nature" which are observable, measurable and repeatable can be QUANTIFIED using research.

Let me quote here from the book "God the failed hypotheses" by Victor J. Stenger, professor emeritus of physics and astronomy at the University of Hawaii.

> *Notice that the main purpose of scientific models is to describe rather than explain. That is, they are deemed successful when they agree with all observations; especially those that would have falsified the model had those observations turned out otherwise.*

i.e. scientific models quantify, they do not explain.

Let me give a few examples of this from various areas of science:

Anatomy is a precise science: the entire human body is observable, measurable and its processes are repeatable in laboratory studies. However, even today many things are still unknown or understood about the processes of the body. How the human egg finds its way into the Fallopian tubes, for example. How the brain converts refracted light into electrical impulses, which are then converted by the brain into vision.

In physics, it is known that four basic forces are acting upon the physical world: gravity, weak and strong nuclear forces and the electromagnetic force. All of these are observable, measurable and are subject to testing in a laboratory in ways that are repeatable. This does not mean that there is a scientist anywhere in the entire world who can explain to you HOW these forces work. Gravity = two masses attract. Why? Don't know. However, I can measure and quantify the extent of the force that is acting between the two masses. In magnetism, opposites attract and like charges repel each other. Why is that? Nobody knows. Nevertheless, it is observable, measurable and subject to repeatable testing in the laboratories. In other words, they just are!

2) Quantification Is Not Equal to Understanding.

As I stated above, the fact that I can quantify something doesn't necessarily mean that I have a very deep understanding of why, or even how it works. I may even be able to make a mathematical algorithm that I can use to effectively based on the quantification of the data at my disposal, and yet that doesn't mean I have a fundamental understanding of the issue being quantified!

The reason for this is that almost all scientific study relies on two sources of reasoning: either by using induction or by using deduction! The difference between the two is as follows:

In induction, I look at and try to quantify, the thing itself. Therefore, all of the information that I gather tells me something about what the thing is. Whereas in deduction I gather all of the information that tells me what the thing is not, therefore I can get an inverse picture which limits my understanding of the item to all information about what the thing is... yet it tells me nothing about what it actually is. Sir Arthur Conan Doyle's character Sherlock Holmes was famed for having said to his sidekick, Watson, concerning deduction, *"When you have eliminated the impossible, whatever remains, however improbable, must be the truth."* That is only true if all that you are left with is a very concise amount of information. 99.9999999999999% of the time that isn't the case.

The only type of "WHY" that science can provide us with is when it pertains to something that can be seen by the human eye. Why does sickness x happen? Because of, let's say, a bacterium that attacks the X-cell. But when it comes to the question of the primal forces of the universe...

nada! They will tell us that they exist, and they can quantify them, yet they have no clue as to why they are the way they are, and they have no means of answering it.

3) "Empirical Evidence" Is Only as Good as The Observer.

In the next chapter, "*In the Beginning*", we will explore this issue more while addressing the topic of the universe and the "multi-verse".

Sorry, you'll just have to wait.

Complexity Is a Sign of Intelligence.

Earlier we discussed the sheer complexity of microorganisms and the difficulties that abiogenesis has because of the second law of thermodynamics. We brought further examples of this in the chapter entitled "World of Care and Wonders". THERE ARE NO INSTANCES OF OBSERVABLE, REPEATABLE AND MEASURABLE COMPLEXITY THAT ARE NOT THE RESULT OF INTELLIGENCE. The fact that I don't know doesn't make them random!

In Summary of This Chapter:

To sum up: There are six, obvious, difficulties with the issue known as abiogenesis which in turn add on to the problems that we stated in the previous lesson concerning biogenesis, better known as "evolution". They are:

Problem A: The time frame in which chemical evolution had in which to take place.

Problem B: The second law of thermodynamics. Systems tend to become less complex over time, never more. This is particularly difficult when applied to abiogenesis, as there is no "system" at all.

Problem C: The environment in which simple life systems could propagate don't seem to support life. Just the opposite! Most of them are antagonistic to life!

Problem D: The complexity of biological systems. The sheer complexity of the individual systems of even cellular life is so great that not even intentional, controlled experiments with today's most cutting-edge technologies can reproduce them.

Problem E: The interconnectedness of biological systems. The systems required to allow for cellular, and therefore biological life are too interdependent to have "developed" separately and then magically synthesized.

Problem F: The Shortcomings of the Scientific method. The science is only as good as the observable phenomenon, the observer and the limits of our human knowledge.

To sum up let me quote here from the book "Fitness of the Cosmos for Life" published by Cambridge University Press, page 12:

> *Understanding how organized living cells emerged from disorganized mixtures of molecules is an entrancingly, seductively difficult problem – so difficult, as we now understand it, that science does not even have well-formulated, testable hypotheses about how it might have happened, only guesses and intuitions.*

This from a book that is coming to explain the fitness of the universe for life!

The Final Difficulty:

Even more challenging than all of the above is that it was said only when we are looking at life on the biological level, however we all know that when we take a closer look at the depth of the reality which we refer to as "biological" and "biochemical" has an even deeper level: the atomic state. All of the reality – as we know it – is made of complex chemical processes based on the known elements of the periodic table. However, we are aware that all known chemical compounds are just atoms, which differ from one another based solely on the amounts of protons, neutrons, and electrons that were bound together using the thing that we call the "nuclear force". This is the name that scientists have given the energy bonds which tie together all of the above components of said atoms.

So, in reality, all of the existence, and hence, all of life, utilize the same components, the exact same building blocks to create everything in existence! Stars, planets, plants, animals and even us! All of the existence is made of the exact same un-living stuff: protons, neutrons, electrons and the energy that binds them!

What, do you think, would be the result of my repeated experiment to build a living breathing dog out of bricks? Try as I might would I ever produce something other than a pile of bricks with the likeness of a dog? Even if I would use clay as the core component of the experiment? Would I ever be able to reproduce with it the splendor of a flower in bloom in any way except its external likeness? Obviously not! Yet these three components and their "binding force", which scientists have aptly dubbed the "nuclear force", are the building blocks of everything, life included. According to certain scientists, there is no other component whatsoever. How is that even possible? Will science ever be able to come up with an explanation for this? Certainly not! At least not in the realm of science.

The answer that any thinking, truthful Human being will have to arrive at, is that there is more to the world than just atoms. You cannot make life from something that is not alive. Also, as much as we all enjoy the story of the Frankenstein monster, the corpse that was revived from death, it just doesn't make any sense whatsoever until a spirit/soul is added to the mix[223].

The Gemara (Babylonian Talmud) in Tractate Berachos gives us insight into the story of the prophet Samuel as described in first Samuel. Samuel's mother was a pious woman, yet for years she was barren. The Prophets describe to us how difficult this was for her and how she finally merited that her wish was granted, and she gave birth to a son, he who eventually became one of our greatest prophets: Samuel. She did so on the merit of her prayers and those of the *Kohein Gadol*, Eli. Sometime after his birth, the Prophet relates to us a song that his mother, Hannah, composed in thanks to G-D for hearing and answering her prayer and granting her a son. One of the things that she says in the song is "there is no *tzur* like our G-D". The Talmud explains that the word *tzur* means a "painter" or "sculptor". We, therefore, understand the praise that Hannah, Samuels's mother, said was "there is no sculptor like our G-D." The Talmud in Tractate Berachos explains like this: a painter can make a very fine likeness of life on the wall or the canvas, but that's where it stops. Whereas G-D renders the image of life (an embryo) inside of life (the womb) and breaths into it life and animation.

So, if we can all agree that the difficulties stated above are indeed difficult, then the only thing that will truly cast the deciding vote in the matter is the following question: What explanation makes the most sense?

Here, I will apply a very specific rule of argument: whichever description explains the most phenomena and does so in the simplest fashion – wins[224]. This is the argument made by Hawkins in his book "The Grand Design" in explaining why M-theory is the correct theoretical model in explaining existence, (we'll talk about that in the next chapter).

If that's the case, the G-D argument is the hands-down winner. Sorry, Professor Stenger. Intelligent Design is the most concise; most

---

[223] G-d willing we'll explore this issue more fully in book 2.
[224] This is a concept in logic also known as "Occam's Razor".

simple explanation there is to address all of the "strange and unexplained phenomena" in the scientific world. Let alone all of the things which are statistically, logically and all around impossible to explain with modern (and future) scientific methods.

Also, there is so much more to consider beyond the issues of Biology and Chemistry. A whole lot more. More on that, G-D willing, in the upcoming chapters (and books).

For a complete summary of the difficulties concerning the field of abiogenesis – please look in the appendix.

8

In the Beginning...

Existence, Time and Multiple Universes in The Eyes of The Torah

Space... the final frontier...

HEN WE LOOK AT THE VASTNESS of the universe there are two thoughts, really two mindsets, which come to mind: Either "Look how infinitesimal I am. How could I be of any importance in the grand scheme of things?" or "Look how vast and infinite the universe is! How great must be He who created them!". Of course, in addition, there is also "Gee! Look at all of that stuff out there that I don't understand! It must be random!", but this is clearly an illogical statement.

These theological points of view concerning the universe have existed since time immemorial. It all comes back to the same thing: is it all happenstance or is it design? Let's take a close look and try to find out, shall we?

It's quite clear that the direct outcome of these two outlooks on existence is vast: am I just an unimportant fluke, here today gone tomorrow and it matters not that I was here at all; or do I hold a purpose in this world for which I was created. Think about it.

I would like to preface that the arguments presented here are open to interpretation. Despite my obvious impartiality, I would like to address the facts being related in the black and white words of the holy Torah without any of the, (many times), extraneous explanation involved in describing creation. The Holy Torah, THE Bible, otherwise known as "The (Old) Testament", has a lot to say about creation. We must ask ourselves "Does the Torah describe a phenomenon which has only been discovered by today's cutting-edge science? And, if so, how could this possibly be a man-made document"? I say this simply because all scientific "facts" are open to debate on some level or another, whereas the Holy Torah is black and white and "set in stone" for thousands of years. It is for this reason that the Torah says (Deuteronomy 4:6)

"And you shall guard and do, (all that is written in it, the Holy Torah), for it is your wisdom and genius in the eyes of the world who shall hear all of these laws and will say 'only a wise and genius people comprise this great nation'."

If we look at the arguments discussed here without context... then there will always remain room for debate. However, if we discover that this Holy Book contains knowledge and details that have only recently been "discovered" by humanity, due to scientific advances, then it can only be because its Author was "in the know." The source of this knowledge could only have been the Creator Himself.

In short: if we see a pattern in the observable scientific data available today, (regardless of some of the details of said scientific evidence, which is debatable), falling into a pattern parallel to those of the Holy Torah then the information of said Torah is no longer up for debate.

Also: I do not claim that everything brought in this chapter constitutes the sum total of the information contained in the first few verses of Genesis. It is clearly not everything. There is yet so much more to learn.

However, I have tried to address in this chapter all of the issues relevant to the scientific knowledge of today which are explicit in the language of the Torah. I also have tried to tie in much of the findings of various sciences to address issues that arise from archaeological evidence and the like. For example, the ice age and the evidence that seems to point to the reversal of earth's magnetic poles. I cannot address, however, issues and findings that are not explicit in the Torah or the language of our holy sages. Which leads us to the next important issue.

Despite the fact that the Torah states most things openly, at the end of the day the entire creation of the universe, the stars, and the essential formation of the entire geo and biospheres that constitute the first four days of creation exist in only 17 verses. The implication is that although these verses, as we will see, contain within them a lot of clear information, they are very limited in their scope. After all, how much detail can be inserted into a paltry 17 verses? Yet despite their paucity – every word of the Torah is gold! Every word was chosen with incalculable intelligence and is significant. So, detail be damned! There clearly are gaps in the story as it is told, which lies at the heart of the arguments as to how we are to understand the story that is told. But that's part of the beauty of the Torah – the discovery that the space in-between the words many times speaks volumes as much as the words themselves.

Well, folks, that is the universe as we see it today! So, what is there to talk about when it comes to the Universe, Time and Multiple Universes? Let's start with a little bit of background information. Towards this end, we will discuss all of the Creation issues related to us in the Genesis narrative from day 1 up until, and including, day 4.

Genesis and the "Big Bang":

The thing about this issue that I find most astounding is that when we compare the description of the first 4 days of creation to the scientific explanation for the "bang" and its outcome, we find some fascinating similarities. We will take note of them as we progress.

The description of creation that I am about to write is not necessarily in "sync" with all modern scientific theories or findings. Having said that, we have to remember that all of the said theories are just that, theories. Almost all of them are based on certain dogmas of the scientific fields. I think it's clear to everyone that there isn't even one person alive today who can testify as to what happened exactly. It's all speculation based on modern-day observations. In other words, "it makes sense to say that...". Many times, the very same information can be read/interpreted in an entirely different way to arrive at completely different conclusions. If there are those who cannot accept this, we will just have to agree to disagree. My dogma comes from a Holy Torah, the truth of which we have only just begun to reveal and the source of all Torah Judaism for thousands of years. For more reasons to accept this – please keep reading.

The first verse of the first chapter of Genesis says

> *In the beginning, (literally "the first thing"), E-lohim created the heavens and the earth".*

From the first five (Hebrew) words of the Holy Torah, we learn the following three things: ex-nihilo, (Latin for "something from nothing"), time and space.

Creation

Before G-D created everything... there was nothing. Everything that is in existence today emanates from nothing. It all came into existence by the command of THE Living G-D. This is the meaning of the word *bara*, "created". Before this act, ... there was nothing. NO thing. This is ratified by Einstein's law of relativity and by the modern theory of the "big bang", which states:

The big bang theory is an attempt to describe the beginning of the universe. Through observation and analysis, astronomers determined that the universe is expanding... They theorized that at one time, all the matter and energy in the universe was contained in an incredibly tiny point. Then, the universe expanded suddenly[225].

This was not always the accepted "scientific" view, but we will get to that later. {Authors note: The issue of the "Big Bang" is also a topic of debate, as we will see as we go on.}

There is a very basic difficulty that lies at the very bottom, or – rather – at the very beginning of time-space as seen through the eyes of science. That question is WHERE DID ALL OF THIS INFINITE ENERGY COME FROM IN THE FIRST PLACE?

"Is there any question that keeps you up at night?

I wish it was just one. There are two that if I allow myself to think about them, make my heart sink. Why is there something rather than nothing? It's a simple question that's been asked for so long, and the idea of nothing seems to me logically sensible. But when I truly imagine nothingness, well, I find it almost scary. Why isn't there nothing?

The other question is the nature of time. Time is with us, every moment. I can't even say a sentence without invoking a temporal word-moment. But what is time? When we look at the mathematics of our current understanding of physics, time is there, but there's no deep explanation of what it is or where it came from"[226].

---

[225] http://science.howstuffworks.com/dictionary/astronomy-terms/space-shape1. htm

[226] New Scientist (5 February 2011 pg. 30 *"Thoughts racing along parallel lines"*, an interview with physicist and author Brian Greene, author of the book *The Hidden*

How about this article from New Scientist July 23rd edition "The Existential Issue" 2011?

> As Douglas Adams once wrote, "The universe is big. Really Big". And yet if our theory of the big bang is right, the universe was once a lot smaller. Indeed, at one point it was non-existent. Around 13.7 billion years ago, time and space spontaneously sprang from the void. How did that happen? Or, to put it another way: why does anything exist at all? It's a big question, perhaps the biggest.

Our answer to this has always been – so told us G-D Himself – that I, (that being THE "I"), made the first energy. It is and was infinite because its source is ME, (that being THE "ME").

Let me quote to you the words of one of our Rabbis, ob"m, from the 13th century, Rabbi Moshe ben Nachman, the RaMBa"N[227] in his commentary on this first verse of Genesis:

> G-d created all that exists from total zero, (total lack of existence). In the Holy Tongue (Hebrew of the Bible), there is no proper word for creating something from nothing except for the word Ba-Ra, ("created"). ... G-d drew out from total non-existence a very fine/thin substance, which had no real substance, but it was the power of existence. ... you should know that the heavens and all that is in them are all made of the same substance, and the land and all that is in it is also made of one substance. The Holy One blessed be He, created both of them, (the heavens and the earth), from nothingness. Both of them, together, were created, and everything is created out of them.

Reality concerning the issues of parallel universes).

[227] **Rav Moshe Ben Nachman**, otherwise known as Nachmanidies, was born in Verona, Spain in 1194. He is one of the foremost commentators on the Torah.

Point 1 for the Holy Torah

Bereishis, Genesis

As opposed to the word *Bara* the first word of the Torah, Bereishit, clearly speaks about time. It's root, *rosh*, (pronounced Roh-shh), means "the head of". With the prefix ב the word literally means "In the beginning", and all beginnings are at the very first moment of whatever is being described.

This issue, however, will always remain a conundrum of the physical sciences. This is because science seeks to explain things without figuring G-D into the picture, as G-d doesn't fit the "observable" criteria. (More on this later in the chapter). So, the only answer at science's disposal as to where the energy came from is using circular logic. "What do you mean 'where did it come from'? The very fact that we are here today is indicative of the fact that it was always there"[228]!

How could it have been "always there"? Look back at the quote from Brian Greene as to the whole issue of modern science and time. Why should there have been time? According to the theory of relativity, if all of the mass and velocity of the universe were squished into something less than even a quantum particle why should there have been time at all? At the very best, seeing as everything was in proximity of the greatest source of energy and mass in existence, time should have slowed to a stop. Worse than that is that, it's more than likely that there just was no time at all! So how in the world can you say that the speck was "always there"?

Listen to the words of Rabbi Ovadiah Seforno[229] in his commentary on the first word of Genesis:

---

[228] A difficult position to defend since we humans are still coping with the proof of our own existence! I mean, if I don't exist – then the whole proof is totally meaningless! Maybe you're not really here?

[229] Rabbi Ovadiah Seforno lived in the 15th century in Italy.

Bereishit, at the beginning of time. This is the first instant, which is indivisible, as no time proceeded it.[230]

Time, itself, is integrally tied to the creation.
If there is no creation – there is also no time.

Point 2 for the Holy Torah.

Existence and The Zeroth Law of Thermodynamics:

This contention of science as to the existence of the quantum point leads us to the next question, which comes from the Zeroth law of thermodynamics. The Law of Thermodynamic Equilibrium. This law states that[231]:

> *In thermodynamics, a thermodynamic system is said to be in thermodynamic equilibrium when it is in thermal equilibrium, (no exchange of heat with another system), mechanical equilibrium, (the net forces acting on the particle is zero), radiative equilibrium, (the object has a constant temperature due to equal loss and gain of temperature), and chemical equilibrium (the concentrations of the reactants and products have not yet changed with time). The word "equilibrium" means "a state of balance". In an equilibrium state, there are no unbalanced potentials (or driving forces) within the system. A system that is in equilibrium experiences no changes when it is isolated from its surroundings.*

---

[230] See also Rav Sa'adiya Gaon *Emunot v'De'ot* chapter 1, pg. 73-74 in the Kappach edition, who states clearly that time is a construct created "in the beginning".
[231] **http://en.wikipedia.org/wiki/Thermodynamic_equilibrium**

I would like to be clear. Even though, technically, the zeroth law of thermodynamics speaks about equilibrium between two or more objects, one should not assume that it wouldn't hold for a single object as well. There is a concept in Hebrew known as a "*kal va chomer*"[232] which is apropos here: if the law of thermal equilibrium is true about the state of equilibrium of two or more objects, then it is most certainly true concerning a single object. Especially if that object is all of the existence!

Therefore, the question is, was this first quantum speck in equilibrium or not? If it was, and according to the definition above there is no reason why it shouldn't have been, (after all it had nothing and no one to exchange anything with!), then what caused its change in equilibrium? Why did it go "bang" at all?

However, if you say that it wasn't in equilibrium, then it was never in such a state and the question that arises is "Why not"? "Because I say so" is never a basis for a logical argument.

According to the above definition, it makes the most sense to say that it *was* in a state of equilibrium for the following reasons:

It was in thermal equilibrium as there was nothing with which to exchange heat.

It was in mechanical equilibrium as there were no outside forces (G-D aside), to act upon it, (and every *re*action must be proceeded by an action).

It was in a state of radiative equilibrium as there was no loss of energy and no gain.

Lastly, it was in chemical equilibrium as there were no reactants or products!

Beyond that: If we are to say that time in the speck had – effectively – stopped, then the energy, which was clearly a closed system, (as stated before, there was nothing else with which it could interact!), should have

---

[232] *Kal va chomer* means "something easy and something hard", this is one of the bases for a logical argument that goes as follows: if, by the comparatively "easy" thing we find a stringency, then it must be that this stringency is equally applicable by the more severe of the two things. This logic stands unless we can find a reason as to why the stringency is applicable only in the "easier" of the two cases.

been in a state of equilibrium and therefore should never have resulted in a "bang"!

The answer of modern scientists to this problem? Quantum Fluctuations. Just what does this mean?

A quantum fluctuation is a temporary change in the amount of energy in a point in space, arising from Werner Heisenberg's uncertainty principle.

> *According to one formulation of the principle, (meaning not all physicists agree to it), energy and time can be related by the relation. That means that conservation of energy can appear to be violated, but only for small times. This allows the creation of particle-antiparticle pairs of virtual particles. The effects of these particles are measurable, for example, in the effective charge of the electron, different from its "naked" charge[233].*

Heisenberg's uncertainty principle states that there is a possibility for particles to "appear" out of nowhere due to the quantum uncertainty of the universe. Therefore, says Stephen Hawking, "Something from Nothing" presents no problem to modern physics.

I have, however, just one little itsy-bitsy problem: what if there is no space? I mean the definition above states "a quantum fluctuation is a temporary change in the amount of energy in a point in space." Can anyone testify, with absolute certainty, as to the existence of space then, at a time during which all of the existence was smooshed into the tiniest of tiny tinys? I can certainly hear how this might not be a problem in regard to the First Law of Thermodynamics, as the theory of probability allows for the switching between energy and mass. However, if that speck were in a state of thermal equilibrium, as we said before, would there still be room for quantum fluctuations to take place? Would Heisenberg's uncertainty principle even apply? Would any of the laws of quantum physics apply, if all that was in existence existed only in the quantum realm? Maybe. (But then again, maybe not). It's true that there are such things as quantum

---

[233] http://en.wikipedia.org/wiki/Quantum_fluctuation

fluctuations in the measured space of today, but that's a long shot from saying that if it's true today - it should be equally true then!

In short: to state that the Uncertainty principle can help us explain how something came to be is beyond hypothetical. It's also beyond scientific, as it is neither Observable, Measurable, nor Repeatable outside of the conditions of nanosecond number one. Even if we could reproduce something in the big Hadron Collider in Geneva which might simulate a point in space similar to the original quantum "dot", it's still not going to prove anything because of the aforementioned lack of reproducing all of the circumstances at point 0.0000000000000000000000000000000000etc1.

In any case, there are those who favor this hypothesis, and we will just have to agree to disagree here.

Just to close the circle here: How do we Jews answer this issue? Why elementary, dear Watson! It's the third word in the Holy Torah! Who created everything? Why is there an "is"? E-lohim! To create – You must precede the creation. G-d, the only Infinity, is the first cause, as we discussed way back in chapter 3. Creation is the effect[234].

Point 3 for the Holy Torah.

The Static Universe

The Classical system: the universe, and time itself, are "eternal", (another word for infinity). This is also called the "Static Universe".

I will not go through the history of how science arrived at the conclusion that the world has a finite beginning because every textbook and whatnot on the topic, (whether pro- or anti- Design), elaborate on this point in depth. Suffice it to say that only recently science caught up with the first verse in the book of Genesis[235], in concluding that the static universe model

---

[234]   For more on this topic please refer back to the chapter *"Logical and Philosophical"*.

[235]   Beginning with the famous experiment of Penzias and Wilson in 1965 using a Bell labs ultra-sensitive microwave receiving system to study radio emissions from the Milky Way discovered an unexpected background of radio noise with no obvious

does not, and cannot, fit the known data. Indeed, the universe had a very definite beginning.

{Author's note: After having written the above, it was called to my attention that the above was written, like much of popular science today, based upon apologetics made upon preconceived notions. This means that although the truly "static" model of the universe is clearly not true, thus refuting the philosopher's creed of a truly "static", meaning un-moving, eternal universe, there is a model of the universe that both adheres to the laws of Newtonian physics and mathematics which denies the continued expansion of the universe thereby making the universe static as far as its size is concerned. However, this model of the universe, known to the world as the "Geocentric Model", in which the entire universe revolves around the Earth, although static in size is not static in its movement. As stated, it holds that the universe revolves around the Earth, which clearly is not "static" in its absolute meaning.[236]}

The Big Crunch

The second model is the expanding-contracting universe, also commonly referred to as the "Big Crunch" model. This model states that at some time in the future everything will collapse upon itself, returning to the primordial energy dot only to explode again and repeat the process, ad-infinitum.

This model states that even though science must concede that there was a beginning it doesn't imply an absolute beginning, just the most recent one in... (Wait for it!) ... an infinite chain. Yes, infinite time is still alive

---

explanation. This was the "leftover" "bang" of the "big bang". For more info see **http://www.bell-labs.com/project/feature/archives/cosmology/**

[236] For more on this topic the reader is urged to read the book "Galileo Was Wrong" by Dr. Robert Sungenis, where the topic of geocentrism and heliocentrism in the eyes of the scientific data is concerned.

and well in the universe. It may not be static, but there is an infinity out there that saves our mathematical bacon, (and "we" prefer "it" to G-D).

It must, however, be pointed out that this is just an avoidance of the question. Even if we suppose that the universe expands and contracts, as it is still, at the end of the day, a finite universe – it had to have begun at some point. So, really it doesn't solve the problem at all, rather it just pushes it off to a distant unclear past. So, the problem remains, why did this process start in the first place?

The rebuttal of the "big crunch" (or "splat")[237] [238]theory, also known as the "yo-yo universe", other than the logical problem above, is based on two facts:

#1> All cosmological observations show conclusively that not only are the billions of galaxies not slowing down, they are picking up speed[239] as they go their separate ways! {Author's note: Again, this issue is debatable if we follow the geocentric model of the universe. However, based on the heliocentric model and the presumption of red-shift, the above observation is true}.

And #2> Because after intense calculations, physicists have concluded that there just isn't enough matter in the universe to create the necessary gravity to "recall" the universe and perform "the big crunch".

The new term for the expanding universe is "The Big Rip", because essentially, over the course of the next few billion years, (don't worry, it's

---

[237] See **http://imagine.gsfc.nasa.gov/docs/ask_astro/answers/980109a.html**

[238] Originally, many scientists hypothesized that there existed "Dark Matter" and similar types of additional matter in the universe. All of which would help to solve the missing matter issue. However, no conclusive proof has been brought to prove its existence. Despite the lack of proof, the current thinking seems to be that the exact opposite is true. Instead of helping the universe to contract the dark energies are actually pushing the universe farther and faster apart! **http://science.howstuffworks.com/dictionary/astronomy-terms/dark-matter6.htm**

[239] See **http://www.nasa.gov/missions/science/f_dkenergy.html** which says this quite clearly! Also, Brian Greene in "the hidden universe" chapter 6 states that the precise *observed phenomenon* that the universe is not only not slowing down, a precursor necessary for a re-crunch of space, but it's *speeding up as the galaxies move further apart.*

not in your lifetime!), the universes will move so far apart that there will be no stars in the sky!

This means that science has only just "come to the conclusion" stated clearly by King David thousands of years ago in Psalms (119:96): "*to all that begins I have seen an ending...*". All that exists in this universe – including time and space – is finite. It has both beginning and an end. Bye-bye static and yo-yo universes!

Let it be noted, however, that both of the models above (and, as we will see later, all other possible models as well), rest on the fulcrum of something called "infinity". This is done to solve much of the realistic mathematical, statistical and physical problems that stem from all physical models that don't take G-d into the picture.

Let's ponder this issue for a moment.

Infinity

Since it is now clear to everyone that the universe had a finite beginning, science is left with only one of two possibilities to explain our existence. Either this universe is on a one-way trip, with finite time and space, (which would agree to the Torah, but raise many of the above problems); or there must be some other infinity out there!

If there is an aspect of existence that is infinite, meaning that it has no beginning and no end, then – to paraphrase the answer – *we don't have to deal with the problem.*

This is a classic case of the "ostrich syndrome".

Effectively, this "answer" says that I don't have an answer, but because I am a true believer in the process called "the no-god creation" I, therefore, don't need one. I am sure that an answer can/will/might, (please G-D!), be provided at some other time(/space) which might have something contained in it which sounds a little bit like an answer. (I also repeat this mantra daily to reinforce it, in light of its total absurdity).

In any case, up until relatively recent history, there were two basic "explanations", both of which utilize the infinity theorem: infinite time-space, ("Always been there... Ha! Ha! Ha! ... Always will!"[240]), now dead, and R.I.P., or the more modern theory of infinite parallel space, which we will come back to later.

Point 4 for the Holy Torah.

Heaven!

...es hashomayim ve'es ha'aretz

The first thing G-D created was the heavens[241] followed by the Earth. This means that the first billion or so years of the universe, (as counted by modern cosmology[242]), fit into the first five words of the first verse of Genesis. Everything that led up to the next stage of creation, the creation of the Earth, is included in the word *hashomayim*, the heavens. How, exactly, G-D did this is irrelevant to us. It is for this reason that The Book doesn't go into further detail in this matter. You are welcome to explore this in the scientific literature. However, the fact remains that that is precisely what happened. Space, i.e. *shomayim*/heavens were created first.

Point 5 for the Holy Torah.

---

[240] A paraphrase of an old 7-up commercial for those of us old enough to remember it.

[241] See Tractate *Tamid* 32a, which states this clearly as well. However, the Gemara in Tractate *Chagiga 11b* relates that this was a topic of debate between Hillel and Shamai. The simple reading of the verse, however, clearly puts the *shomayim*, the heavens, first.

[242] I reiterate: I disagree with this issue completely. I am bringing it up to use it as a "devil's advocate". The rebuttal of the entire premise can be found in chapter 9.

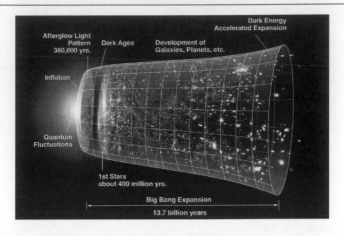

Universal Expansion and the 6 Days of Creation

Modern cosmology and physics make a claim similar to that of the Torah concerning the matter of universal expansion: that a lot of creation was crammed into a very short time. They do this to solve a very basic difficulty with the universe: the uniformity of background thermal radiation.

Cosmologists refer to this problem as "the horizon quandary/problem". Which asks, how can the entire universe have a common thermal (=temperature) background when the extreme "right" side of the universe never "communicated" with its polar opposite "left"?

> *"If you make one part of an object hotter than its surroundings and then wait, the hot spot will grow cooler and its surroundings warmer until the temperature of the object is uniform. Similarly, one would expect the universe to eventually have a uniform temperature. But this process takes time, and if inflation hadn't occurred, there wouldn't have been enough time in the history of the universe for heat at widely separated regions to equalize, assuming that the speed of such heat transfer is limited by the speed of light".*

"A period of very rapid expansion, (much faster than light speed, somehow, (we have no idea as to how)), remedies that because there would have been enough time for the equalization to happen in the extremely time pre-inflationary early universe."

"...According to even conservative estimates, during this cosmological inflation, the universe expanded by a factor of 1, 000,000,000,000,000,000,000,000,000,000 (that's 10 to the 29th power) in 0.00000000000000000000000000000000 0000001 (that's 10 to the -32nd power) seconds. It was as if a coin 1 centimeter in diameter suddenly blew up to ten million times the width of the Milky Way"[243].

From here, we see clearly that even modern science recognizes the need for "creation" to occur in tremendously fast bursts. Albeit at specific junctions of creation.

In addition to the above problem, there are also[244]:

• The Flatness Problem:
WMAP has determined the geometry of the universe to be nearly flat. However, under Big Bang cosmology, curvature grows with time. A universe as flat as we see it today would require an extreme fine-tuning of conditions in the past, which would be an unbelievable coincidence.

• The Monopole Problem:
Big Bang cosmology predicts that a very large number of heavy, stable "magnetic monopoles"[245] should have been produced in the early universe. However, magnetic monopoles have never

---

[243] Hawking *"The Grand Design"* pg. 203-4. Listen also to Professor Brian Greene, in his book "The Hidden Reality" lesson 2 (around 44 minutes into the recording) concerning this issue.

[244] Quoted verbatim from **http://map.gsfc.nasa.gov/universe/bb_cosmo_infl.html**

[245] As opposed to all magnetic-fields of today, all of which are bi-polar, (i.e. North and South poles), a Monopole magnetic-field is one that only has one pole.

been observed. So, if they exist at all, they are much rarer than
the Big Bang theory predicts.

Let me quote from Stephen Hawking here as he addresses the issue of universal expansion in the July 23, 2011, edition of New Scientist.

Inflation made the universe very large and very smooth and
flat. However, it was not completely smooth: there were tiny
variations from place to place. These variations caused minute
differences in the temperature of the early universe, which we
can see in the microwave background. The variations mean
that some regions will be expanding slightly less fast. The
slower regions eventually stop expanding and collapse again
to form galaxies and stars. And, in turn, solar systems. We owe
our existence to these variations. If the early universe had been
completely smooth, there would be no stars and so life could not
have developed. We are the product of primordial quantum
fluctuations.

Isn't it incredible how there were these tiny "variations" which slowed down pockets of the universal expansion enough to form galaxies?

However, even though science recognizes the necessity of cosmological inflation it doesn't mean that it's all smooth sailing when the issues of cosmological inflation are scrutinized!

Cosmological Inflation: How Necessary Is It to The Universe's Creation and How Precisely Does It Have to Be?

The following is a quote from Scientific American (April 2011) in an article entitled "The Inflation Debate" (pg. 36-43). After stating the reasons above for expansion, the article then says the following:

...The case against inflation challenges the logical foundations of the theory. ...

[Problem #1] ...bad inflation is more likely than good inflation. ... Only an extremely narrow range of values could produce the observed temperature variation. ....

[Problem #2] ...no inflation is more likely than either. ... Some ... configurations lead to inflation ... Other ...lead to a uniform, flat universe directly—without inflation. [However] Both sets of configurations are rare, so obtaining a flat universe is unlikely overall[246].

Another approach ... showed that an overwhelming number of extrapolations have insignificant amounts of inflation. ... a flat and smooth universe is unlikely, and inflation is a powerful mechanism for obtaining the needed smoothing and flattening. Yet this advantage appears to be completely offset by the fact that the conditions for starting inflation are so improbable. When all factors are taken into account, the universe is more likely to have achieved its current conditions without inflation than with it[247].

---

[246] Penrose's shocking conclusion, though, was that obtaining a flat universe without inflation is much more likely than with inflation—by a factor of 10 to the googol (10 to the power of 100)!

[247] In addition, this doesn't take into account that we have absolutely zero examples of any explosion ever creating anything at all, let alone something as amazingly organized as a universe. It also doesn't mention that one of the main proofs of the "bang" is the issue called "redshift", which refers to how light, when moving away from an object, tends to shift more towards the red end of the light-spectrum. As Keppler noticed that the starlight visible from the earth tended to be shifted towards the red-light spectrum he therefore concluded that this meant that all of the stars are moving away from the earth. This "conclusion" was jumped on by scientists in the hope that it could allow them to continue saying the universe just happened. However, it fails to take into account that we don't have enough clear information to

The crux of the problem here is that the two positions stated above cannot, scientifically, live hand-in-hand. Well, I ask, WHY NOT? What really is the problem noted above with the inflationary hypothesis? That if events are truly random then the likelihood of the inflationary universe ever occurring is next to nothing.

Once again: the science is only as good as the scientist! If we were not to suppose that the world is random... then what? Well, basically, what comes out is that the reasons for inflation stated earlier, and the explanations that it provides as to the universe's expansion and uniformity make a whole lot of sense!

But that's just the tip of the proverbial iceberg! Listen to the words of the prophet Isaiah, (Yes, from THE (Old) Testament) (42:5)

> *"Thus, spoke The G-D, HaShem, He who created the heavens and spread them out."*

Clearly, the prophet was "in the know" about how the heavens were spread.

Do our sages, of blessed memory, have anything else to add concerning the inflationary epoch? You bet your sweet petuti they do! Listen to the words of our sages in tractate Chagigah 12a:

> *Rav Yehuda said in the name of Rav "At the time that the The Holy One, blessed be He, created the world[248] (i.e. existence) it was spreading and going like two spindles of warp[249] until the*

---

actually say that. After all, it could be that all starlight is naturally red-shifted in the first place!

[248] Even though the word עולם is translated literally as "the world", clearly here it is not being used in that meaning, because the verse brought in support is not talking about the עולם rather it's talking about the שמים, the heavens.

[249] In weaving cloth, one sets up two types of strings: the warp and the weft. The warp is the basis for the cloth, it's set up on the loom first by arranging the strings in a parallel. Afterwards the weft is woven into the strings of the warp in an up and down fashion. It should be noted, however, that warp and weft are flat, just like the universe.

Holy One, blessed be He, chastised them and made them to stop, as it is written (Job 26:11) "the pillars of the world were weakened (נתרופפו, at the time of the creation) and they became firm from His chastise".

Our sages also tell us[250] that it was this act of stopping the expansions of the heavens for which we call G-D by the name שד-י, (Sha-dai in Hebrew). This name means, "Who said 'Enough!'", (a composite of the words שאמר די).

In truth, however, there are two ways of interpreting the words of our sages, who themselves were interpreting the words of Isaiah. It could be that they speak of an ever-expanding universe, like the one described in the Big-Bang model, in which HaShem said "Enough" to the incalculable speed of the inflation bringing it down to the levels that scientists claim today. It could also mean that He told them to literally stop their expansion, which is in-sync with the geocentric model of the universe. Regardless of the model and the corresponding interpretation[251] of the words of our sages, there is one clear thing that is agreed upon. The universe was created and spread out at an incredibly rapid rate, and that without HaShem's intervention, they would not have stopped.

Wow! Even according to the most skeptical views of the age of the oral Torah, (the Talmud), HOW COULD THOSE RABBIS HAVE POSSIBLY KNOW THAT TWO THOUSAND YEARS AGO[252]? Unless... they got the information from Someone Who Knows!

---

[250] See Tractate *Chagigah* ibid. See also *Midrash Rabbah* on this verse in Genesis

[251] I will state that the simple understanding of the words of our sages, ob"m, in Tractate Chagigah is that He told them to stop entirely. However, that does not mean that the universe is not in constant motion, as all of our holy Rabbis, ob"m, speak of constantly. See, for example the Rambam in the Laws of the Foundations of the Torah in the first chapter.

[252] In reality the Oral Torah is much older than that. In Jewish tradition we say that it was given to us on Sinai over 3300 years ago and handed down from Rabbi to student orally until a standard model was made and put into written form about 2000 years

In any case, we see clearly from the first verse of Genesis that the first thing created was the *shomayim*, the heavens. No stars just yet, just lots and lots (and lots) of ... heavens. It's important to note that science tells us that all of this occurred in just fractions of fractions of seconds. Much less then a day, (even less time than it takes to say *shomayim*!)

Point 6 for the Holy Torah.

Genesis and the "Big Bang" Continued: The Earth

Planet Earth, *ha'aretz*, is then created... and it is a mess!

Please note: the entire narrative of the Genesis story is told over from the perspective of the Earth. Everything after the word "*Shomayim*", (the heavens), is described from the face of the "*Aretz*", (literally "the land"). In this instance, the word *aretz* is not referring to the land as opposed to the seas, as there was no land mass until day three. Rather it refers to the planet that we call "Earth".

Having said that, it becomes apparent that the *aretz* is used here to accentuate that the planet was, at its inception, a world without water. It was composed of the same *aretz* of which the land mass, (see day 3), was made. Yet it is not called *yabasha*, which means "that which became dry," (the term used on day three to describe the land that jutted out of the waters and therefore had to "dry off") because originally there was no water at all. This teaches us that during "stage 1" of the planet it was decidedly not wet or watery.

Point 7 for the holy Torah.

ago. For more on this topic the reader is urged to look on my website www.rabbibz. com for the blogs "The Torah, The Massorah"

Verse 2 States

And the land (Earth) was tohu and bohu, (more on what they are in a moment

RaSh"I explains *tohu* and *bohu* as a sort of phrase, meaning that everything, all of the elements of the earth, were mixed together and covered with water), and it was dark on the face of the water and the ruach of G-D, (whatever that is), was hovering over the face of the waters".

Tohu and Bohu

The first thing that the Holy Torah tells us after the creation of the earth is that it, (*Ha'aretz*, i.e. the world), is tohu and bohu, (*Tohu va Bohu*). Clearly, these things pertain to the Earth. But just what are they?

The Oral Torah in tractate Chagigah 12a states the following:

> *It has been taught (by our sages) Tohu is a green line that encircles the entire world, from which emanates the darkness [to the world], as it says (Psalms 18) "He places His hidden darkness around it ([the Earth], from here we learn that the line of darkness surrounds (or encircles) the heavens – RaSh"I)". Bohu, those are the damp stones, which are embedded in the depths from which the water comes out. As it is written (Isiah 34) "And he rested upon it a line of Tohu and stones of Bohu." (From which we see that Tohu is a line, and Bohu is stones – RaSh"I[253])*

From the order of the words in the verse, we see that *Tohu* and *Bohu* preceded the stage when the Earth became a water planet, (more on this shortly).

---

[253] Rabbi Shlomo ben Itzchak, one of our most prolific sages. He lived in France in the 10th century.

Tohu

I am not sure what our sages, ob"m, meant when they said that "the Earth is surrounded by a green line from which darkness emanates". I believe, however, that this refers to the earth's electromagnetic field, which is like a "line[254]" that surrounds the planet. Although plainly, from the way our sages use the word, it's not referring to an actual line, but rather a "line" which separates between the darkness of space and the planet.

The reason that I say this is based on a verse in Job (20:7) which states *"The tilt (or "leaning") to the north is because of,* (literally על means "rests on"), *Tohu"*. Although Tohu, in almost every other inference in the Bible means "emptiness", here it is clearly referring to a force that causes things to tilt to the North, (צפון in Hebrew). If that is, indeed, what the word נטה means.

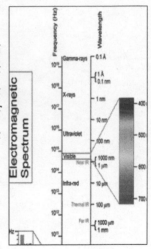

One of the interesting things concerning what our sages say about this line, Tohu, is that it is green. In all of the other sources brought relevant to "Tohu", there is no explicit mention of it being green. So why did our sages, ob"m, go out on a limb to give it a color?

One thing, though, before we can go on. We must establish that although in modern language "green" is only the color of the leaves and the grass in spring[255], our sages use it to include some shades of what we call "Yellow" as well[256]. What I

---

254 Many scientists describe the electro-magnetic spectrum as a "band" of energy frequencies, which, in Hebrew translates as קו, the exact word that our sages used above!

255 The reason that we see them as green being that they absorb all other types of light of the electro-magnetic spectrum except for green, which then registers on the receptors in our eyes.

256 See, for example, the laws concerning an Esrog, one of the four species which we are commanded to "wave" during the festival of Sukkos.

find interesting in this is that the colors green-yellow make up almost the exact "middle" of the visible electromagnetic spectrum. (See picture of the electromagnetic spectrum).

However, it does not make sense to say that this is the interpretation. This is because on day one the Earth still lacked an atmosphere, (only on day two). It is the atmosphere, which reflects most of the electromagnetic spectrum, but not the visible spectrum.

It is also a color frequently seen regarding the phenomenon known as the "Aurora Borealis", (see picture at right), a side product of Earth's magnetosphere. The interesting thing about the magnetosphere of the Earth

is that modern scientific theory is that the magnetosphere keeps the solar winds from the sun at bay, which could certainly fit the description mentioned above about the "green line" that keeps the darkness of space at bay.

This includes, as well, that which is known as the "Van Allen Belt", a belt made up of charged solar particles that are trapped within the layers of earth's magnetosphere, (see the yellowish area in the picture below).

It seems clear from the verses that this was necessary in preparation for the further stages of the earth's development, as will quickly become apparent.

It would seem, therefore, that the Torah is telling us is that the function of Tohu is to separate the darkness that is space from the earth. This is also the simple understanding of what the verse says later, "and the dark, (of space was touching), upon the face of the depths, (of water)."

The Darkness that Precedes the Light

As I noted in the verse above there is "dark" that was touching the face of the waters, we learn that dark is not the opposite of light. Dark itself is one of the creations. In truth, we say this quite clearly in the *Ma'ariv* prayer that we say daily. "Blessed are You, the Lord, our G-d! King of everything! Who forms light and creates darkness...". It is the dark of space, (i.e. dark matter or aether), that was touching the face of the waters[257]. This is because there was not, as yet, an atmosphere of the planet to separate space from the waters that were now covering the earth, (more on this in a moment). That only came to be on day two, (more on this on day two).

In any case, I, personally, cannot claim with absolute certainty that the above is the definitive explanation as to what tohu is. However, it sounds amazingly close.

---

[257] This issue becomes especially obvious when compared to the later verses. Only after the creation of light does the Torah say that the light is renamed "day" and the darkness is renamed "night". Night is a time-period measured by a lack of light. *Choshech,* (חשך in Hebrew), is not night nor a lack of light. It was a separate creation that of light and it was a noun.

The Wobbly World?

If we are to suppose that Tohu is the electromagnetic force, we do not have to say that this line of magnetic force – at this point in time, as opposed to in Job's time – was necessarily pointing North, as described in the (later) verse of Job. Just the opposite! We must take note that there was no moon in a stable orbit around the Earth at this time, (more on this later). It, therefore, makes sense that there was no clear "Magnetic North" at that time, even in a very broad sense. There was only the molten core of the Earth randomly churning according to its haphazard "boil". This does not imply, however, that the Earth was not already turning on an axis, {or that the sum-total of the universal forces around the geocentric world were pulling on the world in all directions} (again, more on this later). If this is true, then it would solve an issue that has been raised against the idea of creation: that of all of the signs pointing to extreme changes, and even "switching" of earth's magnetic poles. The Holy Torah tells us that the moon was not in geosynchronous orbit around the Earth until day 4. That means that there were almost 4 whole days during which the earth's magnetosphere was lacking something to stabilize it. This could account for the multiple "flips" in the magnetic poles for which there is some evidence.

However, as the above is, like much of science, the interpretation of the data, the real question that we need to ask ourselves is this: Could there be something else that caused the changes in the magnetic forces? After all, during the time of the flood, there were massive changes occurring to the planet by means of tectonic and volcanic activity. As the verse itself describes (Genesis 7:11) the deep wellsprings of the deep were torn asunder, (tectonic forces) expressing the deep-earth waters to above-ground levels. Not to mention the massive amounts of water that our sages, ob"m, tell us were brought to earth in order to make the flood into *THE flood*. As the gravitational pull of the earth certainly increased as a result of the flood[258] it makes a lot of sense to say that all of these factors wreaked havoc on the magnetics of planet earth, *ha'aretz*[259]. Much of the above is my own speculation based on my understanding of the data and the Book. It might be wrong. But then again, it could be right as well.

Still, I would say point 8 for the Holy Torah!

What I do know is that Bohu, the moist stones at the lowest levels of what is today the sea, and from which the waters came, is certainly something that we can find analogous in the scientific theories of the early earth!

Once again, I would like to stress that I do not write the above as apologetics. I do so to show that the observable evidence does not argue with the simple understanding and order of the words of the Torah.

Bohu And Earth, The Water Planet

Here the verse tells us that Earth became a water planet. As it says, *"and there was dark on the face of the depths* (of water)." Let's ask the question: does science ratify this? Was the Early Earth a water planet? This is one of the more puzzling issues in science today, for clearly the planet today is a water planet[260], and all evidence seems to point to the fact that it also was in its earliest stages of development as well.

---

[258] Our sages, ob"m, in the Midrash tell us that the configuration of the Chimea star cluster was played with, thereby affecting the gravitational forces working on the earth. It sounds like that this is what "pulled" the waters out from the deep springs in the first place.

[259] For more on this topic please check out my blog at www.rabbibz.wordpress.com and read the article "Noah and Tectonic Movement".

[260] A little bit more than 70% of the Earth is covered by oceans today.

Recent evidence suggests the oceans may have begun forming by 4.2 Ga, or as early as 4.4 Ga. In any event, by the start of the Archaean eon, the Earth was already covered with oceans[261].

Yet, according to virtually all scenarios concerning the early earth, no one seems to have a genuinely plausible explanation as to how! If the early earth was a phenomenally hot, volcanic planet, then the liquid water cannot have come from the planet itself!

The large amount of water on Earth can never have been produced by volcanism and degassing alone. (This is true even were we to assume that at the time of the original accretion of the earth there was a significant amount of water in the form of meteorites and the like). It is assumed the water was derived (later) from impacting comets that contained ice. Though most comets are today in orbits farther away from the Sun than Neptune, computer simulations show they were originally far more common in the inner parts of the solar system. However, most of the water on Earth was probably derived from small impacting protoplanets, objects comparable with today's small icy moons of the outer planets. Impacts of these objects could have enriched the terrestrial planets, (Mercury, Venus the Earth and Mars), with water, carbon dioxide, methane, ammonia, nitrogen and other volatiles. If all water on Earth was derived from comets alone, millions of comet impacts would be required to support this theory. Computer simulations illustrate that this is not an unreasonable number[262].

---

[261] http://en.wikipedia.org/wiki/History_of_Earth#4.3_Ga:_Oceans_and_atmosphere

[262] http://en.wikipedia.org/wiki/History_of_Earth#4.3_Ga:_Oceans_and_atmosphere see also New Scientist Oct. 29, 2011 pg. 14 an article entitled *"Comets may Douse Nw Worlds into Life"*

The cometary and asteroidal delivery of water to accreting Earth and Mars has significant caveats, (the wrong term, they mean "difficulties"), even though it is favored by D/H isotopic ratios. Key issues include:

The higher D/H ratios in Martian meteorites could be a consequence of biased sampling since Mars may have never had an effective crustal recycling process. (Meaning since Mars has no tectonic plate recycling, unlike Earth, therefore it has a higher reading for D/H because every gram that ever slammed down on the planet stayed right where it landed).

(In) Earth's Primitive Upper Mantle, (the layer of the earth that resides below the Earth's "crust"), (we have discovered an), estimate of the $187_{Os}/188_{Os}$ isotopic ratio exceeds 0.129. (This is) significantly greater than that of carbonaceous chondrites, (the less common type of meteorite fragment, comprising only about 5% of all chondrites), but similar to anhydrous, (meaning "having all water removed"), ordinary chondrites, (the more common (80%) type of meteorite). This makes it unlikely that planetary embryos, (the "protoplanets" described above), compositionally similar to carbonaceous chondrites, supplied water to Earth.

(i.e. if meteorites were responsible for bringing the water to earth, they didn't seem to leave behind a footprint in the various strata of having done so! Just the opposite! The trace minerals found are more like the water-free chondrites, which are common even today)

Earth's atmospheric content of Ne is significantly higher than would be expected had all the rare gasses and H_2O been accreted from planetary embryos with carbonaceous chondritic compositions. (As above: if meteorites were the source of said *water they also didn't leave behind a "footprint" in the atmospheric gasses).*[263]

SO... where the water came from remains a conundrum in science. However, apparently, we are in agreement that at a very early stage during the earth's history it was a water planet. If we consider, as described in the previous lesson on abiogenesis, that the Earth itself, according to science, is 4.5 billion (GA) years old, (again, not a fan), that means that the Earth was – effectively – covered with water almost immediately... and became a water planet.

Where did the water come from? Well, from *Bohu*, of course! As our Sages of blessed memory have told us clearly, these are some forms of rock that reside at the depths of the oceans, and they are responsible for the production and synthesis of all of the Earth's water. What type of rocks are they exactly? I don't know. Do I have to know? No, I don't. Perhaps they are the aforementioned "Protoplanets", but even science doesn't seem to agree with that. But if they are...*then how did the holy Torah know this if it's a human made document?*

In any case, we see here clearly that the Torah holds that (1) in its initial stages the Earth was a barren world until (2) the processes of the Bohu rocks "kicked in" and produced all of the water, turning the world into a water world[264].

Points 9 and 10 for the Genesis description of the Torah.

---

[263] http://en.wikipedia.org/wiki/Evolution_of_water_on_Mars_and_Earth

[264] At a later time, there was an incredible amount of water that was "delivered" to earth, which is most likely the source for continental drift and earth's tectonic plates. For more information on this – see the article "Noah and Continental Drift" at my blog on www.rabbibz.com .

A World Shrouded in Darkness

Aside from being a water planet, the Holy Torah says that it was shrouded in darkness, "*dark on the face of the depths (Tehom).*" The reason for this? Let's look at the next verse:

Verse 3

And E-lohim (G-D) said 'Let there be light', and there was light."

This verse is clearly stated from G-D's perspective, as the previous verse noted the "*Ruach of E-lohim*" was hovering on the face of the waters before He said, "Let there be light." It is evident from the narrative that there was nothing that produced light before this point in time. Indeed, there was no light at all.

Then G-d creates light. "And there shall be light! And there was light".

The narrative clearly describes to us that the light in the verse is not starlight, as the Genesis narrative distinctly states, (Genesis 1:14-19), that the sun, the moon, and the other stars were only created on the fourth day. (More on this later in the chapter). As such, this was light which came not from stars, but rather it, itself was light.

This is evident from the language of the Torah as well. As at this point, the Torah uses the word "*Or*", which means "light," as opposed to the language used on day four when the celestial bodies are called "*Ma'or,*" things from which light shines.

Science agrees with this, that the stars were formed a long time after the "bang." The scientific theories of today put the creation of stars at anywhere between 150 million to a billion years *after* the "bang". Whereas the light that itself has no light source is called "photons" in the scientific literature. Our sages, ob"m[265], state this clearly when they tell us that this

---

[265]   This is mentioned in RaSh"I in explanation of the events of the fourth day, based on the gemara in Tractate *Chullin 60b*

was a special light that was "hidden away for the future" and therefore was not the classic star-light.

Point 11 for the Genesis description of the Torah.

Furthermore, it is clear from the Genesis narrative that the "day" being discussed at the end of verse 5 is, of course, not one judged by one full revolution of the Earth around itself in its journey relative to the sun, as the earth was not in geosynchronous orbit around the sun at that time. {Or not judged by one revolution of the sun around the Earth, as in the geocentric view, as the sun was not yet in its present orbit around the Earth.}

The Oral Torah[266], however, tells us that all of the stars were created on day 1. But it wasn't until day 4 that they were arranged into set orbits. So clearly, our sages were "in the know" as to the very early creation of the stars even in the face of the simple understanding of the verses.

Point 12 for the Genesis description of the Torah.

Light and Darkness Intertwined

SO, there were no stars. The Torah tells us clearly that the universe, at its inception, began in darkness, ("...*and darkness over the face of the depths*"), and was followed by a period of time in which light and darkness existed intertwined. This continues until verse 4, where the Torah states:

> "*And E-lohim (one of G-D'-s names) saw the light, for it (was) good, and E-lohim then separated between the light and between the darkness.*"

This description sounds hauntingly like the following narrative of an epoch called "the dark age" that occurred during the "bang" timeline.

---

[266]   Tractate *Chagiga 12a*. See also Rashi *al loc.*

"Before decoupling occurs most of the photons in the universe are interacting with electrons and protons in the photon-baryon fluid. The universe is opaque or "foggy" as a result. There is light, but not light we could observe through telescopes. The baryonic matter in the universe consisted of ionized plasma, and it only became neutral when it gained free electrons during "recombination," thereby releasing the photons creating the CMB (cosmic microwave background)".

Loosely translated this means that before the universe achieved opacity the available light in the universe was trapped in the stuff of the universe and was therefore not visible to the human eye. There was light, but it was mixed in with the darkness. This continued until the universe went opaque (clear) and only then did the light of the atomic reactions taking place "shine out". "Let there be light... separated from the darkness..." and yet, somehow, it's emitted light, but not by stars[267]!

Point 13 for the Holy Torah.

Scientific Conundrum:

The Natural Forces Created in the "Bang":

The natural forces that were "born" with that "bang", those fundamental forces which act upon all matter, as described by physicists today are: A) Gravity, (called *Blima* by the prophets. More on this later); B) Electromagnetism; C) Strong nuclear force; and D) Weak nuclear force.

According to Hawking in his book, "The Grand Design", today most physicists, (string theorists), to simplify and solve inconsistencies, unify the electromagnetic force together with the weak nuclear force. The result is the electro-weak force. So really, there are only three natural forces.

---

[267]   However, when the Torah says that "they will be for signs and festivals etc." that IS referring to the creation of the celestial planetary bodies, by which we DO calculate the signs, festivals and whatnot.

No matter how we cut it, there are at least three major forces that bind together the universe. The question is just how precise did they have to be to allow the universe to exist?

> *"One of the deepest questions of all of physics is why nature's particles have the properties they do? Why, for example, does the electron have its particular mass and charge? Had the molecular weight of the electron been different, i.e. slightly heavier or lighter, and if its attractive/repulsive force been slightly stronger or weaker how would that have affected the universe as we know it?"* (Brian Greene – the Hidden Universe)

Why is this so important? It is because we have to get an idea of just how much of a margin for error there is in these primary forces before we can conclude that they are, indeed, "random"!

We have already mentioned in regards the issue of inflation that the likelihood of that occurring randomly is nil. So, let's just continue to see just how far we can "push the envelope"!

Let me quote a little more Hawking on this subject[268]:

> *"By examining the model universes, we generate when the theories of physics are altered in certain ways, one can study the effect of changes to physical law in a methodical manner. It turns out that it is not only the strengths of the strong nuclear force and the electromagnetic force that are made to order for our existence. Most of the fundamental constants in our theories appear fine-tuned in the sense that if they were altered by only modest amounts, the universe would be qualitatively different, and in many (= "almost all") cases unsuitable for the development of life.*

---

[268] Ibid. Chapter 7 pg. 250-1

He then goes on to bring many examples of "fine tuning" in these primal forces. I'm only going to mention a few:

- A weaker nuclear weak force would not have allowed for the production of hydrogen, only the lighter element, helium. This would have prevented the formation of stars.
- A stronger nuclear weak force would have prevented the seeding of the galaxy with heavy elements when stars blew their outer envelopes upon going super-nova.
- A change in the molecular weight of protons, (even 0.2%), would cause them to decay into neutrons, destabilizing atoms.
- If the quarks that make up a proton would have even only a 10% change in mass, it would destabilize almost all atomic nuclei. Truly, the atomic mass that they do have is optimal for the largest number of stable nuclei.
- Lastly, the fine-tuning of the cosmological constant is such that if it were even slightly larger:

"our universe would have blown itself apart before galaxies could form and -once again- life as we know it would be impossible".

I find it very hard to believe, despite the fact that Hawking goes on to state this explicitly; that any thinking person can conclude that this is only happenstance! It just goes to show you human nature: we are capable of looking truth in the face... and denying it anyway!

Let's take a look at the bold answers of staunch antagonists of "fine tuning" (New Scientist July 23rd, 2011, *"Why is the Universe just right?"* pg. 34)

Although many people like this (G-D) explanation, scientists see no evidence that a supernatural entity is orchestrating the cosmos. (More on this later). (1) The known laws of physics can

explain the existence of the universe that we observe. ... (2)
Another possibility is that it simply couldn't be any other way.
... This could seem to imply that our existence is an incredible
slice of luck ... (3) another possibility is that there is nothing to
explain. (4) Some argue that the whole idea of fine-tuning is
wrong. One vocal critic is Victor Stenger of the University of
Colorado at Boulder, author of The Fallacy of Fine-tuning. ...

... One example of fine-tuning, however, remains difficult
to dismiss: the accelerating expansion of the universe by dark
energy. Quantum theory predicts that the strength of this
mysterious force should be about 10 to the 120th-degree times
larger than the value we observe. This discrepancy seems
extraordinarily fortuitous. According to Nobel Prize winner
Steven Weinberg, if dark energy were not so tiny, galaxies
could never have formed, and we would never be here. ...

So, without getting into the Multiverse argument, which we will get
to soon, Hawking and others propose to answer the apparent "fine-tuning"
problem with the following four counter-arguments, which I paraphrase
as (according to numbers above):

(1) We're here, aren't we? Therefore, it must be possible[269]!
(2) Despite the odds, we must have beat them. We're here after all[270].

---

[269] In reality this "answer" is on par with the first one, as they are basically saying the
same thing. This is one of the most ridiculous arguments that I have ever heard! The
thinking goes as follows: Once we got the "winning" hand, who cares what the odds
are of getting it? The analogy used with this argument is that it's like getting dealt a
hand in cards: what are the odds of me getting this hand specifically? 1 in a billion.
But, you see, I got this hand, didn't I? So, once I got the hand the odds against me
getting it are irrelevant.

[270] My 9-year-old son saw how ridiculous this argument is. The question here is not "*did*
we beat the odds?", that much is clear. The question is *how did* we beat the odds. To
say, "because we did" is an answer only if you are talking to anyone younger than my

(3) I don't see a problem here. Do you see a problem here? (Again the "ostrich syndrome", or, even worse, the "Trust me, I'm a professional" claim). Lastly:

(4) This isn't a problem! Maybe there's a solution somewhere? (Stress on "maybe")

All of the above "explanations" take us back to the definition of "Emunah" that we discussed in the first chapter, "Emunah vs. Faith". There we discussed how King Solomon said, "A fool will believe all things, whereas a crafty (wise) person will understand thoroughly." They all answer the question... by avoiding it and then saying "There! Answered!"

Even so, I would like to point out that the "happenstance" of fine-tuning doesn't stop there, at the four/three primal universal forces! Oh NO! There is a whole universe of cosmological and physical information that we need to consider carefully before jumping to the conclusion that there is room for the word "random" in explaining our existence!

What Makes Our Universe and The Earth So Fit for Life?

I would like to address two more issues before considering the rebuttal of Hawking and his ilk. Obviously, this will follow the heliocentric (sun in the middle) view of the universe, so bear this in mind. The first is the readiness of our universe for life and the second is the preparation of our planet itself for life.

For our universe to facilitate life, it must have the following qualities:

- Be positioned in an area of the universe hospitable to life, as opposed, say, to being in the spiral arm of the galaxy;

9-year-old apparently. Only if you can explain to me how we beat impossible odds in order to get this stage called existence can we begin to consider this as an answer.

- Have only 3 dimensions which allow for gravitational force of "just the right" strength to allow for the existence of stars and stable orbits around them[271]; (string theory says there are more dimensions than this. More on this later).

- A single sun, which allows for a stable circular orbit around its star, (as opposed to, say a "figure 8", or an oval orbit)[272];

All of which is certainly helped by the existence of several large planets in the world's galactic orbit which protect our planet from bombardment by most large space objects.

For our world, Earth, to facilitate life it has to have the following qualities:

- An orbit of "just the right" distance from a central star, of "just the right" mass, so that the planet is "not too hot" and "not too cold", but "just right"[273];

- It's "just the right" size to allow for the stabilization of a gravitational field capable of keeping "just the right" gasses required to make a breathable atmosphere while allowing the "wrong" gasses to escape.

- An orbiting moon of "just the right size" to stabilize the rotation of the planet so that the whole planet experiences day and night and allows for temperature equilibrium[274];

- An orbiting moon of "just the right size" and "just the right" distance so that its own gravitational field doesn't wreak havoc on the planet it's orbiting.

---

[271] Hawking, ibid pg. 251.

[272] Hawking, in his book (pg. 234) states that it is likely that if we were in a binary, 2 suns, system that it would be inhospitable to life because of the temperature extremes and due to exposure to the sun followed by periods of time far away which would result from either a large circular orbit around the double suns or a "figure 8" orbit.

[273] Hawking ibid pg. 237-8

[274] http://www.swri.org/3pubs/ttoday/spring99/moon.ht

- An orbiting moon in just the right orbit to allow for the precise tilt that the Earth requires to facilitate a relatively constant global temperature and to prevent tilt fluctuations because of the gravity of other planets in the solar system;

- A rotational speed that is "not too fast" and "not too slow", but rather "just right".

- A molten core that, because of said planetary {or universal} rotation, produces a magnetic field. This, in turn, protects the Earth from radioactive cosmic rays, produced from the sun[275].

- Liquid water, which is "the source of all life", as we learned about in the last lesson concerning abiogenesis;

- An atmosphere, as all carbon-based life forms require oxygen. However, it cannot be just any atmosphere! It, too, must be "just right", containing a very particular mix of oxygen and carbon dioxide[276].

In getting back to the Genesis description, we must recall that most of these things occurred later during the planet's facial reconstruction.

How fine-tuned are we so far? I would venture a very modest estimate of Very, Very, VERY, VERY, VERY (I could go on for a few pages, just for emphasis, but I'll spare you if you consider it as if I wrote it!) fine-tuned. Seems indicative of intentional creation, just like it says in the first verse of Genesis!

Point 14 for the Holy Torah.

String Theory, M Theory, and the 11 Dimensions

Quantum theory, string theory, and M-theory all hold that there are 10 dimensions + 1 (time). Dawkins, in chapter 6 of his book *The Grand Design*

---

[275] http://sec.gsfc.nasa.gov/popscise.jpg

[276] We discussed this issue at length in chapter 5, *"World of Care and Wonders"*.

states that there is no known reason as to why only three dimensions, (width, height, and depth), were developed at the time of creation if there are so many to choose from. However, he notes, it's a good thing that it happened. Had it been otherwise, in all likelihood, nothing would be here at all!

Compare this to *Sefer Yetzira*[277], which states, (Chapter 1 mishnayos 2-9) that the world was created with 10 Sefirot of *Bli Mah*.

When it says that there are 10 Sefirot of *Bli Mah*, it is referring to the verse in Job (Chapter 26 verse 7)

> *"He [causes] the Northern incline on TOHU (?); He hangs the land on BLIMA, (of Bli Mah)".*

Our great sage RaSh"I translates the words *Bli Mah* as

> *"There is nothing, (bli=without, mah=something), [physical] upon which the world rests because they, (the world and planets), stand in the air [resting] on the arms of G-D."*

It's not just RaSh"I, who lived over 1000 years ago, long before the discovery of the laws of Newtonian physics and the law of gravity, who explains this verse in this manner. Listen to the words of an even earlier source from among our sages in the Midrash on Job (chapter 50):

> *G-D said to him (Job) "Gird yourself as a man (for war, to answer) for I will ask you a question like a student asking of his master. Where were you when I laid the foundations of the world? Perhaps you gave me advice as to how the world should have been created, or how to make the ground upon which you stand? Who told me to prepare the world for the sake of man?".*
> *He said to him (G-d continued saying to Job) "Upon what is*

---

[277] Sefer Yetzira is a very, very old Torah text, but no one knows for sure just how old. Jewish tradition names it's author as being the one and only Abraham, our father.

the land supported? On the pillars. And the pillars (on what do they stand)? On the ledges. And the ledges (on what do they stand)? On "Mah", as the verse says, "He hangs the world on Bli–Mah" (Job 26:7). And if you do not believe in this, (that the Earth itself is supported using Mah), then "Raise your eyes to the Heavens" (Isaiah 40:26) and learn about the subject! For I (also) created the lower (celestial) bodies. Upon what are they resting? The sun, the moon, and the constellations, what are they hanging from? On something which has no substance and no form, (so too) on the land (the earth) the land is also held by that (same force).

From G-d's rebuke of Job, we are told that the POWER that holds up the Earth and all of the celestial heavens is called *Bli Mah*, literally "without substance".

In *Sefer Yetzira* we are told that there are ten SEFIROT of *Bli mah*, which, according to the verse above, is apparently referring to the POWER that affects all of the celestial bodies.

Therefore, the next question is what in the world is a SEFIRA, (singular of *SEFIROT*)?

Well, clearly, it is one of the three types of Creation G-D utilized in creating the world and all of the existence. *Sefer Yetzira* teaches us, (Chapter 1, Mishna 1), that there were thirty-two paths of unfathomable wisdom used by G-D to create the world and that all of them are contained in three "*Sefarim*", (the plural of the word "Sefer", which is the root of the word SEFIROT). In the Mishnayot that follows, we understand the three *Sefarim* like this[278]:

---

[278] As all classical Hebrew writing has no vowels therefore the proper pronunciation of the word is derived either by oral tradition, (the most common), or by the context.

One *sefer* refers to counting, ("Sa-fer", "to count", is the root for the word "Mispar" (=number)). This teaches us that the universe/existence is mathematically sound and mathematically quantifiable[279]);

One *sefer* refers to the written word, (the word "Se-fer", means "book", =the written Torah); and lastly

One *sefer* refers to the spoken word, ("Sa-per" means "to tell"). This relates to the ten utterances of G-d listed in the Genesis narrative.

All of the above words, are made using the 22 letters of the Hebrew alphabet. In Jewish tradition, there is more meaning to the Hebrew alphabet than just a word. All Hebrew words are multifaceted. They have a face value, (writing), a phonetic value, (pronunciation) and a numerical value, (*gematria*, otherwise called "numeration" or "numerology").

Now, the interesting thing about the aforementioned scientific theories is that even though they have deduced that there are other dimensions outside of height, width, and depth, they have no clue as to what the 10 dimensions, (=the remaining 7), are!

Let me let you in on a little secret: they are all listed explicitly in the *Sefer Yetzirah*, Chapter 1 Mishna 5!

OK, it's not explicit in Genesis, but seeing as it is pertinent, and its source is the ORAL Torah – I'm awarding yet another point.

Point 15 for the Holy Torah.

The Infinite Dimension Hypothesis.

So, just how do scientists today, who want to cling to the understanding that the world, and indeed existence, is just a fluke, just how *do* they justify their rationale? The Infinite Dimension theory.

---

[279] This refers to the amazing fact that all aspects of the creation make sense numerically, mathematically and in all other respects. It is this order of creation that allows us to quantify and formulate all aspects of science, as all sciences are built on mathematical principles.

It is a hypothesis that is debated more and more nowadays by the most prominent scientific minds.

It is also the only explanation that has any logical basis. Essentially, it's not new. All previous models also utilized an infinity to escape from the difficulties that the physical world presents in any logical model.

Infinite dimensions mean that – hypothetically – our evidently finite universe was "copied" an infinite number of times.

The logic is as follows: in the known universe, there is a limited number of variables, no matter how numerous they may be. It follows therefore that if we were to jumble those variables an infinite number of times then unquestionably the same patterns will repeat. For example, if I have the variables 1, 2, 3 and 4 then I can combine them in many different configurations. However, there are a finite number of patterns in which they can be arranged. The total possible variables are 4 to the second power or 16. Therefore, if I combine the integers randomly 1000 times, it is clear that I will chance across the same combination of variables more than once. It follows, therefore, that if I would combine them an infinite number of times, then the same patterns would repeat infinitely.

Effectively even if the universe itself is finite and its variables are finite, as long as the possibility of these variables repeating infinitely exist, then the same pattern will, mathematically and statistically, repeat an infinite number of times, regardless of how slim the odds are that occurring.

It is for this reason that scientists can still hold that existence is, essentially, a "loaded deck". Despite the fact that the science seems to show overwhelmingly that there is no possible way for the universe to have come into existence without any intelligent guidance, as long as I can presume that the universe's variables exist in an infinite number of parallel universes then there must be universes in which the dice were rolled just so.

This is the basis behind Stephen Hawking's book "*The Grand Design*" and also behind Brian Greene's book "*The Hidden Reality*".

To this end, these books bring theoretical proof based on string theory and M-theory (the unified string theory) to provide the basis for the infinite universe scenario.

Let's assume for a moment that Hawking and Greene are correct and that there are, in fact, an infinite number of realities, does that prove – in any shape, way or form – that there is no G-D?

ABSOLUTELY NOT! The following are two reasons why this "claim" is irrelevant:

Theologically is there a problem with multiple universes?

Let's say that we were to find empirical proof as to the existence of multiple universes[280]. What of it? Why is there an assumption that the Holy Torah has any problem with the existence of multiple universes? Just the opposite! The Torah has no problem whatsoever with multiple universes! The reason for that being that the world was created with a free choice: to do good or to do evil. How does that affect the issue of multiple universes? It is because the correct "weight" of a person's good or bad deeds can only be measured by his or her actual potential. In other words: only if G-D knows what and who I would/could be if I made all of the "correct", (i.e. GOOD), choices vs. what I would/could be if I made all of the "wrong", (i.e. BAD), choices will I be able to tell where I am, relatively, on my path in life. Those correspond with the knowledge of, and the creation of, multiple universes. It's just that the one in which we live in is the one that we are judged for, not the one where we did everything wrong, and not the one in which we do everything right, unless that happens to be the reality in which I chose to live my life, and I actually did them!

The story goes that Rav Zusia, (zt"l), a student of the Holy *Chozeh* (seer) of Lublin, was once asked what he was afraid would happen after his death. He replied, "I'm not scared that after 120 years on this earth that I will be asked why I wasn't like Moses or like Yosef, the Tzadik. I'm worried that G-D will ask me "Zusia! Why weren't you Zusia?" (the potential Zusia)".

---

[280] A very difficult thing to do, according to Max Tegmark at MIT, who has worked out that to find "your closest identical copy you would have to travel 10 to the 10th to the 28th power meters. That corresponds to 1 followed by 10 billion billion billion zeroes". (New Scientist July 23rd, pg. 38) In short: It's never, ever going to happen!

Realistically is there any real proof here as to G-D's non-existence?

The entire claim here is that I don't see G-D's hand in the works upon scrutiny of the empirical evidence. Therefore, if I, (this being the holy "I", namely some hotshot know-it-all), don't see G-D ergo there is no G-D. Let me bring you a quote from the book "God, the Failed Hypothesis" by Victor J. Stenger: (in the Preface, pg. 13-14)

> *My analysis will be based on the contention that God should be detectable by scientific means simply by virtue of the fact that he is supposed to play such a central role in the operation of the universe and the lives of humans. ...*

> *... Science does not explain everything, so there is always room for other explanations, and the believer is easily convinced that the explanation is God. However, the "God of the gaps" argument by itself fails ...unless the phenomenon in question is not only currently scientifically inexplicable but can be shown to forever defy natural description. God can only show up by proving to be necessary, with science equally proven to be incapable of providing a plausible account of the phenomenon based on natural or material processes alone.*

> *...As far as we can tell from current scientific knowledge, the universe we observe with our senses and scientific instruments can be described in terms of matter and material processes alone.*

In a nutshell: if I can't see it with my eyes or test it with the scientific apparatus and methodology available today – it doesn't exist.

This is pure hypocrisy in action, and I will bring a few issues as proof.

The Scientific Method Is Only as Good as The Means of Observation and The Observer.

First, during my investigation in a previous chapter, "Abraham and Abiogenesis", I discovered that only very recently, due to the development of new imaging apparatus and techniques, scientists discovered that the prokaryotes have a cytoskeleton. Up until recently, science didn't see it and therefore immediately assumed that there wasn't one!

Similarly, there was once a neurosurgeon, (unfortunately, I can't remember his name, but I'm sure you can find it if you want!), who decided that – once and for all – he was going to disprove the existence of a soul. How so? During neurosurgery, he was going to do "exploratory surgery" all around the brain with the most sophisticated technology and techniques available, and he did! Guess what? He didn't observe a soul! So, therefore, it's clear that there is no soul! So, too, Stenger in his book "The Failed Hypotheses", brings up all of the available scientific data and searches made to try and find the soul, all of which failed miserably. "See!", says Stenger, "No soul"!

This claim, "I didn't find one!", is sheer lunacy! To assume that because I cannot detect something that that is a clear proof of its non-existence is ridiculous! As the joke goes:

Once upon a time, a Science Teacher wanted to prove to his students that G-D doesn't exist. What did he do? He took them outside, showed them around, and said "Children! Do you see the sun? That's because it exists! Do you see the trees? That's because they exist! Do you see the birds in the trees? That's because they exist! Now, children, can anyone show me G-D? NO! That's because HE doesn't exist!". He then turned around smugly, feeling that he had made his point. Suddenly, he heard one of the students say "Hey kids! How about the teacher's brains? Can you see them? No? THAT'S BECAUSE THEY DON'T EXIST!"

Sorry Charlie, just because you can't see something doesn't prove your point. As our Sages, of blessed memory, said so succinctly "[If you claim proof just because] we haven't seen it – is not a proof [at all]". Maybe tomorrow you'll develop the technology to see it yet! Maybe you're looking in the wrong place? Or maybe you're using the wrong device? This is, once again, one of the key issues in understanding the actual value of the scientific method: IT'S ONLY AS GOOD AS THE OBSERVER.

Science Itself and The Scientific Method Acknowledge the Existence of Things That Cannot Be Detected by Observation.

The second issue with this ridiculous claim is that in all fields of science it is acknowledged that there are things we believe in even though we can't see them. Let's bring a few examples of this.

String theory practitioners have come to accept that there are more than 3 dimensions, (4 with time). The current calculations point to 10 dimensions, (11 with time, we discussed earlier). Yet, somehow, even though the other 7 dimensions are not visible to the eye or detectable using today's scientific machinery and methodology, they still hold that they exist! Similarly, to quote Hawking in his book:

> *"The concept of quarks is a vital element of our theories of fundamental physics even though individual quarks cannot be observed"*[281].

In truth, even the atom was thought of as semi-fictional for many years until technology capable of gleaning an object that small became available. Dark Matter and Dark Energy also fall into the category of "inferred but not seen", (Stenger, ibid, pg. 38).

But maybe they will say, "Yes, that's true. But string theory gives us a mathematical model based on which we must conclude that there are more

---

[281] *The Grand Design*" pg. 36. See also Stengar *"The Failed Hypotheses"* pg. 37 who also admits to this.

than three (or four with time) dimensions". To that I respond that last time I checked statistics is a science as well and that all statistical projections tell me that statistically, life is not possible unless something "infinite" intervenes, (or is a factor in the universe in some way, shape or form).

Is Life Explainable Using Modern Scientific Models?

Despite the above argument about the existence of a soul[282], I feel that Dr. Stenger here has raised an issue that even for him is a problem, and which will forever remain scientifically inexplicable. That is the issue of how a bunch of protons, neutrons, and electrons made up of quarks, bosons and any other type of non-living, inanimate atoms can come together ... and create life.

Does science present us with a model, even a hypothetical one, which can rationally explain how this happened? I think that we both agree that not only it HAS NOT but it also CAN NOT. Is this not a glaring hole in the physical model that cannot be explained away by science? I'm pretty sure that it is.

But that's alright. The physicists and their ilk of the no-god persuasion can go ahead and do what Dr. Kukonis did by evolution. Just say "Great question! I'm sure that someone has an answer to this issue, but that's really a problem for the field of chemistry/biology/cosmology/some-other-ology, that just isn't my -ology" (Ostrich Syndrome alert! Is that you, Dr. Stenger, with your head in the sand?). However, this one really does "hit the fan" because although we have a working knowledge of the chemical world, and we can explain how certain atoms form chemical bonds with others... at the end of the day we're not 100% sure *why* that is, just *that it is*! So, it's really just blaming someone else for an issue for which there is no real explanation either in physics or in chemistry or any other field.

---

[282]   I discuss this topic in the second volume of the series, Core Emunah 2 "G-d and Me".

The Main Focus of Science is To Quantify, Not to Explain

This brings us back to the crucial issue regarding science that I already mentioned a few times in the book. The vast majority of all science is never really about the *why* of a thing, (unless it can be determined by observational data), but rather it's all about measuring and describing physical, observable phenomenon. It's about quantifying the observational data. Physics cannot explain to us why there is gravity. It can tell us its strength, and it can tell us what is affected by it, but never WHY it is affected in this way. Physics cannot explain to us why there is a nuclear weak or strong force, (or why they have the values that they do), just that they do. Therefore, we must accept the following truth about the various fields of science: Essentially any explanation as to the "why" of things offered in the field of science is almost always pure, unadulterated *science fiction*. Think about it.

The Scientific Fallacy of Infinity

Getting back to the multiple universe hypothesis, there remains one great big glaring problem that needs to be addressed. For it, like all of its predecessors, relies on the existence of that strange and elusive thing called "Infinity".

As we have mentioned previously in this chapter, and also in the chapter entitled "Logical and Philosophical," there just ain't none of that known to man in our finite universe! Infinity is not observable, repeatable or measurable and therefore lacks the most basic criteria of scientific data, and it also is not subject to scrutiny. The fact that we have infinities in our mathematics is illogical, not philosophically sound, and even mathematicians have severe doubts as to whether there should be infinities in math.

It follows, therefore, that if there is no infinity, there is also no infinite repetition of the variables. If there isn't an infinite repetition of the variables, there is no chance of the infinitesimally small chance of existence having occurred. And if it couldn't occur by chance... then it must have been planned.

Let's state this another way: if you're going to have to rely on an infinity, who in their right mind would choose a run-of-the-mill one over G-d? Does any other infinity solve the vast list of problems which arise based on the scientific models of the no-god variety?

In this regard, the simplest explanation that can be invoked, which answers all of the statistical, mathematical, chemical, physical and biological problems is called "G-D". I will take G-D any day, even though – like the other seven dimensions – I cannot see, hear, smell, touch or otherwise detect HIM using present-day scientific machinations. (Although personally, I don't feel any need for this at all). This is particularly the case because to invoke any other infinity doesn't fit the scientific bill either. The most unscientific claim that a person can make to solve their mathematical problem is to insert an "infinity".

Let me quote from the book "Fitness of the Cosmos for Life" published by Cambridge University Press, page 12:

> The origin of life is one of the biggest of the big questions about the nature of existence. Origin tends to occur frequently in these big questions: the origin of the universe, the origin of matter, the origin of life, the origin of sentience. We, scientists and non-scientists alike, have troubles with such "origins" – we were not there watching when the first events happened, we can never replicate them, and, when those first events happened, there was, in fact, no "we." I believe that one day we will be able to describe life in physical terms   that is, we will rationalize life satisfactorily in molecular detail based on accepted scientific

law and scientific theory using the scientific method. But we
certainly do not know yet how to do it.

Meaning, we will never be able to know the answer to this scientifically, we may be able to come up with a plausible fiction about it that gives us a warm and fuzzy feeling, but in a moment of honesty the writer above states clearly: it's all just rationalization.

Day, Night and The Round Earth

And the Lord separated between the light and the darkness, and
He called the light "day" and the darkness he called "night". And
it was evening, and it was morning, day one. (Genesis ibid)

The verse teaches us that on day one, the day-night cycle was arranged... but was it? How is that possible if the sun, moon and stars were only created on day four?

Our sages in the Oral Torah, the Babylonian Talmud Tractate *Chagigah 12a*, tell us that this refers to the length (i.e. the time period) of a day. That is what the Torah is describing[283], that day one had the exact same amount of time as all of the other days, in that it also was the equivalent of one present-day 24-hour day. Yet practically, how can this be?

There are only two ways to explain the above statement. Either, it means that an arbitrary limit of a day was set for the first days of creation, as there was no real way to measure it (unlikely, as the verse itself states "it was evening and it was morning," which doesn't lend itself to this interpretation); or it means that it was somehow already measurable on day one.

---

[283] The language of the Talmud there is *middas yom ve middas laylah*, which translates as "the length of the day and the length of the night", meaning a full 24-hour period. See RaSh"I ad loc.

Assuming that it is measurable, there are only two ways, to my understanding that are plausible: either because the universe revolves around the planet and does so at a constant speed, at the same rate that the present-day Sun-Earth does to create a 24-hour day-night cycle, as in the geocentric view[284]; or that the "day" of day one was measured by one revolution of the earth around its axis, and it teaches us that already on day one the earth's velocity was the same as that which it revolves today. Either of these interpretations fit the information, although the geocentric view has more appeal, as everyone agrees that if the earth has a special place in the universe – it says something about our relationship with the Creator.

Let's add more depth to the picture.

Why is Earth Called Aretz?

The planet is called *aretz* in Hebrew, the root of which is the word *ratz*, which means "to run". Meaning that the planet's name is "I will run." The world was given this name either as a description of what the planet, itself, does (it is running on its axis), or to describe the relationship of the world to the universe that surrounds it. Meaning, that the universe is running (=revolving) around the Earth[285].

It was this revolution, either around an axis or around the world, despite the lack of our present-day sun as the source of light, which led to a measured 24-hour day. No actual light source is even necessary for there to be a "measured" day, even though the simple understanding of the verse

---

[284] A similar interpretation can be found in the words of the RaLBaG, (Rabbi Levi Ben Gershon), in his explanation of the verse in Genesis. He also supposes a different – yet similar – explanation: that it wasn't a day-night cycle, per se, that made for a 24-hour day. It was a full revolution, which, in the future, would constitute a day-night cycle.

[285] This interpretation is found in many of our holy Rishonim, for example the RaDaK (Rabbi David ben Kimchi) in his *Sefer haShorashim*. The Abarbanel, (Rabbi Yitzchak Abarbanel), in his explanation on the verse and others. Although they interpret it according to the Geocentrical model, that the earth was the axis for the heavenly spheres, that the universe was running around it..

seems to say so. That was written for us, not for the Genesis narrative. In fact, our sages[286], ob"m, tell us that during the first days of creation there was no real day-night cycle as the celestial bodies were not stable in their orbits, regardless of which "centric" model we follow.

Our sages also tell us that this teaches us two other things.

First, it teaches us that all of the commandments concerning which we are to perform during the day, refer to the period when there is light, whereas all things commanded to be done at night occur during the period when it is dark out[287].

Second, it teaches us that a day, according to Torah law, begins at nightfall and ends at sundown the next day[288].

Now, because there is some argument as to just how old the claim of the round earth is in history, I will therefore not quote from the Holy Zohar, which says this quite clearly. I will say, however, that, as opposed to non-Jewish and secular sources, the Jewish tradition is that the 5 books of Moses are over 3300 years old. That being the case it's clear that, once again, the Holy Torah was clearly in possession of knowledge and understanding about the reality of the world long before the rest of the world got their act together[289].

Point 15 for the Genesis description of the Torah.

Genesis 1:6-8, Day Two:

6 And E-lohim said, "There should be a rakiya (translated "firmament") amidst the water, and it should separate between

---

[286] See Rashi on the verses of the creation on day 4, where he quotes our sages as saying that for the first 3 days of creation the light and the darkness had no real set pattern, as they have today.

[287] See Tractate *Pesachim* 2a which states this clearly. See also Tractate *Berachos* 2a which also alludes to this.

[288] See Tractate *Berachos 2a*

[289] The earliest findings concerning the Earth being round date back to the 6th century BC at best.

water and (other) water. 7 And E-lohim made the Rakiya, and
He separated between the water, which is under the Rakiya,
and between the water, which is above the Rakiya, and it
was so. 8 And E-lohim then called the Rakiya "Shamayim"
(Heavens), and it was evening, and it was morning the second
day.

Here the Holy Torah is describing the creation new level of creation on planet Earth. The water planet, whose gravitational and electromagnetic field held the water close to its surface, now acquired an additional boon: a *Rakiya*. But what *is* that?

The *Rakiya*[290], according to the simplest translation of the above verses, is the atmosphere. Literally, we find this word used in regard to the layering of a thing, as the verse says (Psalms 136:6) "*To He who layered (rokah) the land on top of the water*". The atmosphere is what separates between the water that is "under it", (the oceans), and between the waters that are "above it", (clouds and other types of atmospheric water, including water emanating from space). The verse then relates that the Creator renamed the *Rakiya* and called it *shamayim*. Although it is translated as "firmament" or "heavens" the literal translation of the word means, "that which lifts the water". (It's a composite word of the words *sah mayim*, based on its literal pronunciation with a "silent" Aleph, where *sah*=lifts and *mayim*=water)[291], which precisely describes what the *Rakiya/Shamayim* does: it raises water, in its gaseous form, into the atmosphere. However, the *Rakiya/Shamayim* is not water, it separates between the water which is "under" it and the water which is "over" it.

At this point in the narrative, there is still no landmass. That only occurs on day three. So even after the separation of waters, the Earth is still a water planet.

---

290 The root of which means "background", which is very fitting when you think about it: because the atmosphere is really the "background" necessary in order for the planet to be life-sustaining.

291 See RaSh"I ibid.

Another detail that the Holy Torah adds in here is that when G-D made the *Rakiya*, it was formed in the midst of the waters. He just *shtupped*[292] it in there! How did this happen? I can think of at least two possibilities that are proffered by the scientists themselves. (This doesn't mean that I endorse them. I don't. I also explained this at length in the chapter "World of Care and Wonders". It's just that the adherents of Evo-science themselves seem to be finding their way into the narrative of Genesis).

First of all, the Great Oxygenation Event[293]:

> *The Great Oxygenation Event (GOE), also called the Oxygen Catastrophe or Oxygen Crisis or Great Oxidation was the biologically caused appearance of free oxygen (O_2) in Earth's atmosphere. This major environmental change happened around 2.4 billion years ago. Photosynthesis was producing oxygen both before and after the GOE. The difference was that before the GOE, organic matter and dissolved iron chemically captured any free oxygen. The GOE was the point when these minerals became saturated and could not capture any more oxygen. The excess free oxygen started to accumulate in the atmosphere. The rising oxygen levels may have wiped out a huge portion of the Earth's anaerobic inhabitants at the time. From their perspective, it was a catastrophe (hence the name). Cyanobacteria, by producing oxygen, were essentially responsible for what was likely the largest extinction event in Earth's history.*

So, cyanobacteria, which can dwell in the ocean up to depths of 200 meters, began production, (truthfully it is really bi-production, as oxygen is a "waste product"), of oxygen, most of which was stored inside of the ocean's waters.

---

[292] Yiddish for "shoved". See, you're not only learning Torah and science here. You're even learning a foreign language

[293] **http://en.wikipedia.org/wiki/Oxygen_catastrophe**

Secondly: another derivative of the word *shamayim*!

As we said before phonetically, the word is *sha-mayim*. Our sages tell us[294] that another derivative from this is *eish–mayim*, ("fire[295]" and "water", which in Hebrew is *mayim, mem-yud-mem*), that fire and water were mixed together to create the *Rakiya* which was later called *Shamayim*. Where exactly did the fire come from? Not that G-d can't do what He wants, when He wants, but the Earth was made with its own ready-made fire heating system: magma. There is extensive evidence as to volcanic activity that took place on the early Earth.

Within 150 million years (of the earth's creation), a solid crust with a basaltic composition must have formed. ... Steam escaped from the crust, and more gasses were released by volcanoes ... The oldest rocks on Earth are found in the North American craton of Canada. They are tonalites from about 4.0 Ga. They show traces of metamorphism by high temperature, but also sedimentary grains that have been rounded by erosion during transport by water, showing rivers and seas existed then.

The abundance of gasses varies considerably from volcano to volcano. Water vapor is consistently the most common volcanic gas, normally comprising more than 60% of total emissions. Carbon dioxide typically accounts for 10 to 40% of emissions[296] [297].

This mixture of fire, (volcanic activity), and water boiled away a significant amount of the water covering the early earth raising the hot

---

[294] Babylonian Talmud Tractate Chagigah 12a. See also Midrash Rabbah on Genesis ibid

[295] If we take the first Hebrew letters of the aforementioned word *sah* (Hebrew letters *shin* and *alef*) and turn them around, they become *eish* (*alef shin*).

[296] http://en.wikipedia.org/wiki/Volcanic_gas

[297] http://www.sciencedaily.com/releases/2007/08/070829143713.ht

mixture above the ocean releasing the trapped oxygen and creating what is today the earth's atmosphere.

There is a lot more depth concerning the issue of the *Rakiya/shomayim,* but this is enough concerning the simple understanding of that which is explicit.

Point 16 for the Genesis narrative of Creation

<u>Genesis Day 3:</u>

---

9 And E-lohim said, "The waters should coalesce from under the Shamayim to one place, and the land should become visible" and it was so. 10 And E-lohim called the dryness "Eretz" (land) and the gathered waters he called, "Yamim" (seas) and E-lohim said that it was good.

A quick side note:

One might note that until now there are two words that have been repeated several times. They are the words *Shamayim* and *Aretz*. The first verse of Genesis spoke about the creation of *Shamayim* and *Aretz*, the second day described how the *Rakiya* was called *Shamayim* and now, on the third day, we find that the dry landmass is called *Aretz*. What's going on here?

Well, although these things utilize the same names, we must differentiate between names that are intrinsic and names that are given. What do I mean by this?

In the first verse of Genesis, the words *Shamayim* and *Aretz* are clearly referring to the first creations: the heavens (space) and the planet (earth). At that time the Earth was comprised entirely of one giant landmass until later when the *Bohu* rocks kicked-in to produce the water, which eventually covered the planet.

After that, on days 2 and 3, further things were created, namely *Rakiya* and *Yabasha*, which were afterward given the names "*Shamayim*" and

"Aretz" respectively. It, therefore, becomes clear that although the words being used are the same, the verses are not talking about the same things. Don't be confused.

The Ancient Land-Mass

Please read the first verse above very carefully and tell me what you understand? Let me point out 2 things: First> all of the waters are to gather in one place; Second> the land mass is to become visible. Just what do these things mean?

Well first, it tells us that the reason the landmass became visible was that the waters covering the planet receded. Perhaps this needs more clarification. It's not just that the waters receded, but rather that the waters should coalesce, which means to be collected inside of something. Because the waters "drained" inside of a something, (an underwater fissure), the landmass, which was – apparently – higher than all of the others became revealed. Secondly, it tells us that the first land was exactly that: one landmass!

Don't believe me? Well other than the simple reading of the verse, then read the words of the Holy Zohar[298], *"Truly one land came out of the waters and from it was created the 7 lands."*

Let's "set the table" here so that we can get our bearings on the information that we are looking for: Earth has already been covered with water. Earth already has an atmosphere, (at first, the *"rakiya"* stage, followed by the *"shamayim"* stage). The latest developments: water receding and land protruding.

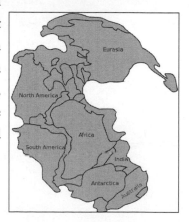

---

[298] New Zohar 12:1

Modern science is in total agreement with all of the above. The reason for this is the discovery and the subsequent study of Earth's plate tectonics. These findings have led to what is commonly known as the "supercontinent cycle." The supercontinent cycle states that all of the known continents of today were once one land mass until the time when they began to drift apart. The first "super-continent" was dubbed "Pangaea", (see artist's rendition on the previous page).

The continents themselves are sitting on what are known as "continental shelves", but the entire crust of the planet is actually broken up into several tectonic plates, which are either:

Moving away from each other, subsequently creating an enormous rift between them, into which the oceans flow;

Colliding with each other, usually forcing one of the colliding sides to "hop on top" of its friend, creating mountains, (called "induction" in the literature), whereas the other plate "subducts", plowing itself under the other plate and back down into the planetary core to be recycled.

Lastly, they can rub against one another, one traveling, for example, north as the opposing one moves south. This is a common source of almost all earthquakes.

Although science today does not really have a clear idea as to how the continents happened based on the information above, I would guess as follows, based on the Genesis description:

First, a very deep fissure appeared on the floor of the ocean in one area[299] (the Marriana Trench, perhaps?) into which the waters immediately flowed. The splitting of the planet's crust caused immense pressure to build up in subsequent areas of the planets crust. This may, or may not have caused some plates to subduct, (to be driven down towards the core), and some to ride on top of the subducting plates. Immediately after the rift occurred, the waters receded into the oceanic rift, (causing the waters to coalesce, as in the first verse above), this then causes the landmass to

---

[299]   In verse 9, the verse itself states that the waters were gathered (coalesced) into one place.

"stick out", *to be revealed*, as the water levels receded. *And the dry landmass should be seen*[300].

Point 17 for the Holy Torah.

Animal Type Dispersion on The Various Continents

According to the above description, it is easy to understand the proliferation of animals throughout the entire planet and the fossil records that we find in them, as they all emanated on the original super-continent. Even after the continents broke apart and drifted, each of the continents continued to retain their indigenous animal population.

However, we are getting ahead of ourselves as, obviously, that did not happen yet, as there still were no animals of any type. It didn't occur until sometime after the flood in Noah's time. Almost all animal life was destroyed during the flood, with the exception of those animals who went on the trip with Noah and then proliferated after the flood. To look at the time schedule for continental drift is not relevant to this chapter. For some ideas as to when this happened check out the blog on my site[301].

The Green Earth:

11 And E-lohim said, "The land should be covered with vegetation: grasses that produce seeds, fruit-bearing trees which produce fruit according to its type, whose seed is inside it, on the land" and so it was. 12 And the land gave forth vegetation: grass which produces seeds according to its type (species), trees bearing fruits whose seed is inside of it, according to its type,

---

[300] After writing the above, I discovered that the Midrash (*Yalkut Shimoni 1:8*) says this explicitly.

[301] Again, see the article at my blog www.rabbibz.com

and E-lohim saw that it was good. 13 And it was evening,
and it was morning day three.

The Torah then tells us that after the emergence of the landmass, now called *Aretz*, vegetation springs up *on the land*. The simple understanding of the verse is that vegetation sprang up on the now dry landmass. It's not talking about the entire planet.

It is therefore very interesting to note two things that science agrees with in this statement:

(1) Technically, there is no vegetation growing in the oceans.

All known oceanic "plants," including kelp, coral, seaweeds, phytoplankton, algae and the like are not comparable to the plants that grow on the land[302]. Technically, they are more sea creatures than sea plants! Land plants all have roots, stems, and leaves of some sort, whereas sea vegetation does not[303].

(2) Another way that distinguishes land plants from sea plants is in the way that they reproduce.

All types of sea vegetation reproduce asexually, either through cell division or by parts breaking off and growing into a new "plant"[304]. This differs tremendously when compared to plant-life growing on land, all of which reproduce using seeds. Either the seed is released from the plant as spores, or they occur in the fruits produced by said plants.

Isn't it amazing? That's exactly what the Torah described above?

Only on land does the vegetation reproduce *by seeds*.

Point 18 for the Holy Torah

---

[302] See, for example, **http://www.naturegrid.org.uk/biodiversity/plants/crypalga. html** or open up Wikipedia and look for "algae".

[303] **http://en.wikipedia.org/wiki/Thallus**

[304] See, for example, **http://www.ehow.com/how-does_4574307_algae-reproduce. html**

The Order of Plant Genesis

Another interesting thing about the Torah's description of this era is the order in which vegetation appears: first simple plant-life, (*de-she*), next grasses, (*esev*), and then fruit-bearing trees, (*etz pri*).

Perhaps we need to specify what the Torah means when it is referring to vegetation. In Halacha, (the practical application of the Oral Torah), there is a distinction made concerning blessing on foods between whether one is eating a fungus, such as a mushroom, a plant, such as lettuce, or the fruit of a tree. Fungus, although a plant of sorts, does not have a blessing like other things that grow from the earth. Although it is attached to the ground, it doesn't grow from nutrients derived directly from the land, via roots, whereas both plants and trees do. There is an intrinsic distinction between what a plant is and what a tree is. For although both plants and trees have roots, a plant has a limited lifespan and has no real branches, whereas a tree has both. However, the Torah here states something quite emphatically: *eisev* and *eitz*, (grasses and trees), have seeds, but *deshe*... does not.

Now that we have this piece of information, we are ready to understand the scientific findings[305]. One issue, however. Although I am quoting the scientific literature, please don't take this as a sign that I agree with the dating of the events or the actual description given. My intent is solely to show that the pattern of events that the scientific literature describes precisely matches the order of events as laid out in the Holy Torah. Now, let's see what they say.

> *By Middle Devonian, shrub-like forests of primitive plants existed: lycophytes, horsetails, ferns, and pro gymnosperms had evolved. Most of these plants had true roots and leaves, and many were quite tall. The earliest known trees, from the genus*

---

[305] **http://en.wikipedia.org/wiki/Devonian#Terrestrial_biota**

Wattieza, appeared in the Late Devonian around 380 Ma. In the Late Devonian, the tree-like ancestral fern Archaeopteris and the giant cladoxylopsid trees grew with true wood. (See also: lignin.) These are the oldest known trees of the world's first forests.

Let's make something clear: all fauna that are like ferns, according to the definition that we gave previously, are not trees or grass. For although they possess attributes similar to a plant, they don't bear seeds, rather they propagate by shedding spores[306].

By the end of the Devonian, the first seed-forming plants had appeared. This rapid appearance of so many plant groups and growth forms has been called the "Devonian Explosion."

Another point that needs to be made is that the scientific literature is full of the word's "tree" and "grass". This is a cause for much confusion. Even though the existence of grasses before ferns, (which scientists call "trees"), as described in the Torah, goes contrary to archaeological findings. (The oldest trees found are from about 360 million years ago[307] whereas the earliest findings of grass are from about 65 million years ago, in the dung of dinosaurs[308]), it is absolutely ridiculous to assume that just because we didn't find it – it didn't exist. This is particularly the case according to evolutionary theory, as it is ridiculous to think that large plant-life preceded small plant-life. This is one of Richard Dawkins favorite mantras: according to the fossil record, one might conclude that worms are a new phenomenon. This is simply the result of the relative fragility of grass, (and worms), and the relative unreliability of the fossilization process.

---

[306] Don't believe me? Look up any of the species mentioned above! OR... continue reading!

[307] http://www.nature.com/news/2007/070416/full/news070416-10.html Please remember: I don't take the scientific age as that actual age. I'm quoting it only for reference and chronological purposes.

[308] http://www.foxnews.com/story/0,2933,176052,00.html see also http://www.livescience.com/3912-dung-reveals-dinosaurs-ate-grass.html

Another factor to consider is the Earth's atmosphere. Remember, according to scientific dogma, the atmosphere was undergoing changes in the process of becoming what it is today. Accordingly, until there was an abundance of plant-life capable of supporting the breathable atmosphere of today the conditions probably didn't exist to allow for the growth of larger types of vegetation[309].

However, having said the above, we must once again state that according to the Torah's definition of a "tree" – ferns are not trees. It, therefore, comes out that everyone agrees that the order of creation is: non-seed vegetation, seed-bearing "grasses" and lastly fruit-bearing trees.

> *The first "spermatophytes" (=seed plants) – that is, the first plants to bear true seeds – are called pteridosperms: literally, "seed ferns," so called because their foliage consisted of fern–like fronds, although they were not closely related to ferns. The oldest fossil evidence of seed plants is of Late Devonian age, and they appear to have evolved out of an earlier group known as the pro gymnosperms. These early seed plants ranged from trees to small, rambling shrubs; like most early pro gymnosperms, they were woody plants with fern–like foliage. They all bore ovules, but no cones, fruit or similar[310].*

Meaning that first "grasses", seed forming, but not fruit-bearing, vegetation came to be, and only at a later time did fruit-bearing trees come into the fossil records.

Point 19 for the Holy Torah

---

[309] "The early Devonian landscape was devoid of vegetation taller than waist height. Without the evolution of a robust vascular system, taller heights could not be attained". From the Wikipedia article on the Evolutionary history of plants.

[310] http://en.wikipedia.org/wiki/Evolutionary_history_of_plants#Seeds

Ice Age:

See day 4, even though chronologically the issue is equally applicable here.

Day 4:

14 And E-lohim said, "There will be luminous (bodies) in the Rakiya, the Shamayim, to separate between the day and between the night, and they will be for signs and for festivals, for days and for years. 15 And they will be for lights in the Rakiya, the Shamayim, to shed light on the land (planet)", and it was so. 16 And E-lohim created the two large luminous bodies, the large luminous body to rule the day and the small luminous body to rule the night and the stars. 17 And E-lohim placed them in the Rakiya, the Shamayim, to shed light on the land. 18 And to rule during the day and during the night and to separate between the light and between the dark. And E-lohim saw that it was good. 19 And it was evening, and it was morning the fourth day.

In the first part of the above passages, the Torah goes out of its way to state the purpose of all the heavenly bodies: *Otot*, (signs), *Moadim*, (festivals), *Yamim*, (days), *Shanim*, (years) and to shine upon the Earth. I will not discuss what the Otot are. *"Moadim"* are the Jewish festivals, Pesach, Shavuos, and Sukkos. *"Yamim"*, days, is clear: the side upon which the sun is shining is the day. *Shanim*, years, refers to the solar calendar. I hope that "lighting up the planet" needs no explanation?

The Universe:

Thus far, I have been trying to show that the narrative of the Holy Torah should be taken quite literally according to its simple understanding and according to the order relayed therein. I intend to continue to do so. However, it should be clear that not all things are written in the Torah explicitly. Some things are only hinted at, and some are better defined by looking elsewhere in the Bible, and some still require segments of the Oral Torah to fully understand them.

So far, in the Bible narrative, we have heard nothing concerning the creation of the stars, the moon or other galaxies. This is the first time that the Torah discusses them and the language itself, (i.e. "there should be" "and it was so"), implies that it was at this point that they were created. Although this clearly contradicts the scientific theory of today and the methods of dating which science employs, I have no problem whatsoever with this. If the Torah says one thing, whereas science says another thing I will choose G-D's word over man's every time. However, as I mentioned previously, the Oral Torah addresses this and tells us that the "creation" here, (*va'ya'as*), refers not to their actual construction, but rather to the stabilization of their orbits. The actual stars say our sages, ob"m, were created on day one.

As to the veracity of scientific dating: I will, G-D willing, address it in chapter 9.

The Sun and the Moon

Now the Torah goes out on a limb: it describes to us the creation of the sun and the moon. Why do I say that it goes out on a limb? Because it says that there was the original creation of the sun and the moon; and then there is what we have today.

The Torah first says that G-d created the two large luminous bodies. Both of them large, both of them radiant, both of them equal. The meaning of this statement is that our galaxy originally was a binary galaxy. We had two suns. Then something happened, and they changed, one becoming the sun and the other becoming the moon. So, what happened? Well, here we are in need of the Oral Torah to explain. The Midrash[311] asks exactly this question, and it answers that what changed things is that the one luminous body entered the boundary, (*techumo*), of its friend.

> *As a... star increases in size during its evolution, it may at some point exceed its "Roche lobe", meaning that some of its matter ventures into a region where the gravitational pull of its companion star is larger than its own. The result is that matter will transfer from one star to another through a process known as Roche Lobe overflow (RLOF), either being absorbed by direct impact or through an accretion disc. The mathematical point through which this transfer happens is called "the first Lagrangian point". It is not uncommon that the accretion disc is the brightest (and thus sometimes the only visible) element of a binary star.*
>
> *If a star grows outside of its Roche lobe too fast for all abundant matter to be transferred to the other component, it is also possible that matter will leave the system through other Lagrange points or as stellar wind, thus being effectively lost to both components[312].*

My understanding of what the Midrash means is the following:

Once upon a time, the moon was really a sun and, in this regard, it was an identical twin to the sun. For whatever reason, the pull of gravity from the sun exceeded that of the moon, and this resulted in the "sunny-ness"

---

[311]   Genesis Rabbah 6:3

[312]   http://en.wikipedia.org/wiki/Binary_star#Orbital_period

of the moon being transferred to the sun. The moon, which suddenly lost both mass and light, uncoupled from its orbit with the present sun and was flung into the galaxy where it eventually was "grabbed" by the earth's gravity and pushed into synchronous rotation around the planet. (G-D's doing, of course).

This is helpful, of course, because science today really has no idea where the moon came from. For sure, there have been many hypotheses forwarded on the subject, but at the end of the day... no idea! The most prevalent of the hypotheses is the "Giant Impact Hypotheses"[313], which states that a long time ago, not in a galaxy far away, something very big plowed into the earth. The impact tore off a hunk of the earth and knocked it into the atmosphere. Eventually, it turned into the moon.

One of the reasons that this hypothesis is so beloved is because it gives some explanation as to why it is we find that almost the entire surface of the moon was covered in a lava ocean. I mean if there was a big collision with earth, so it makes sense that there would be a lot of molten material as a result, no?

Well, the Torah here is giving us another option: it was molten because the moon is made from the heart of a star that was quickly depleted of its hydrogen and helium.

Another issue, which might be the result of the transfer of mass from the moon to the sun, is the apparent lopsidedness of the moon's crust[314]. The side of the moon that is not facing the earth has a thicker crust and is made of a different composition. This could be a result of the Roche Lobe effect mentioned earlier as the side closest to the sun would experience the most severe effects of the pull of the sun's gravity, "shifting" the mass of the molten moon to the one side and packing it more densely.

Although my description is debatable, in my opinion:

Point 20 for the Holy Torah.

---

[313] http://en.wikipedia.org/wiki/Giant_impact_hypothesis
[314] See *New Scientist* August 6, 2011 pg. 9 *"Transformer: dark side of the moon"* which presents a new hypothesis in this issue.

The Milky Way Galaxy

I have already made a distinction between the *Shamayim* of the first verse of Genesis, as opposed to the *Rakiya*, which was renamed *Shamayim*. Elsewhere in the Bible, the following is related: there is the *Shamayim* and then there is *Shemei haShamayim*[315], (literally the *Shamayim* of the *Shamayim*). I say this to stress the following: the verse here is not coming to tell us that the sun, the moon and stars are "hung" in earth's upper atmosphere, which was called both *Rakiya* and *Shamayim*. How do I know this? Because I looked very carefully at the words! The *Rakiya* of the Earth, the one mentioned on day two, its purpose is to separate between the waters that are below it and the waters that are above it. That *Rakiya* was also called *Shamayim*. Here the Torah is telling us that the sun, the moon, and the stars reside in something else entirely: the *Rakiya* of the *Shamayim*. This means that there exists a second *Rakiya*, which was not mentioned previously, at least not explicitly. This is the *Rakiya* that separates the *Shamayim* of the Earth, (also called *Rakiya*), from the *Shamayim* of the *Shamayim*, the one discussed in the first verse of Genesis.

So, if we are to look at it the order, (from the ground up), goes like this: *Eretz*, water, land, *rakiya/shamayim*, water, *rakiya* of the *shamayim* and then the *shamayim*, (followed by *shemei ha shamayim*).

Therefore, when the Torah talks about the *Rakiya* of the *Shamayim*, it is referring to the area of space in which our sun, the moon, and the visible stars reside. It's what we call the Milky Way!

Point 21 for the Holy Torah.

In addition, the above, there is a whole lot to say about the findings of modern science and what they say about the configuration of the universe.

---

[315] The verse is in Nehemiah 9:6 "You, alone, are the Lord. You made the Shamayim, Shemei haShamayim and all of their hosts, the land and all that is on it, the seas and all that is in them. And You grant life to all and the hosts of heaven (השמים) bow down to You".

I'm referring to whether it is helio- (sun) or geo- (earth) centered. Many of science's greatest minds of both today and yesteryear have admitted that there really is no way of mathematically or geometrically discounting the organization of the stars, the moon, the sun and the rest of the universe in either of the aforementioned configurations. Both schemes can meet and match the math. However, there are a number of experiments that have been done over the past 200 years that seem to show clearly that the earth is not in motion. For example, the Michelson-Morley experiment[316] of the late 19th century and the experiment known as "Airey's Failure"[317], (because he failed to detect in the hundred-odd experiments that he conducted, the speed of motion of the earth). In addition, much of the information streaming in from today's most advanced satellites also seem to confirm that what the Torah states simply … is simply true. The earth, *ha'aretz*, is standing smack-dab in the middle of the universe, as its centerpiece.

As this topic is beyond the scope of this book the reader is urged to look up the books *"Galileo Was Wrong"* by Dr. Robert Sungenis and also the information on his website and blog. Although Dr. Sungenis is a believing Christian, and there are so many reasons why that part of his understanding is wrong, but the math and science he clearly knows and has what to say about[318]. I am not endorsing his opinion. In truth, I am not sure which is the correct interpretation of reality. I am only pointing out that the data, and therefore the topic, is open to interpretation and that Dr. Sungenis presents a very strong argument. Realistically, whichever point

---

[316] See, for example, https://en.wikipedia.org/wiki/Michelson%E2%80%93Morley_experiment#Most_famous_%22failed%22_experiment and also http://scienceworld.wolfram.com/physics/Michelson-MorleyExperiment.html

[317] See http://rspl.royalsocietypublishing.org/content/20/130-138/35.full.pdf+html f or a pdf scan of the initial publication from 1872. See also http://articles.adsabs.harvard.edu//full/1873GOAMM..33C..17A/0000132.000.html

[318] If you peruse the link at http://blogs.discovermagazine.com/badastronomy/2010/09/14/geocentrism-seriously/#.Wi2w-zdx02w you will find that everyone agrees that at least on a purely mathematical level there is no way to show definitively that one model is better than the other. As both of these models can be read into the text – I brought both. In truth though, only HaShem knows which of these is the right one.

of view is correct isn't a fundamental issue for me, or for the Torah for that matter, as it was written for those of us living on planet earth, for whom this isn't a truly earth-shattering topic.

Ice Age Revisited

As we saw earlier, the earth and the sun became set in their orbits only on this day, day 4. This means that prior to this time the following had occurred:

As there was no moon to stabilize the earth's "spin", a flux factor was acting on the earth's magnetic core.

Winter and all the other seasons are regulated based on the earth's proximity and relative angle to the sun. When there is no set orbit of the earth-sun, there is also less control over the temperature. As I mentioned before, we know that the earth exists in "the Goldi-lox, (we're Jewish, after all!), Zone," meaning the relative distance between earth and the sun places it in just the right area so that it's "not too hot and not too cold." That zone doesn't exist unless there is a stable orbit of earth-sun. The result is that this leads to extreme temperature variations until the orbits stabilize. This could certainly be a source of the ice age.

Included in the first four days is the creation of the land and vegetation. This also occurred before the creation of any animals. Therefore, evidence of an ice age could be found on the landmass.

I'm sure that the correlation of the above information is clear: evidence for an ice-age is not contradictory to the Torah in any shape, way or form.

This is just another one of the many issues in which we find that the written and oral Torah's describe how, where and when the evidence somehow, miraculously just "fits" into the Torah's narrative when we take the time to piece the pieces together.

Having said that, we must also consider the following. The flood story is mentioned explicitly, as opposed to the ice age, as it has something to teach us that is relevant to us. Whether it is the lesson of the rainbow, the continued chronology of the generations, or any other side of the flood story, there is a lesson there for us. The ice age, however, is entirely irrelevant.

How many verses did it take the Holy Torah to describe to us the creation of the universe and the world? 19 verses in total.

Think about this very, very deeply.

Due to the very technical nature of the narrative concerning the last days of creation, I have decided not to include them in this book. With HaShem's help, I will find the time and strength to figure out how that is best taught later.

9

The Timeframe of Creation and Anything Homo...

Torah And the Age of The Universe:

HE AGE OF THE EARTH according to modern scientific methodology is 4.54 billion years (4.54 × 109 years ± 1%). This age is based on evidence from radiometric age dating of meteorite material and is consistent with the ages of the oldest-known terrestrial and lunar samples[319].

Following the scientific revolution and the development of radiometric age dating, measurements of lead in uranium-rich minerals showed that some were in excess of a billion years old. The oldest such minerals analyzed to date – small crystals of

---

[319]   This information is based mainly on NASA's Wilkinson Microwave Anisotropy Probe (WMAP) project's seven-year data release in 2010. (Wikipedia "Age of the Universe").

zircon from the Jack Hills of Western Australia – are at least 4.404 billion years old. Comparing the mass and luminosity of the Sun to the multitudes of other stars, it appears that the solar system, (i.e. the Milky Way), cannot be much older than those rocks. Ca-Al-rich inclusions (inclusions rich in calcium and aluminum) – the oldest known solid constituents within meteorites that are formed within the solar system – are 4.567 billion years old, giving an age for the solar system and an upper limit for the age of Earth.

The estimated age of the universe is 13.75 ± 0.11 billion years (alternatively Gigayears or 10 to the ninth power years), the time since the Big Bang. The uncertainty range has been obtained by the agreement of a number of scientific research projects. These projects included microwave background radiation measurements by Wilkinson Microwave Anisotropy Probe and other probes and more ways to measure the expansion of the universe. Background radiation measurements give the cooling time of the universe since the Big Bang. Expansion of the universe measurements gives accurate data to calculate the age of the universe[320].

Many people feel that there is a tremendous inconsistency between the above age of existence as compared to the Jewish dating system. The Jewish/Torah dating system counts the date – as of this writing – from creation as being only 5782 (and 6 days) years ago. "How can it be?" say the critics. Clearly one of us is a few years off!

The question that we need to ask ourselves, therefore, is what are the means of calculating the age of the earth/universe; and does the data really imply what is being promoted in popular literature?

---

[320] http://en.wikipedia.org/wiki/Age_of_the_universe

A Fundamental Piece of Food for Thought

There are two types of evidence that we are dealing with when it comes to dating: there is evidence that is observable, and then there is evidence which is *not* observed, but it is implied.

Whenever we are talking about dating methods that are of the observable, measurable, and repeatable category, meaning that it from it's beginning to its conclusion the entire process can be seen, measured, and we can repeat the process many times to verify its accuracy, then we are dealing with fact. However, when it comes to deep-time, which really is anything older than 100 years or so, as it is beyond our scope of fully being observed, and measured; and it most assuredly is beyond repeatability, we are no longer talking about evidence. We are talking about projection/ Extrapolation. Which means that there are fundamental issues which are presumed to be true from the outset.

Let me bring a few reasons to better understand this issue.

The Problem with Projected/Extrapolated Data

Let me quote from a NASA response to one fellow concerning the waning power of the Earth's magnetic field[321]:

> *The magnetic field of the Earth changes all the time, and yes, magnetic charts have to be redrawn from time to time (this was first found in 1641, by an Englishman named Gillibrand). And yes, in the century and a half since the first careful mapping of the Earth's field, the dipole has become weaker by about 8% (the rate may have speeded up in 1970). If you draw a straight*

---

[321]   http://www-spof.gsfc.nasa.gov/Education/FAQs1.html#q1 question 1d

line through the points, you will find that perhaps 1200 years from now, the line goes through zero.

Extending straight lines too far beyond the present, however, is risky business, as noted by no less a scientific authority than Mark Twain. (See below) …

It is not impossible that the magnetic field will go through zero 1200 years from now, but (judging by the past record of reversals) not likely.

In "Life on the Mississippi", Twain, upon noting that the Mississippi river was getting progressively shorter, wrote the following:

"Now, if I wanted to be one of those scientific people, and "let on" to prove what had occurred in the remote past by what had occurred at a given time in the recent past, or what will occur in the far future by what has occurred in late years, what an opportunity is here! … Please observe:

In the space of one hundred and seventy-six years, the Lower Mississippi has shortened itself two hundred and forty-two miles. That is an average over a mile and a third per year. Therefore, any calm person, who is not blind or idiotic, can see that in the lower Oolitic Silurian Period, just a million years ago next November, the Lower Mississippi was upward of one million three hundred thousand miles long, and stuck out over the Gulf of Mexico like a fishing rod. And by the same token, any person can see that seven hundred and forty years from now the Lower Mississippi will be only a mile and three-quarters long, and Cairo and New Orleans will have joined their streets together and will be plodding comfortably along under a single mayor... There is something fascinating about science. One gets such wholesale returns of conjecture out of such a trifling investment in fact."

Which brings us to one of the basic flaws in the logic behind the science involved in the calculation of deep time: the projection of a decay rate beyond testable experience.

Radiocarbon Dating

"All organisms absorb carbon from their environment. Those that absorb their carbon directly or indirectly from the surface atmosphere have about 1 ppt (part per trillion) of their carbon content as ^{14}C. ... When an organism dies, carbon stops being absorbed. Hence after 5730 years, about half of its ^{14}C will have radioactively decayed (to nitrogen): only about 0.5 ppt of the carbon of the organism's remains will be ^{14}C. And if the carbon of the remains is found to be 0.25 ppt ^{14}C, then the organism would be assumed to have died about 11 460 years ago. Thus, a simple calculation can find the age, since death, from any ^{14}C concentration."[322]

A close reading of the above will show that it is based on the following assumptions:

(1) That as a base measurement there is 1 ppt of ^{14}C in every living creature/plant.
(2) That the only way there is ^{14}C present is by absorption from the atmosphere.
(3) That the rate of decay, in and of itself, is constant or near constant.
(4) That there is nothing that in any way affects the rate of decay.

---

[322] *Basics of Radiocarbon Dating* pdf, from www.informath.org

All of these assumptions are testable, and the question is: how much of these premises have been shown to be true?

Concerning points 1 and 2

It is very clear that this is an educated guess. It presumes that since there is, on average, in the breathable atmosphere 1 ppt of ^{14}C in the atmosphere, and all living things "breath" in the atmosphere, including the aforementioned unstable carbon, therefore the entire saturation available should be 1 ppt at any given time. Is that actually true? Just because there is 1 ppt in the atmosphere in no way says that the saturation in our bodies, for example, or in the vegetation around us actually absorbs an amount of 1 ppt. Perhaps the actual levels of ^{14}C saturation varies according to species, according to oxygen levels, according to elevation, or many other variables that the above equation cannot take into account?

It also presupposes that the saturation levels that we find in today's atmosphere (the aforementioned 1 ppt), is a constant, and that also in ancient times the ^{14}C levels of the atmosphere were the same.

In addition, as the amounts that we are talking about in the calculations are incredibly small (1 part per trillion) therefore even a small variation in the initial saturation level changes the entire result of the equation!

Premise 3: Radioactive Decay is Constant

As stated above, carbon-14 has a calculated half-life of around 5730 years before it decays into nitrogen, and all of the math is based on that. This "half-life" is an extrapolation made based on measuring two or more points and making an estimated guess based on these points as to what the half-life is.

Let me be more specific. The thinking is as follows: because I can demonstrate half-life in action, using a radioactive isotope that has an incredibly short half-life, say a month, for example, so too when we are talking about isotopes with very long half-lives, say carbon-14, then the underlaying assumption is that the principal is the same. Therefore, despite my not having ever actually observed or fully measured the half-life of a carbon-14 isotope, as the logic is demonstratable and the math can back it up, so it must be true. Except that it isn't.

First of all, there is no such thing as a "constant rate of decay" or any other "constant rate". In all experimentation, there is a form of a curve. In all speed testing, a thing gets its initial speed and then grows faster until it reaches a point that it peaks and then starts to decelerate. All movement eventually must come to a stop when the body in motion meets up with resistance of some sort which then produces a counter motion. So why should the rate of decay of a radioactive isotope be any different? Even projected fluctuations in the rate of decay, which would allow for some "level of error" in the projected decay rate, suffer from the same fundamental flaw[323]!

In addition to the above, there have been numerous examples of conundrums arising from this fundamental premise in measuring time in this way.

The above proposes that the older a thing is, the less radioactive isotopes, (referred to as the "parent" element) as they have already "decayed" into the "daughter," non-radioactive isotopes. Accordingly, the lower the find in the older earth strata – the fewer isotopes should be found. However, there have been many instances of deeper (=supposedly older) earth strata being measured and having a larger carbon-14 content than those in younger earth strata, which seems to fly in the face of the underlying assumption that the rate of radioactive decay is constant. Similarly, discrepancies have been noted while measuring findings in more recent strata, as some of the finds have less carbon-14 than those found in older strata. Both of these fly in the face of the premise that the rate of decay is constant (and the same holds true for any other type of radioisotope dating)!

---

[323] [2012.00153] Anomalies in Radioactive Decay Rates: A Bibliography of Measurements and Theory (arxiv.org)

They also take us back to points 1 and 2, as the calculations presuppose that the strata being measured at first had an equal amount of saturation, and that they also had NO "daughter" element in them initially. This is just a guess. If this is not true, and in all likelihood it isn't, then in reality the rate of decay is actually much faster than what is claimed. As evidence that this is incorrect it should be noted that even the adherents of "radioactive isotope" theory themselves admit that readings that are done on "new strata" and on "new remains" tend to be wildly incorrect[324]. Why would this happen unless they also have either more "daughter" non-radioactive elements in their makeup initially, or that the initial premise of 1 ppt of ^{14}C is simply not correct?

In addition, we must take into account the vast discrepancies that are measured in isotope dating, despite the fact that they are all using the exact same instrumentation and calculations. In virtually all instances of isotope dating, there is a wide spectrum of opinions as to the actual date that is measured. In some instances, the range of error is in the billions of years. This means that when an actual date is quoted it usually follows the one the "presenter" is most comfortable with, not because all measurements agree.

Premise 3 and The Uncertainty Principal

Another crucial issue comes from the results of the many tests done in various "colliders" around the world. The following is an excerpt from the March 2011 issue of Discover Magazine (pg. 50):

One of the results of the uncertainty principle is

---

[324] For example, rock samples that were collected from Mt. Saint Helens, which erupted in Washington State in 1980, were sent to various labs in the year 2010 for radiometric dating. The labs were not informed that the samples were from an eruption that happened 30 years ago. The results that came back were wildly differing, but for the most part the age of the rocks was set at 350,000 years old, which is ridiculous. https://www.icr.org/article/argon-mount-saint-helens/

> *"...that you can never predict the outcome of a quantum experiment with certainty; you can only calculate the probability of getting a particular result. ... This fundamental indeterminism has been repeatedly confirmed in the lab. For instance, physicists have shown that two identical radioactive atoms will decay at different times. There is no way to explain why they behave or to predict the precise time of decay".*

Although this might supply a possible answer to the some of the problems mentioned above, clearly this problem lies at the heart of the calculated rates of radioactive decay! If the above is true and there is no way of calculating or knowing when and how the radioactive atoms decay with any accuracy, then how can we predict, based on said decay rate, the guesstimated time of anything?

Premise 4: Nothing Affects the Rate of Radioactive Decay

In addition, who is to say that there are no outside factors that have an effect on the rate of radioactive decay? For example, it has been noted that sun flares have a direct impact on the decay rates of radioactive isotopes[325]. If this is true, then who can say in what way this affects the half-life of radioactive dating of deep time?

Lastly, directly concerning this issue is the following:

> *"This age (of the universe 13.7 billion years) is based on the assumption that the (WMAP) project's underlying model is correct; other methods of estimating the age of the universe could give different ages. Assuming an extra background of*

---

[325] See Radioactive decay rates vary with the sun's rotation: research (phys.org) for example.

relativistic particles, for example, can enlarge the error bars
of the WMAP constraint by one order of magnitude" (ibid.)

Meaning that it is recognized that the calculations involved in these dating methods are based on assumptions. The term "model" which is mentioned in the above article, doesn't meant that the underlying principals of the model are sacrosanct or even based on undisputable facts. The model is presumed correct because it fits the observable data, but it is by no means the only explanation that fits the data. It's just the one that is promoted more publicly, that has received more PR than any other model.

If we take into account that practically every deep time related calculation rests in some way on either the carbon clock, or the potassium-argon clock, (including the issue of dendrology[326] which we will talk about later in this chapter), so the same problems arise concerning the validity of the dates supplied by these systems.

But it's not only the measurement of isotopes that is problematic. There are many other forms of "time measurement" that we are told of which "prove" that the age of the universe is positively more ancient than the age that the Torah tells us! For example Dinosaur bones, Dendrology, the measurement of the oceans salt content, the movement of the continents based on tectonics, and, of course, the ever-popular calculations of the age of the universe based on starlight. What do we say to these things, Rabbi?

The answer is quite simple as all of the above suffer from most of, if not *all* of, the aforementioned problems. Let's quickly discuss the issues above.

---

[326] Dendrology is the science of dating wooden objects by means of matching up tree-rings. There is much debate concerning the accuracy of such dating methods, especially in light of the fact that much of the field is not open for peer-review, but rather is given over from private institutions that have the wood samples in their possession.

Dinosaur Bones

I am not going to discuss the issue of dinosaurs in this book. The reason for this is that they are not a theological issue at all. The Torahs, both written and oral, do not provide us with an explicitly detailed description of creation, (as we mentioned previously in chapter 8). Did dinosaurs live before humans, or side-by-side with them is a topic of great debate and I'll leave it at that[327]. However, concerning the topic of the age of the universe, when we are told, "How could it possibly be that we found a dinosaur in strata that is 500,000,000 years old?" there I have *plenty* to say. There are two reasons why this is claimed. Either based on the aforementioned, problematic, issue of isotope dating or because we date the strata based on the dinosaur. Meaning because I, the evolutionary-believing scientist, have true-faith in evolution, and according to my faith this dinosaur should have lived – I don't know – say, 500 million years ago, therefore when I discover the bones – it's clear that the strata are also 500 million years old! After all, how could a 500-million-year-old dinosaur be found in 5000-year-old strata? The logic is clearly circular!

Dendrology

The issue of dendrology is based on the measurement and comparison of rings that a tree makes during its growth. As trees *from the same area*

---

[327] This topic essentially boils down to evolutionary adherents claiming, "we've never found any dinosaur and human bones together in the same strata" vs. adherents in the church claiming that they did anyway. Realistically, there is no absolute proof on either side, however, there is a *sevara*, a logical inference in the church literature, in that there are many ancient stories of man and dragons, which would be just another name for a very large lizard. See, for example http://toptenproofs. com/article.php?id=3 or https://www.intellihub.com/scientist-terminated-proving-dinosaurs-humans-walked-earth-together.html for the proofs "for", vs. https://www. tor.com/2013/03/25/10-dinosaur-myths-that-need-to-go-extinct/ for the "against".

experience the same rate of growth and, roughly, the same amount of rainfall, therefore, if we compare the "rings" that a tree has in it, we should be able to detect a pattern that will create a "tree-history" allowing us to show a time-line extending from the present day back to ancient history.

The problems with this are manifold. First of which is because in order to actually date many of the trees we need to rely on isotope dating. However, for further problems, please be patient... this issue will be torn apart later in the chapter.

Oceanic Salt Content

This issue was discussed at length back in chapter 5, *World of Care and Wonders*. The premise is that all the saltiness of the sea is due to the salt outflow of the freshwater rivers. Therefore, if we divide the salt outflow of river X based on ocean X's level of salinity per square meter of water we'll arrive at... a very long time.

This method is a total mess as it has many of the same fallacies of isotope dating. It pre-supposes a constant rate of salt flow from rivers into the ocean; it pre-supposes that there was no salt already present in the oceans, and worst of all it doesn't address that fact that there is something that is keeping the salinity levels of the ocean at livable levels, a state that has clearly been – according to them – a virtual constant for millions of years.

Tectonic Movement.

This issue was addressed already in chapter 8, *In the Beginning*. The premise of the calculation is based on our understanding of tectonic movement, and that today's continents were once-upon-a-time all part of one, big "supercontinent" which split-up until it became the globe that we see today. Therefore, if we take the distance between, say, Africa and South

America, which at one time were close neighbors on the supercontinent, and we divide that by the present rate of tectonic movement we get... a very long time!

Here also, we find that the same problems persist. This pre-supposes constant rates of movement. It also doesn't take into account the varying amounts of resistance which two continental plates could experience when running into each other. In addition, it also doesn't take into account the mechanism which drives tectonics, which is not really known today. For more on this topic, the reader is urged to look on my blog <u>www.rabbibz.com</u> in the article entitled "Noah and Tectonic Movement".

Star Light

This is probably the most fun of all the above issues. It is argued that because we measure starlight at 300,000 km per second (about 186,000 miles per second) therefore, if we can see the light of a star that is 15 million light-years away then the universe must be at least 15 million years old, as that's how long it would take the light to reach us from that far away.

This argument presupposes the following.

1> That light travels at a constant 300,000 k/ps everywhere in the universe. While it is true that we measure that speed on earth and in our galaxy, and that there is technically nothing in space that causes "air friction" to reduce its speed, it is only an assumption that this holds true during interstellar travel.

2> This doesn't take into account that beyond a certain point in space, referred to as "parallax", we cannot measure with any accuracy the real distance of that star from earth. Within parallax, where we can measure changes in movement, we can, therefore, use geometry to help us understand the actual distance from the earth. However, beyond parallax, we cannot measure movement and therefore the numbers offered are... figments of the astronomer's imagination only. The extent of "parallax" is only a modest 400 light years away[328].

However, in addition to "parallax" we are told that there is another means of measuring the distance between the earth and the stars and that is:

> There is no direct method currently available to measure the distance to stars farther than 400 light years from Earth, so astronomers instead use **brightness measurements**. It turns out that a star's **color spectrum** is a good indication of its actual brightness. The relationship between color and brightness was proven using the several thousand stars close enough to earth to have their distances measured directly. Astronomers can, therefore, look at a distant star and determine its color spectrum. From the color, they can determine the star's actual brightness. By knowing the actual brightness and comparing it to the apparent brightness seen from Earth (that is, by looking at how dim the star has become once its light reaches Earth), they can determine the distance to the star[329].

The proper name for this in the literature is "red-shift", and its premise is based on the observed phenomenon that the farther away an observed light source is – the more its light shifts towards the "red" part of the light spectrum. The problem with this is that it suffers from all of the same maladies as all of the other postulations. It assumes that the natural

---

[328] "The first technique uses **triangulation** (a.k.a. **parallax**). The Earth's orbit around the sun has a diameter of about 186 million miles (300 million kilometers). By looking at a star one day and then looking at it again 6 months later, an astronomer can see a difference in the viewing angle for the star. With a little trigonometry, the different angles yield a distance. This technique works for stars within about 400 light years of earth". Quoted from https://science.howstuffworks.com/question224.htm

[329] https://science.howstuffworks.com/question224.htm

light of the stars that we see is not naturally red-shifted. It assumes that the extrapolation of the red-shifting visible within parallax is a constant throughout the universe. It also "glosses" over the fact that even if we assumed that the above two premises are true it doesn't mention that the "conclusions" are still only gross estimations.

So, if *I* tell you that this star is "20 billion light years away, how can *we, today*, see it's light *unless the light has traveled for 20 billion years*", then if you buy it – it's only because I succeeded in fooling you.

Based on the very same logic I can, in fact, prove to you that the world is 300 million google-plex years old, because in truth we see the light from stars that are 300 million google-plex light years away! Just do the math and you'll see I'm right. After all, the math never lies, does it?

Well... yeah, it does! IF the initial integers are fictitious!

Measurement of Creation

However, let's assume, for argument's sake, that carbon dating and any other type of dating is correct. Now, what Torah?

To get an understanding, let's lay down a few Torah facts:

First, it must be clear that our counting of 5782 years is calculated from the time that has passed since the creation of Adam plus the first days of Creation, as stated explicitly in the first chapter of Genesis. Second, also explicit in Genesis, the first six days is all the time that it took G-D to make everything. This explicit information is all we need to understand why this is not a dilemma for the Torah.

The Jewish position describing creation is stated clearly in the Oral Torah, (Tractate *Rosh HaShanna* 11a), there the Talmud states that all of existence was created *bekomatan*, literally "erect". This means that yes, the chicken came first. The entire creation was created "standing", meaning that the trees had fruits on them, the grass was long and green, etc. All of this is explicit in the Torah.

The Torah says that the land is to *"give forth trees which make fruit"* and it did (Genesis 1:12-13). It says that *"fish should appear in the waters"* and they did (ibid. 20-21)[330]. The "funny thing" about the Torah saying this is that from an entirely objective view, or a data-based view, if you will, ... that's exactly what the archaeological and paleontological records show! Not only did biological life of different complexity suddenly "appear" in the archaeological record, but it does so precisely according to the "schedule" detailed in the first verses of Genesis (as we described in detail in the previous chapter)! First land-based grass and plant-life, then fishes, followed by avian life[331], then animal life etcetera, exactly as the Torah describes it.

However, this, in no way, is to say that the actual physical creation would not show the "wear and tear" of however long is required to create a natural world. The world itself, was set up to mask G-D's presence, (as will be discussed at length in book 3 of this series, with G-D's help!), yet because it is the creation of G-D, it is consistent with G-D's Truth. If it looks that old, it's because naturally, it should take that long to make... but for G-D, it happens a lot quicker!

So, either we say that the tallies are still not in on this subject, and we wait another 100 years or so until science gets it right, or we assume that it is possible to "cram" 13 billion years into 6 days of creation.

Noted physicist and lecturer Dr. Gerald Schroeder, Ph.D. in his books *"Genesis and the Big Bang"* and *"The Science of G-D"*, who read the first draft

---

[330] This is also the position of all of our sages, ob"m. For example, Rav Sa'adiya Gaon in his book *Emunot v'De'ot* second ma'amar point 5 (page 93 in the Kappach edition).

[331] Although there is still some debate on this, as until recently avian findings were quite rare and seemed to come only "after" dinosaurs, this is just another case of "didn't find it", which is proof of lack of looking only. Like in most of these issues, as time goes on more and more fossilized birds are found and the silliness of the "educated conclusions" becomes obvious to anyone who wants to pay attention. See, for example, https://news.nationalgeographic.com/2017/06/baby-bird-dinosaur-burmese-amber-fossil/ or http://www.ucmp.berkeley.edu/diapsids/birds/birdfr.html where it sounds like that the university of Berkley has finally decided that Archaeopteryx really is a bird, not a dino-bird.

of this book, first advanced this position. In both books, he makes the claim, based on Einstein's theory of Relativity, that it is possible to cram billions of years into six 24-hour days if the clock measuring the days is not based on Earth's present mass and gravity, but rather the universal clock of radioactive background (CMB) emission.

Another possibility, however, which also is more in-sync with the simple and classical understanding of the verses stated above, is that the velocity at which the original creation occurred was much faster than what we presently experience. Accordingly, it would leave signs of growth that correspond with much of the data that we mentioned above. As a result of the speed at which the world was created it shows signs of the "wear and tear" of billions of years without actually having experienced the actual flow of time. I do not mean to say that the world revolved at a faster pace, as our sages tell us, quite clearly, that that was a constant since day one. I mean to say that velocity of growth and change experienced on earth were different than those of today. Let me explain what I mean.

Since E(nergy)=M(ass)xC(speed of light)^2 and the speed of light is a factor of velocity, it follows that just as much as mass has an effect on time, so too does a things velocity. After all, V(elocity)=D(istance) traveled divided by the T(ime) it took to travel. So, if we assume that T = 6 days of 24 hours, just like those of today, therefore, the "Distance" that the universe had to "travel", (i.e. the "wear and tear" of the universe), in order to get where it is in that very short time was very, very great. MEANING that if creation occurred fast enough, it would look like it was a long time in the making. This is akin to what the scientific data tells us about wormholes: You can fold time-space and within an instant, you can travel, say, from one end of the universe to the other, (a very great distance indeed!). All that is needed is enough Energy, (which G-d, of course, isn't lacking). This, however, utilizes no velocity whatsoever.

Let's understand it with the following parable. If you were sitting around in your backyard one day, not doing anything, in particular, just looking at the grass and enjoying the fine weather. All of a sudden, before your very eyes, a green sprout pokes out of the ground right in front of you.

To your disbelief, it continues to grow bigger and higher until it is standing 30 feet tall, looking to all the world like a tree that has been around for 100 years. Now, for the crux of the issue. Let me ask you: if you would cut down that tree, how many rings would it have? Probably 100, just like any other tree that it took 100 years to grow! This is because the rings of the tree, the layers of rock sediment/ice/tundra or any other type of layering, are not indicative of time passing. True, in modern observation we see that as a rule the rings or the layering corresponds with one year of growth, however, realistically they are more a sign of growth and change more than they are a sign of time. Many times, growth and change intersect/are parallel with the amount of time that passes, however, that does not mean that it is the time or the phenomena that we see today occurring during that time that is the sole cause of the layering or that caused the tree-rings to occur. Tree-rings occur due to the growth of the tree, which is based on many factors, including (to name a few) the amount of rain that falls and the amount of oxidation available in the air. Ice layers are the result of not just the seasons, but rather the phenomena that occur during the time that passes. If there were varying weather patterns that occurred with great intensity at different times, then the result would be that numerous layers would be created over a very short time. Although water can cause erosion, that does not necessarily mean that the rate of erosion is constant. It, like all physical phenomena, is subject to change and fluctuation.

What I am trying to say is that the presumption that I can make a good and proper (gu)estimation concerning the passage of time-based on observable phenomena of today, does not, and cannot truly prove that the rates of yesterday were those we see today.

The same applies to the earth and the universe. Despite their relative newness, (as opposed to the secular world's opinion), they would seem to display evidence of being quite older. But they are not. They are only 5782 years old (as of this writing) + 6 regular days of 24 hours, which are measured by one revolution of the earth around itself, and as described in the Holy Torah quite clearly at the beginning of The Book.

At any rate, both THEOLOGICALLY and SCIENTIFICALLY this issue presents us with no difficulty *at all*.

Genesis and Anything "Homo":

At this point, I would like to address the issues relevant to the timeline of earth based on the findings of "Human evolution". Obviously, when we say that the world "came to be" and that man "came to be", the question arises, how does this jive with all of the various "Homo"-species that archaeologists and paleontologists have been finding for years? How can the Torah count 5782 years since Adam if there were people who pre-existed him?

Let's make some quantifying statements here:

First of all, archaeological findings in existence today that bear the markings of modern human society are no older than 5782 years.

The Torah itself, in describing the creation of man, tells us that there was one unique attribute that G-D Himself bestowed upon him and not on any other creature and that is (Genesis 2:7) *nishmas chaim*, literally "living breath". The Oral Torah[332] explains that this refers to man's powers of wisdom and communication. All artifacts found left by civilizations belaying both advanced intelligence and communicated abilities are no older than 5782 years. This is uncontested.

Having said that: cave paintings, crude "tools" and other such findings are not considered evidence of human civilization.

Only scientists, who – according to their world-view, based as it is on evolution – who see man as an advanced monkey, will conclude that the older the monkey the older the evidence of human existence. I mean on this point we all agree: the monkeys came first!

---

[332] See the translation of Onkelos on that verse, who translates it into Aramaic as רוח ממללא, meaning the spirit of speech. It is clear that we are not talking about grunts and whistles here as Adam goes on to have intelligent conversations with G-D. Clearly it refers to the power of speech and wisdom.

We have already discussed the issue of skeletons and paleontological "evidence" in a previous chapter, (chapter 6, "The Emperor's New Clothes"). There we discussed the fallacy and failure of anthropology to categorize correctly ancient findings based on modern ones. Proficiency in the contemporary does not give any credence concerning the ancient. To say that we have conclusive proof of something for which we have only partial evidence and no actual present knowledge of is about as irrefutable as saying, "This is the absolute truth... I think". It's either conclusive proof or its conjecture. There is no middle-of-the-road.

Any and all skeletons found are a long-shot from bringing conclusive proof as to the existence of actual modern humans pre-dating Adam. Especially since these less-than corpses cannot sit up and have a conversation, which is the only way to really know whether they could even have an intelligent conversation at all! The only way today that we can testify about an ancient civilization, and claim with any certainty that it was one of both intelligence and communicative abilities is because they left behind writings that we can translate and study.

Maybe these skeletons left behind were ancient gorillas or some other large simians, which are not considered human, and certainly not more than human, even by evolution's standards, except in the comic books. New Zealand and their ilk aside, although chimps and other monkeys have been taught sign language and some computer language skills, virtually no one considers them to be an actual Human.

However, beyond the above – listen to words of our holy sages, ob"m, in the Midrash Rabba, (Genesis 23:9). The Midrash there tells us that because of their promiscuity, that during the times of the generations of *Enosh*, (Adam's grandson), the visage of the peoples of the time changed so that they looked like monkeys! In addition to the above, the Midrash also teaches us that there was an immense tidal wave that occurred during that same period that wiped out the vast majority of life on the supercontinent[333].

---

[333] As we pointed out in the chapter "In the Beginning" the Torah states, matter-of-factly that the world was, at first, a single super-continent. This only began to change at a much later stage, during the generation of Peleg.

According to the Midrash, (Ibid. 23:10), the "super wave" washed out over one-third of the world. This would certainly account for the finding of monkey-like humanoids in very old earth strata, preceding even those strata that were formed by the flood during the times of Noah.

I wish to stress that the Midrash Rabbah is not some apologetic book that was written recently, trying to address today's archeology, or even the archeology of the time in which it was written. It was, and is, according to all opinions, an ancient book, (around the 6th century CE, even according to the most skeptical opinions)[334].

In any case, it should be clear that the only source of argument in this regard is the definition of what is a human. That being the case we religious therefore rely on the definition supplied to us in our Holy Torah, (Bible, THE (old) Testament), whereas scientists depend on the definition provided by their bible, ("The Origin of the Species", by the prophet Charles Darwin)! As that is the case, we will either have to establish the validity of the Holy Torah, as we have already begun to do in this volume, and which we will – G-D willing – continue doing in the next volume of the series; or … we will just have to agree to disagree on this issue. I leave that up to the reader.

Do you have the fortitude, the desire, to know the truth?

---

[334] https://en.wikipedia.org/wiki/Genesis_Rabbah#Date

10

Parting Shots

A S WE STATED AT THE BEGINNING the purpose of this book is to explore with the reader the relevant fields of science that pertain to the world's creation. It is via the exploration of creation and existence that we must face the ever-so-basic question of life: "Is there a G-d that created all of this... and me"?

The contention of many scientists today is that we have the ability to give a plausible explanation as to the question, "where does existence, and where do *I* come from" according to the understanding of modern science. This model does not invoke the name of... oops! I mean does not mention the name of, or supposedly require, that there be a G-d there to make it happen. "It's all there," the scientists tell us "At the very worst there are just a few little teeny, tiny little itsy-bitsy gaps. Much too small for G-d to hide in. Yup! We're all hunky-dory!" they say. Yes, "Nature" can do it... all... by... Itself! It's not G-d if we call it "Nature", right?

I hope that in our exploration of the varying fields of science that we have seen together the absolute fallacy of these notions.

Not only are there "gaps" in the scientific models posited to "explain" and to "rationalize" existence, there are also chasms, canyons and interstellar galaxy-sized holes in the logic, the philosophy, and even in all of the facets of the science involved.

Nothing is easier for a man to hide his lack of knowledge and understanding in than mounds of information and years of theoretical and practical knowledge. As long as the "answer" lies in areas of human endeavor that YOU don't have. In other words, since I am considered to have knowledge in some area in which you DON'T, it is therefore quite easy for me to hide my fallacies in your ignorance.

Archeology and Anthropology, despite having amassed hundreds of thousands, if not millions, of man-hours overturning the rocks and the dust, examining the bones and the fossils of the past, cataloging, weighing and measuring, cannot give us more than an estimated guess when it comes to anything older than modern man. But this lack of knowledge concerning the ancient doesn't stop them from trying to sell us some amazing science fiction as to what "it" was, what "it" looked like and what "it" did.

We can "Ooh" and we can "Ahh" at their conclusions but we must look at them with a critical eye, as well, and assign them no more credit than their actual value. Guesstimation.

Can the sciences of chemistry or biology account for the physical and biological make-up of life? I think that we have shown, rather conclusively, that they not only *do* not, but that they never will... ever.

Biology cannot account for why the non-living, albeit organic, compounds in our cells are alive, whereas all other amalgams of chemical compounds are not.

It also cannot account for where intelligence comes from, or why, indeed, we can think at all.

It cannot even account for where DNA came from in the first place. Especially since it seems that you need a strand of DNA in the first place to get the next one! Let's also not forget that DNA is useless in and of itself! It needs many other systems to utilize the data that it contains to get stuff done.

All of the above sciences tell us not to worry as after millions of years and an infinite number of biological interactions and reactions there is no problem, scientifically or statistically/mathematically to achieve the end-result: both biologically simple and advanced life forms.
Nothing could be further from the truth.

Chemistry cannot even begin to explain to us what would need to transpire, or even give us a plausible theory, (not a hypothesis, as they are a dime-a-dozen, however, in my opinion there isn't even a plausible hypothesis either), as to how, chemically, DNA came into existence. Nor can it explain to us why it is that the number of protons, neutrons, and electrons an atom have changed so drastically the chemical properties of anything. It just does.
"No problem", they tell us, "After 'untold millions', (a euphemism for "infinite"), of chemical reactions, it just happens/ed."

Physics cannot explain to us why the four/three fundamental energies in existence, (gravity, electromagnetism and the nuclear strong and weak forces), have the values that they do or even where these energies emanate from. Just that they just do. Thank G-d for their existence! As we mentioned in the fourth chapter, "Logical and Philosophical", there is no such thing as a perpetual motion machine and if not for the constant influx of these energies there would be no existence of any sort to speak of.

Cosmology is only on the cusp of understanding the concepts that our Holy Torah spelled out to us so many thousands of years ago in black and white. And as far as the incredible unlikelihood of any planet anywhere ever becoming, or having, the requirements necessary for sustaining life we are told, "Don't worry! In an infinite [universe/time/space/whatever] there is plenty of room for things to work their way out"!

At the end of the day, we find that any and all sciences that want to invoke a model that can/might/somehow, (please G-d!), explain/rationalize existence without G-d will always – without fail – invoke the "infinite". Time, space, matter, what-have-you. SOMETHING IN THE MODEL MUST, BY NECESSITY, BE INFINITE for this universe to make any sense whatsoever.

All-in-all, if in the end there is a need to "hide" behind something infinite – I'll choose G-d every time!

Now that we have seen all of the information that pertains to THE question, that being every man's fundamental life question "Is there a G-d?" I think that we can answer unequivocally "YES! HALLELUJAH!"

Truth be told if the information in this book was all of the information that I had at my disposal or even all of the proof of existence, I feel that it is enough for me to reach this conclusion. However, that is not the case at all. This is only the tip of the iceberg! There is plenty more information in existence that shows, unequivocally, that there is a G-d out there.

With G-d's help, we will explore this more fully in the next volume in the series, Core Emunah 2 "G-d & Me", where we begin to tackle question number 2, "Does G-d know me?"

As I stated all the way at the beginning of the book – although the information presented here shows clearly the existence of a Divine Entity who is responsible for, and continues to, keep this ball of wax known as "existence" in existence, IT DOES NOT, HOWEVER, TELL US ANYTHING ABOUT WHO HE IS!

G-d willing we'll get to that topic in the next volume of the series.

The reason that I say this is because there are at least two of the major religions in the world today, (for example "Illustra media", also known as "the Discovery Foundation", (Christian), and Harun Yahya, (Moslem), and their ilk), who then conclude, after bringing, (similar), claims and proofs from science, that "now you must believe in [X]". You fill in the blanks.

WHAT? Dude! All you did is show that there IS a G-d! None of this proves WHO He is! (Or that He agrees with anything that you say!)

Do you want to know who He is?

Wait for volume 2!

IN LIEU OF A BIBLIOGRAPHY

A S I HAVE TRIED while writing this book, to use source material that is readily available to all, the true extent of the research that went into this book is vast.

Most of the books that I read dealt with one specific issue in science and many others, periodicals, for example, covered a broad range of topics not necessarily dealing with any one issue in particular, but relevant nonetheless.

As evidenced in my footnotes and in my citations, I have found many scientific periodicals of invaluable help in understanding many issues. The following is a list of some of the sources that I used (listed alphabetically):

Answers magazine (2015) Available at http://answersmagazine.com.

Carroll, R. L. *The Rise of Amphibians: 365 Million Years of Evolution*. The Johns Hopkins University Press 2009

Dawkins, R. (1986) *The blind watchmaker*. Burnt Mill, Harlow, Essex, England: Longman Scientific & Technical.

Dawkins, R. (2006) *The god delusion*. Johannesburg: Bantam, London.

Dawkins, R. (2010) *The Greatest Show on Earth: The Evidence for Evolution*. London: Black Swan.

Drees, W.B. (1990) *Beyond the big bang: Quantum Cosmologies and God.* United States: Open Court Publishing Co, U.S.

Freel, S.J., and Harper, C.L. (2012) *Fitness of the Cosmos for Life: Biochemistry and fine-tuning.* Edited by John D. Barrow, Simon Conway Morris, Stephen J. Freeland, and Charles L. Cambridge: Cambridge University Press.

Greene, B. (2011) *The hidden reality: Parallel universes and the deep laws of the cosmos.* New York: Knopf Doubleday Publishing Group.

Hawking, S.W., and Mlodinow, L. (2010) *The grand design.* New York: Random House Publishing Group.

Hazen, R. (2005) *The Teaching Company's Origins of life.* Available at: http://www.thegreatcourses.com/courses/origins-of-life.html.

Krukonis, G., and Barr, T. (2008) *Evolution for dummies.* Hoboken, NJ: Wiley, John & Sons.

Overman, D.L., Kaita, R. and Nicholi, A. (2008) *A case for the existence of God.* United States: Rowman & Littlefield.

Peacocke, A. (2009) *Evolution: The Disguised Friend of faith?* United States: Templeton Foundation Press.

Schroeder, G.L. (1994) *The science of God: The convergence of scientific and biblical wisdom.* New York: Simon & Schuster.

Schroeder, G.L. (1996) *Genesis and the big bang theory: The discovery of harmony between modern science and the Bible.* New York: Random House Publishing Group.

Schroeder, G.L. (2002) *The hidden face of God: Science reveals the ultimate truth.* New York: Simon & Schuster Adult Publishing Group.

Schroeder, G.L. (2009) *God according to God: A physicist proves we've been wrong about God all along.* New York, NY: HarperCollins Publishers.

ScienceDaily: Your source for the latest research news (2016) Available at http://www.sciencedaily.com.

Seriously, science? (2016) Available at: http://discovermagazine.com.

Stenger, V.J. (2007) *God -- the failed hypothesis: How science shows that God does not exist.* United States: Prometheus Books.

Wikipedia (no date) Available at http://wikipedia.com.

Magazines like New Science, Discover, Science and Popular Science have been treasure-troves of up-to-date information. Much of which is written in a down-to-earth way and is therefore readily accessible to non-professionals as well as professionals. They also happen to be available at almost any public library.

Also, I am including a list of some source material that the reader is welcome to read to add to his/her knowledge of these issues.

Not by Chance by Dr. Lee Spetner. (Biology and Evolution)
Permission to Believe and *Permission to Receive* by Rabbi Lawrence Kellerman.
Darwin's Black Box by Dr. Michael Behe.

All the controversy on the topics is readily available online, (not that I would suggest that people live their life online).

Jewish titles relevant to this topic (although the science is outdated, the logic and the philosophy isn't):
Guide for the Perplexed and *The Laws of the Foundations of the Torah* by Rabbi Moses Ben Maimon (Ramabam)
Ha'Emmunot v'ha'de'ot Rabbi Sa'adiah Gaon
Sefer Ha'Kuzari Rabbi Yehuda Ha'Levi
Sefer Ha'Ikkarim Rabbi Yosef Elbaz
Chovos Ha'Levavos Rabbi Bacha'yeh Ben Yosef

APPENDIX I

HE INFORMATION IN THIS APPENDIX is to more fully explore the information and the logical progression described in chapter three, "Into the Twilight Zone".

The premise that I posited there was that the reasoning given behind the engine of evolution, "survival of the fittest", has taken root in the public consciousness due to its publicity. As a result, this idea has been slowly but surely going through its own logical evolution until we arrive at where we are today.

When taking into consideration the full ramifications of the effects of Darwinism and the "No-G-d" world we need to look at the decline of morality in general as expressed in the areas of man's connection with other people and with his mate. We then must compare it to the general world and the religious world to get a full appreciation for the information presented.

To this end, I will divide the topic into the following categories: marriage and divorce, violence and lastly suicide.

<u>Marriage and Divorce</u>

The decline of the connection between man and his mate can be viewed as a direct result of the philosophy of "survival of the fittest".

After all, if life is about "survival", then the whole reason for procreation is the survival of the "fittest" species, (which, I'm sure, most people are convinced means "me"). Why should there be a profound and abiding relationship between mates? After all, the more man can spread his seed, the more likely he is to ensure the survival of the "superior" seed! Looked at in another way since the sexual drive is to ensure the survival of the species it therefore, is an animalistic drive just like any other. So why should a man behave differently than an animal would in this realm? After all, he's only just another animal!

Is it any wonder, then, that we find that the more "progress" that man makes as he lives through the 20th century into the 21st, that we discover that the rate of marriages is in decline whereas the rate of divorce among married couples is steadily climbing?

Take, for example, the following statistics from The Guardian, (an English publication), concerning the rates of the above as it affects the English[335]. Following through the data presented we find that marriages in England rose steadily from 1930, (a little more than 315,000 recorded marriages[336]), until during the beginning of WW2, (1940) when it reached a record high of about 470,000 recorded marriages. During this entire period of time, the recorded rates of divorces remained a statistical constant, (always a little less than 1%). During the years of WW2 and its aftermath,

---

[335]   http://www.theguardian.com/news/datablog/2010/jan/28/divorce-rates-marriage-ons

[336]   By "recorded marriages", I mean to say those English residents who applied for a marriage license in that year. These numbers don't include those who married without such a license. Similarly, the divorce rates are calculated by the amount of people who filed for divorce during that year. It doesn't really take into account the age of couples the number of years married etc. (Although there are statistics for that as well).

(1941-1947), the rates of marriage dropped, (389,000 (1941) – 401,000 (1947)), whereas the rates of divorce rose (6,000+ (1941) – 60,000+ (1947)) significantly[337]. From that point in time and on, (excluding the "peace and love", years of the late 1960's till the early 1970's), the rates of marriage have been in severe decline, (from 397,000 in 1948 to 241,000 in 2010). Whereas statistically, the rate of divorce has been rising severely, (from 28,700 in 1951, peaking at 165,000 in 1993 at "resting" presently at about 120,000 in 2010[338]).

All of this while the rate of England's population has been on a steady rise going from about 42,000,000 people in 1940 to today's population of some 62,000,000 people[339]. What this means in real numbers is that the actual rate of marriage has been in a state of considerable decline for quite some time[340].

Accordingly, the percentage of recorded divorces takes on a different perspective as well. If in 1940, the rate of divorce was a little less than 1% today it's around 11%. That's a 110% increase in percentage! It doesn't reflect the relative rates of marriage and divorce, which knocks the statistics into the stratosphere!

---

[337] Which is most likely the aftermath of dealing with the effects of the war.

[338] Although this represents a statistical drop in the sheer amounts of divorce since its highest point in 1993 (165,000) to 2010 (120,000), which is a drop from 13.8% to 11.1% - that's all it is: statistical. We must remember that the world's population has been rising consistently as well.

[339] http://www.populstat.info/Europe/unkingdc.html which represents almost a 50% increase.

[340] If in 1940, when there was a population of roughly 42 million there were 470,000 recorded marriages that's 470,000/42,000,000 or 0.011 (1.1% percent) of the population with _recorded_ marriages. I am not sure as to how accurate the records of England were then and, in my opinion, there were probably many more marriages than there was on record at the time. Whereas in 2011 with a population of 62,000,000 there were only 241,000 recorded marriages, which is 241,000/62,000,000, or 0.00388, (a little more than 1/3rd of 1%)! If the percentage were to have remained a constant, then there should have been around 650,000 recorded marriages per annum.

	1960	1970	1980	1990	2000	2009	2010	2011
EU-27		7.9	6.8	6.3	5.2	4.5	4.4	
Belgium	7.1	7.6	6.7	6.5	4.4	4.0	3.9	4.1
Bulgaria	8.8	8.6	7.9	6.9	4.3	3.4	3.2	2.9
Czech Republic	7.7	9.2	7.6	8.8	5.4	4.6	4.4	4.3
Denmark	7.8	7.4	5.2	6.1	7.2	6.0	5.6	4.9
Germany	9.5	7.4	6.3	6.5	5.1	4.6	4.7	4.6
Estonia	10.0	9.1	8.8	7.5	4.0	4.0	3.8	4.1
Ireland	5.5	7.0	6.4	5.1	5.0	4.9	4.6	4.3
Greece	7.0	7.7	6.5	5.8	4.5	5.2	5.0	4.9
Spain	7.8	7.3	5.9	5.7	5.4	3.8	3.6	3.4
France (1)	7.0	7.8	6.2	5.1	5.0	3.9	3.9	3.7
Italy	7.7	7.3	5.7	5.6	5.0	3.8	3.6	3.4
Cyprus (2)		8.6	7.7	9.7	13.4	7.9	7.3	7.3
Latvia	11.0	10.2	9.8	8.9	3.9	4.4	4.1	5.2
Lithuania	10.1	9.5	9.2	9.8	4.8	6.2	5.7	6.3
Luxembourg	7.1	6.4	5.9	6.1	4.9	3.5	3.5	3.3
Hungary	8.9	9.3	7.5	6.4	4.7	3.7	3.6	3.6
Malta	6.0	7.9	8.8	7.1	6.7	5.7	6.2	6.2
Netherlands	7.7	9.5	6.4	6.5	5.5	4.4	4.5	4.3
Austria	8.3	7.1	6.2	5.9	4.9	4.2	4.5	4.3
Poland	8.2	8.6	8.6	6.7	5.5	6.6	6.0	5.4
Portugal	7.8	9.4	7.4	7.2	6.2	3.8	3.8	3.4
Romania	10.7	7.2	8.2	8.3	6.1	6.3	5.4	4.9
Slovenia	8.8	8.3	6.5	4.3	3.6	3.2	3.2	3.2
Slovakia	7.9	7.9	7.9	7.6	4.8	4.9	4.7	4.7
Finland	7.4	8.8	6.1	5.0	5.1	5.6	5.6	5.3
Sweden	6.7	5.4	4.5	4.7	4.5	5.1	5.3	5.0
United Kingdom	7.5	8.5	7.4	6.6	5.2	4.3	4.5	
Iceland	7.5	7.8	5.7	4.5	6.3	4.6	4.9	4.6
Liechtenstein	5.7	5.9	7.1	5.6	7.2	4.3	5.0	4.5
Norway	6.6	7.6	5.4	5.2	5.0	5.0	4.8	4.6
Switzerland	7.8	7.6	5.7	6.9	5.5	5.4	5.5	5.3
Montenegro						6.1	6.0	
Croatia	8.9	8.5	7.2	5.8	4.9	5.1	4.8	4.6
FYR of Macedonia	8.6	9.0	8.5	8.3	7.0	7.3	6.9	7.2
Turkey			8.2			8.2	8.0	8.0

(1) Excluding French overseas departments for 1960 to 1990.
(2) Up to and including 2002, data refer to total marriages contracted in the country, including marriages between non-residents; from 2003 onwards, data refer to marriages in which at least one spouse was resident in the country.
Source: Eurostat (online data code: demo_nind)

When we look at the general statistics of the European Union, we find the exact same trend[341]. The following is a list of crude marriage rates in the EU during the allotted years (per 1000 people)

Compare that to the following chart of crude divorce rates in the EU

---

[341] The following chart is taken from the site of the European Union that can be found at http://epp.eurostat.ec.europa.eu/statistics_explained/index.php?title=File:Crude_marriage_rate,_seleted_years,_1960-2011_(per_1_000_inhabitants).png&filetimestamp=20130130111229

	1960	1970	1980	1990	2000	2009	2010	2011
EU-27 (2)		1.0	1.5	1.6	1.8	1.9		
Belgium	0.5	0.7	1.5	2.0	2.6	3.0	2.7	2.9
Bulgaria	:	1.2	1.5	1.3	1.3	1.5	1.5	1.4
Czech Republic	1.4	2.2	2.6	3.1	2.9	2.8	2.9	2.7
Denmark	1.5	1.9	2.7	2.7	2.7	2.7	2.6	2.6
Germany	1.0	1.3	1.8	1.9	2.4	2.3	2.3	2.3
Estonia	2.1	3.2	4.1	3.7	3.1	2.4	2.2	2.3
Ireland	-	-	-	-	0.7	0.7	0.7	0.7
Greece	0.3	0.4	0.7	0.6	1.0	1.2	:	:
Spain	-	-	-	0.6	0.9	2.1	2.2	2.2
France (3)	0.7	0.8	1.5	1.9	1.9	2.0	2.1	2.0
Italy (2)	-	0.3	0.2	0.5	0.7	0.9	0.9	:
Cyprus	:	0.2	0.3	0.6	1.7	2.2	2.3	2.3
Latvia	2.4	4.6	5.0	4.0	2.6	2.3	2.2	4.0
Lithuania	0.9	2.2	3.2	3.4	3.1	2.8	3.0	3.4
Luxembourg	0.5	0.6	1.6	2.0	2.4	2.1	2.1	:
Hungary	1.7	2.2	2.6	2.4	2.3	2.4	2.4	2.3
Malta	-	-	-	-	-	-	-	0.1
Netherlands	0.5	0.8	1.8	1.9	2.2	1.9	2.0	2.0
Austria	1.1	1.4	1.8	2.1	2.4	2.2	2.1	2.1
Poland	0.5	1.1	1.1	1.1	1.1	1.7	1.6	1.7
Portugal	0.1	0.1	0.6	0.9	1.9	2.5	2.6	2.5
Romania	2.0	0.4	1.5	1.4	1.4	1.5	1.5	1.7
Slovenia	1.0	1.1	1.2	0.9	1.1	1.1	1.2	1.1
Slovakia	0.6	0.8	1.3	1.7	1.7	2.3	2.2	2.1
Finland	0.8	1.3	2.0	2.6	2.7	2.5	2.5	2.5
Sweden	1.2	1.6	2.4	2.3	2.4	2.4	2.5	2.5
United Kingdom	:	1.0	2.6	2.7	2.6	2.0	2.1	:
Iceland	0.7	1.2	1.9	1.9	1.9	1.7	1.8	1.6
Liechtenstein	-	-	:	:	3.9	2.7	2.4	2.5
Norway	0.7	0.9	1.6	2.4	2.2	2.1	2.1	2.1
Switzerland	0.9	1.0	1.7	2.0	1.5	2.5	2.8	2.2
Montenegro	:	:	:	:	:	0.7	0.8	:
Croatia	1.2	1.2	1.2	1.1	1.0	1.1	1.1	1.3
FYR of Macedonia	0.7	0.3	0.5	0.4	0.7	0.6	0.8	0.9
Turkey	:	:	:	:	:	1.6	1.6	1.6

(1) Divorce was not possible by law in Italy until 1970, in Spain until 1981, in Ireland until 1995 and in Malta until 2011.

(2) 1971 instead of 1970.

(3) Excluding French overseas departments for 1960 to 1990.

Source: Eurostat (online data code: demo_ndivind)

Or, in visual terms[342]:

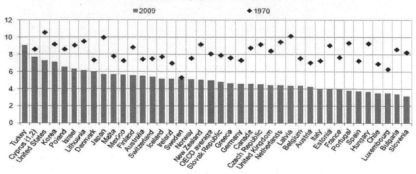

Chart SF3.1.A: The decline in crude marriage rates between 1970 and 2009*

Number of marriages per 1000 population

---

342 http://www.oecd.org/social/family/SF3.1%20Marriage%20and%20divorce%20
rate%20-%20updated%20240212.pdf

Or

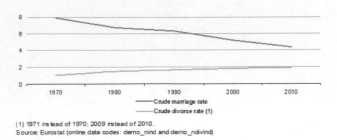

8					
6					
4					
2					
0					
	1970	1980	1990	2000	2010

———— Crude marriage rate
———— Crude divorce rate (1)

(1) 1971 instead of 1970; 2009 instead of 2010.
Source: Eurostat (online data codes: demo_nind and demo_ndivind)

Compare that to the percentage of births out of wedlock and we quickly see that it's only the concept of marriage that is in decline.

	1960	1970	1980	1990	2000	2009	2010	2011
EU-27 (1)		:		17.4	27.4	37.3	38.3	:
Belgium	2.1	2.8	4.1	11.6	28.0	45.5	46.2	49.2
Bulgaria	8.0	8.5	10.9	12.4	38.4	53.4	54.1	56.1
Czech Republic	4.9	5.4	5.6	8.6	21.8	38.8	40.3	41.8
Denmark	7.8	11.0	33.2	46.4	44.6	46.8	47.3	49.0
Germany	7.6	7.2	11.9	15.3	23.4	32.7	33.3	33.9
Estonia	:	:	:	27.2	54.5	59.2	59.1	59.7
Ireland	1.6	2.7	5.9	14.6	31.5	33.3	33.8	33.7
Greece	1.2	1.1	1.5	2.2	4.0	6.6	7.3	7.4
Spain	2.3	1.4	3.9	9.6	17.7	34.5	35.5	33.8
France (2)	6.1	6.8	11.4	30.1	43.6	53.7	55.0	:
Italy	2.4	2.2	4.3	6.5	9.7	19.8	21.5	26.3
Cyprus	:	0.2	0.6	0.7	2.3	11.7	15.2	16.9
Latvia	11.9	11.4	12.5	16.9	40.3	43.5	44.1	44.6
Lithuania	:	3.7	6.3	7.0	22.6	27.9	28.7	30.0
Luxembourg	3.2	4.0	6.0	12.8	21.9	32.1	34.0	34.1
Hungary	5.5	5.4	7.1	13.1	29.0	40.8	40.8	42.3
Malta	0.7	1.5	1.1	1.8	10.6	27.4	25.2	22.7
Netherlands	1.4	2.1	4.1	11.4	24.9	43.3	44.3	45.3
Austria	13.0	12.8	17.8	23.6	31.3	39.3	40.1	40.4
Poland	:	5.0	4.8	6.2	12.1	20.2	20.6	21.2
Portugal	9.5	7.3	9.2	14.7	22.2	38.1	41.3	42.8
Romania	:	:	:	:	25.5	28.0	27.7	30.0
Slovenia	9.1	8.5	13.1	24.5	37.1	53.6	55.7	56.8
Slovakia	4.7	6.2	5.7	7.6	18.3	31.6	33.0	34.0
Finland	4.0	5.8	13.1	25.2	39.2	40.9	41.1	40.9
Sweden	11.3	18.6	39.7	47.0	55.3	54.4	54.2	54.3
United Kingdom	5.2	8.0	11.5	27.9	39.5	46.3	46.9	47.3
Iceland	25.3	29.9	39.7	55.2	65.2	64.4	64.3	65.0
Liechtenstein	3.7	4.5	5.3	6.9	15.7	18.5	21.3	23.5
Norway	3.7	6.9	14.5	38.6	49.6	55.1	54.8	55.0
Switzerland	3.8	3.8	4.7	6.1	10.7	17.9	18.6	19.3
Montenegro	:	:	:	:	:	15.7	:	:
Croatia	7.4	5.4	5.1	7.0	9.0	12.9	13.3	14.0
FYR of Macedonia	5.1	6.2	6.1	7.1	9.8	12.2	12.2	11.6
Turkey	:	:	:	:	:	:	2.6	:

(1) Excluding French overseas departments and Romania for 1990.
(2) Excluding French overseas departments for 1960 to 1990.
Source: Eurostat (online data code: demo_find)

When looking elsewhere, we find the same statistical trend as well. Take the United States, for example[343]:

---

[343] http://www.infoplease.com/ipa/A0005044.html

Year	Marriage Number	Divorce[1] Rate[2]	Number	Rate[2]	Year	Marriage Number	Rate[2]	Divorce[1] Number	Rate[2]
1900	709,000	9.3	55,751	0.7	1991	2,371,000	9.4	1,187,000	4.7
1910	948,166	10.3	83,045	0.9	1992	2,362,000	9.2	1,215,000	4.8
1920	1,274,476	12.0	170,505	1.6	1993	2,334,000	9.0	1,187,000	4.6
1930	1,126,856	9.2	195,961	1.6	1994	2,362,000	9.1	1,191,000	4.6
1940	1,595,879	12.1	264,000	2.0	1995	2,336,000	8.9	1,169,000	4.4
1950	1,667,231	11.1	385,144	2.6	1996	2,344,000	8.8	1,150,000	4.3
1960	1,523,000	8.5	393,000	2.2	1997	2,384,000	8.9	1,163,000	4.3
1965	1,800,000	9.3	479,000	2.5	1998	2,256,000	8.4	1,135,000	4.2
1970	2,158,802	10.6	708,000	3.5	1999	2,358,000	8.6	—	4.1
1975	2,152,662	10.1	1,036,000	4.9	2000	2,329,000	8.5	—	4.2
1980	2,406,708	10.6	1,182,000	5.2	2001	2,327,000	8.4	—	4.0
1981	2,438,000	10.6	1,219,000	5.3	2002	2,254,000	7.8	—	4.0
1982	2,495,000	10.8	1,180,000	5.1	2003	2,187,000	7.5	—	3.8
1983	2,444,000	10.5	1,179,000	5.0	2004	2,279,000	7.8	—	3.7
1984	2,487,000	10.5	1,155,000	4.9	2005	2,230,000	7.5	—	3.6
1985	2,425,000	10.2	1,187,000	5.0	2006	2,193,000	7.6	—	3.6
1986	2,400,000	10.0	1,159,000	4.8	2007	2,208,000	7.4	—	3.7
1987	2,421,000	9.9	1,157,000	4.8	2008	2,208,000	7.3	—	3.6
1988	2,389,000	9.7	1,183,000	4.8	2009	2,080,000	6.8	840,000[3]	3.5[3]
1989	2,404,000	9.7	1,163,000	4.7					
1990	2,448,000	9.8	1,175,000	4.7					

Compare that with the number of Americans who never married, and an interesting picture emerges:

Percent Never Married, 1970–2010

The following table shows the percent of men and women in the United States ages 20 to 44 who never married from 1970 to 2010[344].

---

[344] http://www.infoplease.com/ipa/A0763219.html

Age	1970	1999	2000	2002	2004	2008	2010
Male:							
20 to 24 years	35.8%	83.2%	83.7%	85.4%	86.7%	86.9%	88.7%
25 to 29 years	10.5	52.1	51.7	53.7	56.6	57.6	62.2
30 to 34 years	6.2	30.7	30.0	34.0	33.4	32.4	36.5
35 to 39 years	5.4	21.1	20.3	21.1	23.4	23.0	23.5
40 to 44 years	4.9	15.8	15.7	16.7	18.5	16.9	20.4
Female:							
20 to 24 years	54.7%	72.3%	72.8%	74.0%	75.4%	76.4%	79.3%
25 to 29 years	19.1	38.9	38.9	40.4	40.8	43.4	47.8
30 to 34 years	9.4	22.1	21.9	23.0	23.7	24.0	27.2
35 to 39 years	7.2	15.2	14.3	14.7	14.6	15.2	17.7
40 to 44 years	6.3	10.9	11.8	11.5	12.2	12.9	13.8

In every regard as we progress further into the 20th century – the more marriage as an institution and marriage as a commitment dissolve. Note the significant change that occurs in all of the above statistics becomes more and more substantial from the 1950's and 1960's. This is not due purely because of the technological advances man has made during this period of time. It is, without a doubt, the result of the relaxing of moral standards, which has been in constant decline from the 1950's and on.

This doesn't need a whole lot of explanation. The disillusion with marriage as a concept is a rejection of the necessity of marriage. Marriage is, (despite its legal benefits, but mainly it remains), a religious institution. The reason for divorces? Whether due to adultery or any other reason, the prime motivator is that we have become more SELF-centered as opposed to OTHER-centered. The reason? Because the more "progress" man makes, the more the "survival of the fittest" becomes ingrained and the more I desire to become the fittest – regardless of who has to pay the price! Just "survive" for your own sake!

How do we know this to be true? Well, let's compare it to how those religious people have been affected as the years have gone by!

One considerable issue that isn't covered by the above statistics is the question as to how much of today's marriages are made up of religious couples as opposed to non-religious couples.

BARNA group, a faith-based statistical group out of California, claims[345] that, at least in the US, 80% of the population has been married[346]. They conducted their study on 3792 adults constituting the "full spectrum", (in their opinion), of the American population.

Their findings were that of the 80% of marriages upon scrutiny we find that there are three base groups: "Christian", "non-Christian" and "atheist/agnostics". Of the Christians, 84% married, from the "non's" 74% are claimed to marry and of the "Ath/Ag's" only 64% married.

They further conclude that fully 1/3 of all couples who married divorced. Relative to that number evangelical Christians are quoted as having a 30% divorce rate, less devote Christians a 33% divorce rate, non-Christians a 38% divorce rate and Ath/Ag's a 30% divorce rate.

These figures were re-examined by USA Today[347] and found to be inaccurate. The following is an excerpt from their website:

> But some scholars and family activists are questioning the oft-cited statistics, saying Christians who attend church regularly are more likely to remain wed.
>
> "It's a useful myth," said Bradley Wright, a University of Connecticut sociologist who recently wrote, "Christians Are Hate-Filled Hypocrites ... and Other Lies You've Been Told."
>
> ... The various findings on religion and divorce hinge on what kind of Christians are being discussed.

---

[345] https://www.barna.org/family-kids-articles/42-new-marriage-and-divorce-statistics-released

[346] Clearly, this is assuming that the average married life span is about 40 years and if we therefore add up the total number of marriages over the past 40 years, we will arrive at a number something like 80% of the total population.

[347] http://usatoday30.usatoday.com/news/religion/2011-03-14-divorce-christians_N.ht

Wright combed through the General Social Survey, a vast demographic study conducted by the National Opinion Research Center at the University of Chicago, and found that Christians, like adherents of other religions, have a divorce rate of about 42%. The rate among religiously unaffiliated Americans is 50%.

When Wright examined the statistics on evangelicals, he found worship attendance has a big influence on the numbers. Six in 10 evangelicals who never attend had been divorced or separated, compared to just 38% of weekly attendees.

What all the above means is that the more one is a practitioner of his/her religion – the less likely it is that they will divorce. Assuming the 6% difference quoted above that differentiates "religious affiliates" from those who "are not" is true, even that, alone, is proof enough as to the effects of some religion on a person's life. The fact that this figure increases significantly when a person is more than just "affiliated" is also clear evidence. But that's not all. Later in the article Brad Wilcox, director of the National Marriage Project at the University of Virginia, is quoted as having:

> ...found that Americans who attend religious services several times a month were about 35% less likely to divorce than those with no religious affiliation.
>
> Nominal conservative Protestants, on the other hand, were 20% more likely to divorce than the religiously unaffiliated.

Those are astronomical numbers!

So really, in order to actually understand the genuine marriage and divorce rates, we have to rely on crude numbers as to who, and how many people there are, of the practicing religiously affiliated as opposed to those people who are either non-practicing or unaffiliated religiously, in order to truly understand the magnitude of the decay caused by the "no-G-d" practitioners[348].

Also, we have to always remember that the number of Ath/Ag's who marry is not only smaller, (64% as opposed to approximately 80%), but many times comes after having already "tried on" several potential mates and having gotten rid of them!

Just to round out the picture, let me show you what the competition, (i.e. Christians), have to say about religious devotion and its effects on marriage and divorce[349]:

Faith Affiliation

% Divorce Likelihood Reduction

Protestant - Nominal	+20
Protestant -Conservative	-10
Protestant - Active Conservative	-35
Catholic	-18
Catholic (nominal)	-5
Catholic – Active	-31
Jewish	+39
Jewish (nominal)	+53
Jewish - Active	**-97**

In conclusion of this part: we see that the institution, commitment and therefore the, (quick and easy), resolution of marriages is in direct correspondence with the loosening of moral standards. It has therefore

---

[348] In my humble opinion it is ridiculous to include in the count of "religious", (= "Yes G-d" practitioners), anyone who is not an actual practitioner of religion. To claim one believes in G-d is one thing, but if you actually believe in Him – it's impossible that it would not express itself in some way in our daily lives! I therefore contend to include these types of individuals in the same basket with the "no-G-d" believers.

[349] http://thegospelcoalition.org/blogs/tgc/2012/09/25/factchecker-divorce-rate-among-christians/

declined steadily since the proliferation of the "no-G-d" Darwinian theory of evolution has become a mainstay in the public awareness. As opposed to this living a religious lifestyle is the polar opposite of said statistics. Wherein, relatively, the institution of marriage is strong, the commitment to the marriage is still strong, and divorce is not as easily considered.

What is it that makes for the difference between the religious vs. the secular attitudes towards marriage and divorce? Isn't it specifically the ethical teachings, by which they try to live and adhere?

Violence

When it comes to the issue of violence, we find a similar trend in society, which has, however, an interesting twist in recent times.

However, before we can properly explore this topic, we first need to make the following assertion:

When we are discussing the issue of violence, we are not referring to wars waged, and we are not talking about hate crimes, per se. What we are talking about is whether or not the average individual is more prone to violence and what his or her background is.

If you would pick the average person up off the street, would he have more of, or less of, a tendency towards violence if he/she were a religious practitioner as opposed to a non-practitioner of religion?

Once again when we are talking about "religious", the meaning is someone who is an actual practitioner of his/her religion, not just someone who claims membership in the local church or what-have-you.

I lump together in the "no-G-d" boat everyone who is not actually a practitioner of a G-d based ethical religion. I do so despite the fact that the secular/atheist/agnostic is in many ways preferable to those who claim to be religious adherents but who do not put into practice the tenets of their religion in any significant way.

What we find, wherever it is that we look, is that between the 1960's and the mid-1990's the levels of violence worldwide escalate. In many places to degrees, that boggle the mind!

Towards the end of the 1990's and into the 21st century, however, we find that these numbers take a steep downturn.

Looking back 50 years, a Pew Research Center study found U.S. gun homicides rose in the 1960s, gained in the 1970s, peaked in the 1980s and the early 1990s, and then plunged and leveled out the past 20 years. ...

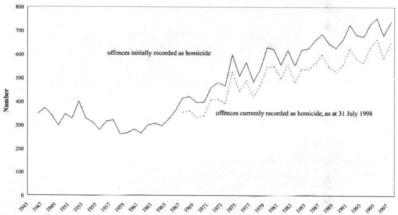

Homicide offences, England & Wales

In fact, gun-related homicide rates in the late 2000s were "equal to those not seen since the early 1960s," the study found[350].[351]

England and Wales clearly experienced a climb in the homicide rates from the 1960's into the late 1990's and even into 2002-2004[352].

---

[350] http://edition.cnn.com/2013/05/08/us/study-gun-homicide

[351] http://www.parliament.uk/documents/commons/lib/research/rp99/rp99-056.pdf page 9

[352] See http://www.theguardian.com/news/datablog/2013/feb/07/crime-statistics-england-wales-violent-sexual-offences

The following chart includes rates for the USA from 1960 until 2012[353]:
Estimated crime in United States-Total

Year	Population	Estimated crime in United States-Total National or state crime Violent crime Total Violent Crime	manslaughter	Forcible Rape	Robbery	Aggravated Assault
1960	179,323,175	288,460	9,110	17,190	107,840	154,320
1961	182,992,000	289,390	8,740	17,220	106,670	156,760
1962	185,771,000	301,510	8,530	17,550	110,860	164,570
1963	188,483,000	316,970	8,640	17,650	116,470	174,210
1964	191,141,000	364,220	9,360	21,420	130,390	203,050
1965	193,526,000	387,390	9,960	23,410	138,690	215,330
1966	195,576,000	430,180	11,040	25,820	157,990	235,330
1967	197,457,000	499,930	12,240	27,620	202,910	257,160
1968	199,399,000	595,010	13,800	31,670	262,840	286,700
1969	201,385,000	661,870	14,760	37,170	298,850	311,090
1970	203,235,298	738,820	16,000	37,990	349,860	334,970
1971	206,212,000	816,500	17,780	42,260	387,700	368,760
1972	208,230,000	834,900	18,670	46,850	376,290	393,090
1973	209,851,000	875,910	19,640	51,400	384,220	420,650
1974	211,392,000	974,720	20,710	55,400	442,400	456,210
1975	213,124,000	1,039,710	20,510	56,090	470,500	492,620
1976	214,659,000	1,004,210	18,780	57,080	427,810	500,530
1977	216,332,000	1,029,580	19,120	63,500	412,610	534,350
1978	218,059,000	1,085,550	19,560	67,610	426,930	571,460
1979	220,099,000	1,208,030	21,460	76,390	480,700	629,480
1980	225,349,264	1,344,520	23,040	82,990	565,840	672,650
1981	229,465,714	1,361,820	22,520	82,500	592,910	663,900
1982	231,664,458	1,322,390	21,010	78,770	553,130	669,480
1983	233,791,994	1,258,087	19,308	78,918	506,567	653,294
1984	235,824,902	1,273,282	18,692	84,233	485,008	685,349
1985	237,923,795	1,327,767	18,976	87,671	497,874	723,246
1986	240,132,887	1,489,169	20,613	91,459	542,775	834,322
1987	242,288,918	1,483,999	20,096	91,111	517,704	855,088
1988	244,498,982	1,566,221	20,675	92,486	542,968	910,092
1989	246,819,230	1,646,037	21,500	94,504	578,326	951,707
1990	249,464,396	1,820,127	23,438	102,555	639,271	1,054,863
1991	252,153,092	1,911,767	24,703	106,593	687,732	1,092,739
1992	255,029,699	1,932,274	23,760	109,062	672,478	1,126,974
1993	257,782,608	1,926,017	24,526	106,014	659,870	1,135,607
1994	260,327,021	1,857,670	23,326	102,216	618,949	1,113,179
1995	262,803,276	1,798,792	21,606	97,470	580,509	1,099,207

353   http://www.ucrdatatool.gov/Search/Crime/State/RunCrimeStatebyState.cfm

1996	265,228,572	1,688,540	19,645	96,252	535,594	1,037,049
1997	267,783,607	1,636,096	18,208	96,153	498,534	1,023,201
1998	270,248,003	1,533,887	16,974	93,144	447,186	976,583
1999	272,690,813	1,426,044	15,522	89,411	409,371	911,740
2000	281,421,906	1,425,486	15,586	90,178	408,016	911,706
2001	285,317,559	1,439,480	16,037	90,863	423,557	909,023
2002	287,973,924	1,423,677	16,229	95,235	420,806	891,407
2003	290,788,976	1,383,676	16,528	93,883	414,235	859,030
2004	293,656,842	1,360,088	16,148	95,089	401,470	847,381
2005	296,507,061	1,390,745	16,740	94,347	417,438	862,220
2006	299,398,484	1,435,123	17,309	94,472	449,246	874,096
2007	301,621,157	1,422,970	17,128	92,160	447,324	866,358
2008	304,059,724	1,394,461	16,465	90,750	443,563	843,683
2009	307,006,550	1,325,896	15,399	89,241	408,742	812,514
2010	309,330,219	1,251,248	14,722	85,593	369,089	781,844
2011	311,587,816	1,206,031	14,661	84,175	354,772	752,423
2012	313,914,040	1,214,464	14,827	84,376	354,522	760,739

Let's compare that with crime statistics from Sweden during this time-period.

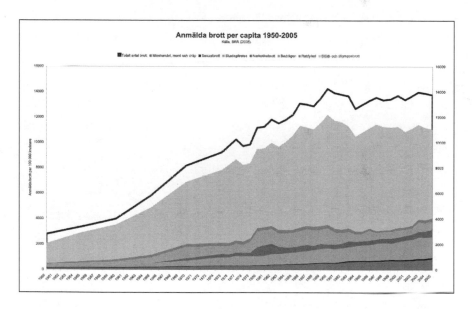

Crime rate statistics of Sweden 1950-2005 (Wikipedia "Crime in Sweden")

Researchers from Linnaeus University compiled statistics that revealed that the number of murders or manslaughters committed in Sweden last year was 62 compared to 127 back in 1989.

Indeed, the 62 murders/manslaughters was the lowest homicides figure since the 1960s, according to statistics from the Swedish National Council for Crime Prevention (Brottsförebyggande rådets statistik, Brå).

Sweden's decreasing murder rate is in keeping with figures compiled for the rest of Europe. France, Germany, and Italy have also had seen the amount of murders decrease by half since the mid-1990s. In Denmark, the murder rate has decreased by a quarter in that same time period[354].

The statistics clearly show the rise in violence and violent crime since the 1960's. The question is, therefore, what brought about this change and what has changed in recent years that has so affected it?

It is my opinion that it is the underlying philosophy of evolution/No G-d that has run rampant since being taught worldwide in the 60's that brought about the initial change and that, in this regard, not that much has really changed.

Why is it that the rates of violent crime have decreased so substantially since the mid-1990? Well, no one seems to really know for sure!

Although it would seem that it is based on a combination of better police work, tougher measures concerning crime and much more sophisticated anti-theft measures[355].

What this means is that there has not necessarily been an internal change in the attitude of the world's populace, but rather the change came about due to outside forces. In you-and-me language, this means that I

---

[354] http://www.thelocal.se/20131016/50824

[355] See http://www.economist.com/news/briefing/21582041-rich-world-seeing-less-and-less-crime-even-face-high-unemployment-and-economic see also http://leftcall.com/4557/u-s-crime-rates-1960-2010-the-facts-might-surprise-you/

didn't do it... because I felt I couldn't get away with it! It would come as no surprise to me to find out that television shows that portray how modern technology and techniques of police work have also added to the lessening of crime rates worldwide – for the reason stated previously. If I am convinced that I can't get away with it – it's much more likely than I am not even going to try to do it! Why? Survival, of course!

Well, if we are going to understand why this is, then one of the things that we will have to explore is this: what is the percentage of those people who are religiously affiliated that make up the statistics above? Does religious practice promote people to lead lives that are less violent than those who don't actively practice their religion or those who claim no religion at all?

The truth is that this is a tough statistic to know for sure! The reason being that there have been no, (to the best of my knowledge), really significant investigations into the aforementioned distinction between religious "affiliation" and people who are religious practitioners to be able to show real conclusions in this regard. Furthermore, there is very little distinction made as to whether we are talking about hate crimes, which can be caused either by religion or by racism, (not necessarily connected to each other), or bar fights and the like.

Remember, we are trying to quantify whether or not the average person is more prone to violence or not. We are not necessarily counting how many crimes were committed as a whole!

When looked at logically it makes more sense that a practitioner of religion, who learns about and speaks about issues of morality as having been decreed by a Higher Being, that an act of "goodness" or "evil" would give him/her more pause than someone who does them "just because". Regardless of the "because", as long as it is not Divine, only "logical" or "societal", then if I don't feel like it – I don't have to listen.

This does not mean, however, that religious practitioners are not liable or capable of ignoring the aforementioned moral teachings. It just means that he/she will have to admit to a moral failure. Whereas someone of only religious affiliation or secular will agree to no such thing. After all, "morality", in their eyes, is only someone else's rules for how he should live!

So, let's try and see what we CAN find.

In studies performed on children of single-parent families, (please remember the statistics of part I, concerning marriage and divorce), the following findings were discovered[356]:

- Neighborhoods with a high degree of religious practice are not high-crime neighborhoods.
- Even in high-crime inner-city neighborhoods, well over 90 percent of children from safe, stable homes do not become delinquents. By contrast, only 10 percent of children from unsafe, unstable homes in these neighborhoods avoid crime.
- Criminals capable of sustaining marriage gradually move away from a life of crime after they get married.
- The mother's strong, affectionate attachment to her child is the child's best buffer against a life of crime.

The father's authority and involvement in raising his children are also a great buffer against a life of crime.

Furthermore, in this issue, we find that[357]:

Can religion help reduce violent crime?

---

[356] http://www.heritage.org/research/reports/1995/03/bg1026nbsp-the-real-root-causes-of-violent-crime I strongly suggest reading the full article as it is full of very pertinent information pertaining to a number of real personal, inter-personal and community wide issues.

[357] http://www.huffingtonpost.com/david-briggs/no-time-for-crime-study-f_b_4384046.html in an article entitled No Time for Crime: Study Finds More Religious Communities Have Lower Rates of Black, White and Latino Violence Posted: 12/04/2013 very worthwhile reading concerning this topic! See also http://www.sciencedaily.com/releases/2013/06/130612144732.htm that quotes the issue as well.

Some new research suggests the answer is yes, both by creating a moral climate that fosters respect among neighbors and by helping to form individual consciences of young adults.

Violent crime decreased as greater numbers of people were religiously active in a community, according to a study analyzing crime and religion data from 182 counties in three states.

The effect was particularly pronounced in black violence in disadvantaged communities that are most likely to have the highest number of victims.

"In the big picture, religious presence seems to matter to the amount of violence and crime in a community," says Jeffery Ulmer, a professor of sociology and crime, law and justice at Pennsylvania State University who led the county-level study. "It matters to blacks, whites, and Latinos."

Just don't expect young men and women who are among the growing numbers of people who consider themselves "spiritual but not religious" to have the same moral inhibitions.

Now I realize that when it comes to the area of statistics, one can quote, and counter quote the studies and the findings that one wants. However, I ask that the reader please keep in mind what it is that we are really looking for here!

The question is not "has or is religion a source of violence". The answer to that everyone knows is "yes". Many wars have been waged in the name of religion and in all likelihood, many more will! The question that we are looking to answer is how the individual is affected by his/her adherence to, or rejection of, religion. When looked at via these criteria much of the data cited as counterclaims become irrelevant, as they do not take this issue into consideration.

Indeed, many times the comparisons made are "apples to oranges" and are irrelevant to each other.

Some prime examples of this are the comparison of crimes of "religious" countries/counties as compared to "irreligious" ones. Clearly, this is done with no calculation whatsoever as to the religious adherence of the populations and with no discrimination as to hate crimes vs. general violence.

Also, the general reference to the BARDA 1999 study into marriage, (mentioned in the previous section), is also misquoted as showing that "religious" are more likely to divorce, and/or be unfaithful than secular. Upon scrutiny, (as mentioned above), we find that it states clearly that religious adherents/practitioners are much less likely to do the above as compared to secular/atheists.

In conclusion of this part: once again, we find that when it comes to levels of violence the less one believes in and lives by a belief in G-d, (which, in my humble opinion, are integrally connected), the more likely that individual is to be prone to violent tendencies and actions.

After all, "survival" is the name of the game, isn't it?

Suicide

The next area of life that we need to explore is the topic of a person's regard as to his/her own life.

As I suggested in the "Twilight Zone" man's search for meaning, the basic psychological need that he has, that his life means something, places him beyond every other creature on the face of G-d's earth!

Every living thing has within it a survival drive. For many creatures, this is an automatic response to a threat to its life. Its body and genetics are "programmed" to keep him alive, (supposedly to ensure the survival of his progeny)!

However, man, in addition to this survival drive, also demands that his life should have meaning! It's not enough to just be alive. That life has to mean something as well. Without meaning man's life is full of suffering. Therefore, man and apparently only man[358], who lives a life without meaning is left with three options available to him: Either to find meaning, to "live" with the pain, or ... to not.

"Living" with the pain does not necessarily mean that we are actually just sitting and suffering. Usually, man will look for "something to do" with his time that helps him to overlook the pain of lack of meaning.

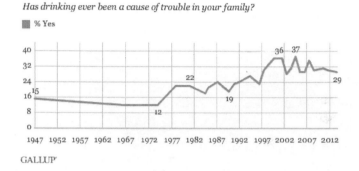

Has drinking ever been a cause of trouble in your family?

GALLUP'

As I mentioned in the "Twilight Zone" this usually is facilitated by distractions, such as video games, movies, TV and many other mind-numbing mediums. It involves substance abuse, whether the substance is food, alcohol, drugs, free sex or what have you. Anything to find a distraction and to "kill time".

Take, for example, this chart from a Gallup poll:

The findings[359] clearly indicate a rise in family-related problems due to alcoholic consumption as increasing steadily from the early 70's into the present day. We are told this despite the fact that, according to the same poll, the amount of alcoholic consumption remained, basically, the same!

---

358   See, for example, http://science.howstuffworks.com/zoology/all-about-animals/
     animals-commit-suicide.htm

359   http://www.gallup.com/poll/1582/Alcohol-Drinking.aspx

*Thinking now about your family and closest friends, how many of them --
drink alcohol -- many, some, only a few, or none?*

	Many	Some	Only a few	None	No opinion
	%	%	%	%	%
2013 Jul 10-14	23	28	36	12	1

GALLUP

However, in the continuation of the same poll, when the people were asked if they felt that their friends consumed alcohol, we find:

What this means is that the consensus of alcoholic consumption is that 88% are drinking. I feel that this is an issue which should be addressed more fully in the data, (they only asked this question in 2013), as it is more likely that people will tell the truth about their friends and alcohol than about themselves and alcohol.

In the Nordic countries, alcohol consumption has grown at a steady rate since the 1960's[360]. In Japan

> *...although alcohol consumption is now decreasing in most industrialized countries, it has quadrupled in Japan since 1960.*
>
> *Drinking is not a moral issue here, since there is no religious prohibition against alcohol consumption, and the temperance movement has never had an impact. And unlike many Westerners, the Japanese don't regard alcohol as a drug.*

In England, we are told in this 2008 article, that

> *Britain is facing a "silent epidemic" of dementia as alcohol consumption has doubled since the 1960s, doctors have warned[361].*

---

[360] http://business.highbeam.com/410209/article-1G1-274409096/trends-alcohol-consumption-and-violence-nordic-countries

[361] http://www.cmaj.ca/content/167/4/388.1.full.pdf

Well, you might be asking, what about other substances, such as drugs? Maybe there we find that things are better? Nope! The following are the results of a Gallup poll in the US on the use of marijuana[362]!

Keeping in mind that all of your answers in this survey are confidential, have you, yourself ever happened to try marijuana?

	Yes, have tried	No, have not	No opinion
	%	%	%
2013 Jul 10-14 ^	38	61	1
1999 Sep 23-26	34	66	*
1985 May 17-20 #	33	67	*
1977 Mar 29 #	24	76	1
1973 Mar 23 #	12	88	1
1972 Feb 29 #	11	88	1
1969 Oct 2-7 #	4	88	8

^ Asked of a half sample
# WORDING: Have you, yourself, ever happened to try marijuana?
* Less than 0.5%

GALLUP

Also, wherever we look concerning drug usage, we find that drugs, in general, is a growing problem. It's true in Australia[363], it's true in the US[364], it's true in Europe and its true most everywhere[365]!

---

[362] http://www.gallup.com/poll/1657/Illegal-Drugs.aspx

[363] http://en.wikipedia.org/wiki/Illicit_drug_use_in_Australia "drug use increased in the 1960s and 1970s... Drug use increased exponentially by the mid-1980s. ... During the 1990s, Australia experienced a heroin "epidemic" ...The Australian Crime Commission's illicit drug data report for 2011–2012 was released in western Sydney on 20 May 2013 and revealed that the seizures of illegal substances during the reporting period were the largest in a decade due to record interceptions of amphetamines, cocaine and steroids".

[364] http://drugabuse.com/library/drug-abuse-statistics/

[365] See also http://www.ncbi.nlm.nih.gov/pmc/articles/PMC2652931/ and http://web.wm.edu/americanstudies/370/2007/sp5/Main_Drugs_Home.html and http://www.drugwarfacts.org/cms/Drug_Usage#sthash.3GV5NKVe.dpbs

Despite some "modest" reduction of some drug use in recent years[366], drugs remain a growing problem worldwide.

Why is that? Why do people use drugs?

One reason often heard from people using drugs is that they do them to feel good[367].

Truthfully, despite there being many reasons as to why people take drugs – this one is usually brought first, and if we really want to face its true scope, it includes all of the other reasons as well.

People have taken mind-altering substances throughout history, whether it is alcohol or drugs and the main reason has always been to feel good and to alleviate stress.

Why do we need help to feel good? Why are we always stressed out?

Because we all have a soul, (more on this in the next book, G-d willing), that keeps telling us to grow! This "nagging voice" that we don't "hear" so much as feel is ever-present, to let us know that we should be making something of ourselves... and more often than not we are not.

That's painful. So, we use mind-altering substances to biologically "relieve" the pain, or we use mind(less) drivel of TV, movies, novels, video games and the like so that we don't "hear" the little voice and to "kill time" – literally!

Either we should be so physically numbed that we can't feel it, or we should be mentally dulled or distracted so that we don't notice that our only real possession in this life – time – is slipping through my fingers and down the cosmic toilet!

---

[366] This is more likely the consequence of stricter security in almost all forms of travel, making the import of drugs more difficult and thereby lowering the amounts of supply.

[367] http://www.addictionireland.ie/faq/article.asp?FID=33 and http://www.drugscope. org.uk/resources/faqs/faqpages/why-do-young-people-take-drugs also http:// www.psychologytoday.com/blog/the-scientific-fundamentalist/201010/why-intelligent-people-use-more-drugs and http://answers.yahoo.com/question/ index?qid=20130801190728AAmqUeb

So, if all of life is just a cosmic accident, then why live it?

Is it any wonder, therefore, that we find the following statistics?

In the USA[368]:

The rate of annual suicides among ages 15-24 has tripled (during the mid- 90's it quintupled!) since the 1950's! And this is only the known amount (based on hospital records) of those who succeeded.

For every successful suicide, there are anywhere between 100-200 attempts[369]!

Once again, we are dealing with information gathered via a poll in which, despite the anonymity, does not always mean that the ones who filled out the form or answered the questions did so truthfully when it came to themselves. If the question asked was about their friends... the outcome might have been even larger.

International Suicide Statistics[370]

Over one million people die by suicide worldwide each year.

The global suicide rate is 16 per 100,000 population.

On average, one person dies by suicide every 40 seconds somewhere in the world.

1.8% of worldwide deaths are suicides.

Global suicide rates have increased 60% in the past 45 years[371].

In Summary:

Having read all of the above data, we are left with a severe question. What is it that caused the world to spiral out of control since the 1960's?

---

[368] http://yellodyno.com/Statistics/statistics_teen_suicides.html it should be noted, however, that there are more conservative amounts. See http://en.wikipedia.org/wiki/Failed_suicide_attempt#cite_note-2

[369] http://www.cdc.gov/ViolencePrevention/pdf/Suicide-DataSheet-a.pdf

[370] http://www.suicide.org/international-suicide-statistics.html

[371] Since the polls listed on the site are from 2002 that means that the information compared here is 2002 to... you guessed it!

Many people say that it is because of the advent of new technologies and the violence and depravity that we find on television. While that may have had some effect, however, when we take a close look at this "claim", we find that that's about all it really is: words.

Why is that? Because, technology aside, in the United States of my childhood, there was a serious level of censorship based on moral values. I remember as a child watching public television when the movie "10" was aired, starring Bo Derek as the female lead. When it came time to show the scenes of the star in her bikini – outside of her hands, her head and a part of her legs – nothing else was visible! It was censored out with a big white dot! My parents tell me that when they were young, the censorship was such that if the male and female leads kissed in the movie it got an "R" rating.

I also remember, as a child, the Saturday Night Live episode when the censorship of the word "penis" was removed and how the entire show of that night focused on that word.

Why did things change in the USA? Not just because of the technology or even as a direct result. It was because of the erosion of morals and morality in the country.

But why do morals erode?

Morals erode when the underpinnings of those morals are weakened.

With the worldwide proliferation of Darwinism in the 1950's and 1960's, so too were the foundations of morality weakened. Once people were taught that there is no G-d and that there is no soul, no Heaven, and no Hell – then what was the point of morals and what was the point of the censorship?

That is the power of an idea: it can literally change the world.

But once that ball was set in motion, it also released all of humanity's negative side as well. For what was there to keep it in check anymore? As a direct result marriages failed, levels of violence soared, and people gave up their hope and their desire to live.

Is it a coincidence? I'm pretty convinced that it is not. Indeed, it is the absolute truth. Is it 100% for sure? No. There always have been and there always will be no way to show conclusively that the one dragged the other in its wake. But does it make sense?

Oh, yes!

APPENDIX II

Summary: The Emperor's New Clothes

HE FOLLOWING IS A SUMMARY of the difficulties inherent in the "proofs" that supposedly verify the "truth" of the theory of evolution.

Archeology	There are no archeological proofs concerning PRE-life (i.e. the chemical bonding that supposedly lead to life) There is no clear record of evolution occurring in the fossil record. New life "appears" out of nowhere.
	Rebuttals: Not all animals fossilize. Therefore, they have no fossil record at all (ex. Worms). Fossilization is iffy and difficult. Very little, in fact, does fossilize. Maybe Macroevolution can occur very quickly (punctuated evolution).

	All this to explain why no fossil record can verify the claims of evolution. Nevertheless, there still IS NO FOSSIL RECORD, which proves evolution either.
Anthropology	Anthropology only has a proven record concerning animals that are alive today. But not so much concerning animals that are no longer in existence. (Example: coelacanth) Even concerning things alive today, the field of "forensic facial reconstruction" is iffy at best. Almost all of the "conclusions" of this field are based on findings of very insubstantial content. There are many things in the world for which these fields cannot bring an explanation (ex. Feathers).
Speciation/ micro-evolution	All of the proofs in this area are based on the same principle: a mutation occurs (antibiotic resistance in bacteria, for ex.), X is introduced (antibiotics) killing off all, or most of, the non-mutants. The surviving mutant repopulates becoming the dominant genetic trait. The weak point, therefore, is the proof that the original change in the genome was caused by mutation, and that it was RANDOM. (If it's due to variation in the DNA then it's a program, not random)
DNA	Whatever is in the DNA – that is what is coming out! For change to occur, new DNA must become available! "Junk" DNA (and vestibular limbs!) is "proof" based on sheer ignorance (*I* don't know what it's for – therefore its junk). The more we explore, the more purpose we seem to find! Mistakes in gene replication have not been shown to have any positive effects on the genome (example: Down syndrome).

Mutations	The chances of a random "mutation" occurring are impossible.
	Despite that – they happen fast and all the time!
	Despite that, they appear to be reversible as well!
	Despite that, they "somehow" can cause many plants and animals to create exact replicas of, or to mimic precisely other plants, insects or body parts.
	Despite that, there are several types of creatures who have "somehow" developed incredibly complex systems, such as sonar, (bats and dolphins), via "convergent evolution".
Genome complexity	Human genome project: we don't have the largest genome by any standard – so why are we more adept?
	Human Genome Project: Human genome is QUALITATIVELY different (one gene codes for many others)
	The actual amount of knowledge of the genome is "nascent" (=next to nothing) due to the sheer size of the genome (3 billion bases) and due to its complexity.
	It can almost never be proven in a court of law what causes a "mutation" (because we truly have no idea whatsoever); therefore, to claim that mutation is the source of variation in any one species is speculative at best, not fact.
	As that is the case, all of the "proofs" from microevolution are worthless.

APPENDIX III

Abraham and Abiogenesis

EFORE EVOLUTION CAN TAKE PLACE – there must first be some form of life! If the premise of evolution is true and there is no need for a G-d for life to become what it is today, then how did it happen? (The order here is different than that of the chapter. It was based on the original chapter which I reorganized)

Evolutionists	Concerning this issue, the evolutionists perform the "ostrich maneuver" by hiding their heads in the sand. "That's not a problem for the field of biology/evolution – it's a chemical thing, and I'm sure, (Please G-d!), that there is an answer".
	Due to the sheer complexity of even the most rudimentary life, (henceforth a "prokaryote") it is impossible that all of the cell's systems "became" at the same time.
	QUESTION:
	CAN they "occur" one at a time?

Timeframe problem	Between the forming of the planet and the first archeological findings of prokaryotes, there are only 300-600 million years[372]. Not much evolutionarily speaking. According to archeological findings, it took an additional 1.65 billion years for the "next step" in evolution, the eukaryotes, to arrive. This despite the fact that the "bigger" step is the actual synthesis of "life" in the first place, not the advancement from type A to type B. So why did step B take so much time?
2nd Law of Thermodynamics	Otherwise known as the "Law of Entropy", states that all systems have a tendency towards *less* organization as time goes on as opposed to *more* as they lose energy as time goes on. Whereas life … keeps getting more complex!
Rebuttal	Sand dunes, snowflakes, and life – following the law of entropy, and because they are "open systems". They become more complex to facilitate more energy loss.
Rebuttal of the Rebuttal	This is like saying that just as water can become more complex when it crystallizes, it can also take upon itself the form and function of a Pentium chip, as that further facilitates energy loss. There is no evidence brought to substantiate this claim either. This also doesn't answer how we find many systems, (glycolysis, for example), which work for maximum energy GAIN in a very sophisticated manner.

---

[372] This is if we calculate from the point of the planet's accretion. In all likelihood it was a very long time after this that the first "life" could have begun as the planet took time to cool before it could begin "generating" life.

The Interconnectedness of biological systems	Cell wall: Majorly complex. NOT impermeable, NOT entirely permeable, but rather SELECTIVELY permeable in both directions. IN – to allow the cell access to the nutrients that it MUST have to function, and OUT to release all things unnecessary so it doesn't explode. The cell wall is PART AND PARCEL OF the reproductive system. There is no cell division without the cell wall. There is no cell without the cell wall. Respiratory and Digestive: Cannot exist independently. One builds the engine but without gas/energy – it's not going anywhere. Respiratory and Digestive: These processes are COMPLEX, successive, and CONTROLLED. Some processes (glycolysis, for example) show clear signs of intelligence as they maximize (despite the 2nd law of quantum mechanics) the production of energy in 5 successive preparatory steps wherein it INVESTS readily usable energy (ATP) to maximize the output of ATP in the *next* 5 consecutive stages. Respiratory and Digestive: cannot exist without a cell wall to protect it from the "outside" and, unless the cell wall is somehow directed by the R&D processes, it can't exist WITH IT either, as it won't get the very specific nutrients that its processes need! Respiratory and Digestive: Cannot be random processes otherwise it would produce unnecessary junk that would quickly deplete the limited energy resources of the cell.

	Respiratory and Digestive: The bio-building (anabolic) process is, however, useless without a building plan (i.e. DNA)! In **ot**her words: NO DNA – NO R&D SYSTEMS.
	DNA: "Central Dogma of Biology" DNA makes RNA that makes PROTEIN. However:
	DNA: replication cannot take place without an existing strand of DNA. Where did the first strand come from?
	DNA: The processes of DNA replication and/or RNA encoding are incredibly complex and require many extremely specific enzymes. Where did these processes come from? How were they subjugated to the replication process?
	DNA: is made up of proteins. Proteins are the product of the anabolic (respiratory/digestive) processes. In other words, if there are no R&D processes – there can be no DNA!
"G-d of the Gaps"	Science "pooh-pooh"s this issue by referring to such discrepancies as "gaps" which G-d then is supposed to "fill".
	These are not "gaps" but rather interstellar sized black holes. I refer to this instead as "the science of grasping at straws".
	Science cannot, and never will be able to account for these tremendous discrepancies in the creation of the "original cell".

The Complexity of biological systems	DNA: In every cell is 6 ft. long when straightened. There is enough DNA in your whole body to make 66 2/3 trips to the sun and back.
	DNA: One cubic cm of DNA can contain the information stored on 250 BILLION dvds.
	DNA has 1,000,000 times more computing power than today's most powerful computers. (It's also one thousandth (or less) the size as well!)
	DNA: processes millions of pieces of information at the same time (parallel processing) as opposed to computers that do so one after the other (sequentially).
	DNA: One of the strongest, most stable molecules in existence. You can extract it from bones that are "millions" of years old.
	HOWEVER: DNA is _useless_ without its enzymes and without a ribosome. Just like a hard-drive is useless without a computer to read its information.
	ENZYMES: All enzymes are _incredibly_ precise.
	ENZYMES: Catalyzation, when done by enzymes, is millions of times faster.
	ENZYMES: The configuration of enzymes is so precise that even a change as small as 10 picometers (0.0000000000001) would render them ineffective.
	ENZYMES: Have a "spell checking" system to ensure the fidelity of the product that they produce, which itself isn't a product of happenstance.

	ENZYMES: All attempts at intentionally, intelligently, and specifically making designer enzymes have produced relatively poor results. They also required a very close inspection to achieve anything at all.
	Yet somehow, blind, random, undirected "nature" does the job!
	FLAGELLA: The flagella's rotary "engine" looks and acts like a jet engine.
	FLAGELLA: Can operate at speeds of 6,000-17,000 RPM. Compared to jet engines that max out at 14,500-15,500 RPM.
	FLAGELLA: Can change spinning direction instantaneously (a jet engine cannot).
	FLAGELLA: Propulsion rate of about 60 body-lengths per second (compared to cheetah, that only does about 25 (110 km/h)).
	Consider this closely: for its size, there is nothing even close to comparable in the man-made world, despite our supposed investment of intelligence, effort, and testing.
Environmental issues related to the "first life".	WATER: Necessary for life, yet should not exist according to quantum physics.
	WATER: Has about 80 properties that baffle science today.
	WATER: Not all water is capable of supporting life. Only on earth have we found liquid water of limited salinity (saltiness) capable of sustaining life.
	WATER: Life needs it, PRE-life – cannot "live" with it! Water is the "universal solvent"; it dissolves all parts of the cell! This despite the fact

that the cell can't do without SOME amount of water for its internal reactions.

CARBON: The basis of all life, yet there shouldn't be any on Earth as it requires temperatures found only in the hearts of stars to bond the necessary electrons together to form it!

CARBON: Just as much as there doesn't seem to be any on Mars – so too there shouldn't be any on earth. Yet there is… in abundance!

OXYGEN: Life couldn't form in today's "oxygen-rich" atmosphere as it "interferes with the reactions that transform simple organic molecules (O"M) into complex ones".

OXYGEN: However, since it is necessary for the proper functioning of cells – there had to have been some amount of oxygen! (Make up your mind!)

Science suggests either we defied the odds… or the universe is "ripe for life" (since when is a stacked deck random)?

OUTER SPACE: Mars, the testing ground of all hypotheses concerning life from space *as it has – essentially – all of the same conditions as earth does.* Yet the Viking lander found no traces of O"M on its surface, no liquid water has been found or any other property which should help support life.

OUTER SPACE: Perhaps comets are the source. Maybe, but maybe not. Mars is impacted by an equivalent number of comets as earth, yet despite this still has no O"M. This could be because they burn up during re-entry or explode upon impact.

	OUTER SPACE: The PAH hypothesis? Maybe, but then again… maybe not! EARTH: The "primordial soup" theory has been dismissed as not viable. EARTH: Hydrothermal vents? Maybe… but maybe not as well! REMEMBER: None of these even *begins* to answer the problems that we raised at the beginning of this chapter!

ABOUT THE AUTHOR

Rabbi Shlomo Ben Zeev

Born in Boston, Mass. Grew up in Atlanta, Ga. I attended the Hebrew Academy of Atlanta.

1984 Moved to Israel where I attended Neve Shmuel Yeshiva High-School.

1988 Attended Yeshiva Ohr David. Followed by Yeshivas Sha'alvim and Ittri. During my 15 years in Sha'alvim, I served in the IDF, received rabbinical ordination from the Chief Rabbinate of Israel (Yoreh-Yoreh), ordination as a Torah scribe and checker from Va'ad Mishmereth STA"M and a BA and MA in Hebrew Letters from Yeshivat Ittri's college program. During this entire time, I taught classes in advanced Talmud studies, Halacha, (the practical application of the oral Talmud), and in many other aspects of Torah learning.

2004 I worked with the Nahal Haredi Project as one of the rabbis. It was there that I began work on the Emunah project, Core Emunah. This book and, with HaShem's help, those that are to follow, are based on the research that I began then and am still working on to this day.

2008 Received ordination as a Certified Mohel (Practitioner of Jewish circumcision).

2014 Finished a degree in Jewish Education (B.Ed.) at the Jerusalem College (Michlala).

Today I am teaching in Yeshivat Ohr David[373] in Jerusalem, (one of my alma maters) and lecturing under the auspices of Nefesh Yehudi[374] and more recently with the organization Hidabroot[375].

I am, with HaShem's help, a lifetime learner. I have been interested in the sciences since I was young and have been an avid reader forever. It is with HaShem's help, the guidance of my teachers and the support of all of my students that I humbly present the reader with this volume and those to follow.

---

[373] **www.ohrdavid.org**

[374] **http://www.nefeshyehudi.org/**

[375] www.hidabroot.org